PRAISE FOR THE STORIES IN 'PUPPY OUT OF BREATH'

"Doug's breadth of experience, memory, and gift for connection are so impressive!"

LOUISE HAGUE Plymouth, Massachusetts

"Each of Doug's stories has a life lesson learned while being presented in a style that speaks to the reader like an old friend."

TONI HANCOCK St. Louis, Missouri

"There is always something enjoyable, thought-provoking, or moving in Doug's stories."

KENT SMITH Hartford, Connecticut

"Doug's stories take me outside myself."

HOLLY FUCHS Ames, Iowa

"*It is good to see that the 'Best of Doug' is now in a book."*

SANDRA BLAKESLEE Santa Fe, New Mexico
(Sandra has authored many books, including: 'The Good Marriage', 'Phantoms in the Brain', and 'The Body Has a Mind of its Own'.)

PUPPY OUT OF BREATH

True-life Stories by
DOUGLAS E SCHNEIDER

Illustrations by Emma Trithart
Cover photo by Eric Geise
Book design by Anne Schonhardt

To my enduring friend —
Enjoy!
Doug

PUPPY OUT OF BREATH

Printed by:

Mira Digital Publishing
1010 Hanley Industrial Court
Brentwood MO 63144

Copyright 2012 by Douglas E Schneider

ISBN 978-0-9885256-1-0

Manufactured in the United States of America

TABLE OF CONTENTS

OPENING
The Little Voice Speaks In Galveston — 3

LIVING IN AFRICA
Slaughtering a Chicken for Lunch — 7
Accused of Smuggling — 9
To Sit, Perchance to Squat — 11
Freezing in Africa — 13
Love and Cholera — 15
Never Squish It, Always Flick It — 17
A Crazed Herd of Stampeding Goats — 19
The Sacred Crocodiles of Zuru — 21
Burning Down the Fire Station — 23

PROUD MOMENTS
Peanut Butter Stew — 27
There Goes the Judge — 29
The Man of the Year Asks Me One Question — 31
The Scourge Raises a Ruckus — 33
Big Ass Beer — 35
Hogan Is Not a Name — 37
Random Acts of Tact — 39
I Used To Be Clever in Mathematics — 41

CHILDHOOD
The Twinkling Lights of Playland — 45
West Egg vs. East Egg — 47
New Jersey Pastoral — 49
Tracing Indelible Journeys — 51
Ketchup and Saltine Sandwiches — 53
Do You Mean That I Was Really Mean? — 55
With a Towel over My Head — 57
The Wrong Island Snail Road — 59
Call It Courage — 61

THE MILITARY
Italy on $6.81 a Day — 65
Protecting South Carolina against the Enemy — 67
Not a Helicopter in Sight — 69
Muhammad Ali Will Feel Welcome — 71
One Eskimo Weeping — 73
My Groin is on File in Little Rock — 75
I Would Never Say Hello to Her — 77
Thank You, Richard Milhous Nixon — 79

FATHER
Buying a Father's Day Card — 83
The Ever-Talking Henry Schneider — 85
I Played Baseball against Lou Gehrig — 87
Squirrels Ruling the Bird Feeder — 89
It Rains Pennies from Heaven — 91

CULTURES
I am a Stupid American — 95
It's No Use Mein Getalking — 97
Life According to Bollywood — 99
Too Much Time on Your Hands — 101
Jewish People Always Show up for Funerals — 103
Seconds Count — 105
Uranium-Crazed Zombies — 107

EATING
The Allure of Sushi — 111
Temptation on the Cob — 113
Lunch with the Duke of Atholl — 115
Because We Eat Our Hamburger Raw — 117
You Can't Live with Us If You Shop at Harrods — 119
A Lifetime in a Lunchtime — 121

PEOPLE IN AFRICA
The House Faced East — 125
The Man in the Blue Veil Sitting on My Porch — 127
A White Man in a Black Neighborhood — 129
Day Tripping with the Pubkeeper's Daughter — 131
A Fish that Lives in a Well — 133
Stranded in My Living Room — 135
A Leper in My Household — 137

CAREER

I Had a Hand in Building It	141
Overcoming the Wrath of My Team Lead	143
Larry, Moe, and Curly at the Bank of America	145
The Standoff at the Jewish Delicatessen	147
The Room Where John F. Kennedy Died	149
Chuck Woke Up and Could Not Find a White Shirt	151
My Childhood Bank Has Disappeared	153
He Shook My Hand a Couple of Times	155

MOTHER

When Edith Met Henry	159
A Little White Duck Doing What He Oughta	161
Bob Hope Made My Mother Cry	163
Saltwater Dreams	165
Edith Learns to Drive at Age 75	167

IN GREAT BRITAIN

Drinking with Walter	171
Breakfast on Pluto	173
We Are Glad You are an Anti-Royalist	175
The Secret of Happiness in England	177
Christmas in Wales	179
Being Caroline's Lodger	181
Rendering People Speechless	183
The Changing of a Guard	185

VOLUNTEERING

Wheat Beer or not Wheat Beer	189
And the Winner Is	191
Spin, LuLu, Spin	193
Massaging Dean Murphy	195
Like No Other Sound	197
Scraping the Easter Plates	199
The Grand Glaize Group	201

IN THE USA

Manure for Sale by Appointment Only	205
The Great Ship Went Down	207
My Heart Will Splurt Out and Land on the Floor	209
I Miss My Marines	211
Christ of the Blue Ridge	213
Omen Spelled Backwards	215

The Waltz Made Me Homesick 217

LUCK
You Have a Nice Catahoula Leopard 221
Crossing the Boundary with Joie De Vivre 223
There Is No Rum in the Life Savers 225
The Ultimate St. Louis Moment 227
You Pull the Duck and Run 229
Blowing in the Narragansett Wind 231
This Weather is Eleven Hours Old 233

FAMILY
The Duke of Windsor Orders a Pizza 237
The Saint and the Wobbly 239
All My Sufferings Are Nothing 241
The Hymn in the Dulcimer 243
My Embarrassing Aunt Margaret 245
We Have No Bishops Here 247

TRAVEL
Like the Arm of a Tattooed Lady 251
Come See My Archeology 253
My Camera as a Passport 255
It Sure Smells Genuine 257
The Volcano Will Blow Tonight 259
I Want a Frigate for My Birthday 261
Seven Floors of Japanese Handicrafts 263
Lining up to Rub Juliet's Right Breast 265
Wiping Yourself with Yesterday's News 267

ANIMALS
Stepping on Horseshoe Crabs 271
Puppies as a Crop 273
An Affinity for Warthogs 275
Still Skittish after All These Years 277
That is Not a Gift from God 279
A Fluffer at the Nationals 281

HOLIDAYS
You are at the Pirate's House 285
Thanksgivings without Turkey 287
Famous as a Holstein Cow 289
First Christmas in Africa 291

Removing Wallpaper without Harsh Chemicals 293
No Better Than a Billy Goat 295

LIFE LESSONS
Black Muddy River 299
Waiting for Intestines 301
Coincidence after Coincidence 303
Centering the Clay 305
Continuous vs. Continual 307
Confession in the Pharmacy 309
In the Fight between You and the World 311
Your Tuna Sandwich Will Be Here at 10:45 313

DEATH
Last Stop, Penn Station 317
The Blue-Eyed Girl Did Her Job Well 319
Taking on Human Form 321
Finding Solace 323
Us Schneiders Always Die on Holidays 325
Sighting a Doe 327
Unspeakable Things at the End of Road K 329

CLOSING
Say Good Night, Not Good-Bye 333

OPENING

2

THE LITTLE VOICE SPEAKS IN GALVESTON

Jokes in Search of an Audience

In those heady days when I first got Internet access, I received a lot of jokes via e-mail. I liked getting jokes; I would save them and pick out two good ones each day to forward to my friends.

I had a hard time predicting how people would react to my two-joke e-mails. Some people said they enjoyed them; some people asked me to never send them e-mails again. Once I sent out a joke about a bar mitzvah, and got differing reactions --- one person warned me that the joke might offend my Jewish friends; another person told me that she couldn't wait to tell the joke to her rabbi.

Then I noticed that the jokes on the Internet started to repeat. It became difficult to find fresh humor. Because the Internet allows jokes to be circulated widely, there was no audience for them anymore because everyone had heard them already.

I decided that I should stop sending my two-joke e-mails. I came to that decision shortly before we left for Christmas in Galveston in 2001.

Every Electric Appliance Imaginable

My buddy Randy and I rented a dog-friendly cottage in Galveston near the Gulf of Mexico.

It was clear that the cottage's owners liked going to antique shops and secondhand stores, and they used the cottage as a place to display their purchases. There was plenty of clutter.

The cottage also had every electric appliance imaginable: waffle iron, food processor, microwave, electric carving knife, coffee maker, and dishwasher. Plus a big-screen TV, which wasn't so common back in the year 2001.

One morning, while I was watching the big-screen TV, CNN announced that there had been a workplace massacre: A disgruntled employee had killed some coworkers at Edgewater Technologies in Wakefield, Massachusetts.

At this point, a little voice spoke to me in Galveston. The little voice told me that I should continue to watch CNN because I needed to hear the details of the massacre. I listened to the little voice and did what it said.

Within an hour, CNN displayed a list of the people killed, seven in all. One of the names displayed by CNN was Louis Javelle. He had been a friend of mine when I was in college.

The gunman was disgruntled because the IRS was planning to garnish his wages in order to pay the back taxes he owed. This is the reason why seven people were killed in cold blood.

Sudden and Senseless Death

Louis Javelle died suddenly. Louis Javelle died senselessly.

When it came time to leave Galveston and go back home to Missouri, I decided that I was going to use e-mail for something other than forwarding jokes. I was going to be personal, sending out my thoughts and my reminiscences. I would e-mail out a weekly vignette, a true-life story, which I called an ELetter.

Louis Javelle's sudden and senseless death showed me that life is very fragile. Sometimes, it seems that the only thing holding us on this planet is gravity.

LIVING IN AFRICA

Living in Africa

Living in Africa

SLAUGHTERING A CHICKEN FOR LUNCH

The Memorable Meringue

Some of my friends couldn't believe that I had a servant when I lived in Africa. They thought that having servants was un-American and elitist. And they definitely thought it was out of character for me. My response, "Everybody in Africa has servants."

When I first moved to Nigeria in 1965, visions of grass huts danced in my head. I saw myself as self-sufficient, living life as the locals did. However, Nigeria had a different vision for me. The government had built housing for teachers, and behind each teacher's house, the government built servants' quarters.

Instead of a grass hut, I wound up in a cement house. Instead of being self-sufficient, I wound up hiring a steward named Musa.

Musa cooked three meals a day for me, six days a week. He had learned to cook when he was in the British Army, fighting against the Japanese in the Burma Campaign in World War II.

My government house had a wood stove, and Musa had it mastered. I was impressed by the nice food he produced from a wood stove: He roasted, fried, boiled, and baked.

The most memorable item he baked was a meringue pie. When I cut into this pie, I expected to find a layer of lemon filling. Instead, I hit a layer of cream-of-wheat. Musa had baked a cream-of-wheat meringue pie.

What was Musa thinking? I guessed that Musa knew I had fruit for breakfast and you make pies with fruit. And I had cream-of-wheat for breakfast...and, therefore, you could make pies with cream-of-wheat. I valiantly ate a slice or two and then asked Musa to stick to fruit.

Off to Washington

A steward does more than cook. A steward does the food shopping, which is almost a daily activity in a tropical climate. He cleans the house, makes the beds, feeds the pets, washes clothes, and does the ironing. Ironing was the most impressive of these tasks because Nigerians use irons heated by charcoal.

In 1966, civil war broke out in Nigeria. Musa, because of his military experience, got an officer's commission and joined the Nigerian Army.

Living in Africa

After Musa, I hired a steward named Tarkwa. He was an excellent steward, and I had no problem when he said he needed to go visit his ailing father for a month. I said OK and asked where his father lived. Answer: in Washington.

I thought I might have misheard, but I checked the map and there really is a town called Washington, Nigeria. Tarkwa had a friend temp for him while he was in Washington. When Tarkwa came back, I did not have the heart to fire his friend, so I actually had two servants working for me.

Because my two servants were friends, they spent a lot of time chatting and not much time keeping my house in order. I learned that having one servant is better than having two.

Two Dry Footprints

Having servants meant that at age twenty-one, I became an employer.

Not only was I a good employer, I was also supporting a Nigerian family. I paid more than the going rate for the weekly wage. I paid on time. I paid extra if a steward had to do extra work.

I paid my servants' head tax. I bought them uniforms as they requested. I paid for one servant's wedding.

It was worth it. Teaching in the tropics was very tiring. When I came home from work, it was wonderful to find my lunch waiting for me, my bed made, my pets fed.

For anyone who thinks I had a servant because I wanted to be pampered, I have a response.

Imagine teaching in 104 degree temperatures, standing at a blackboard, and then noticing that there is a pool of sweat on the floor with two dry spots in it: Two spots showing where your feet were. Next, imagine arriving home hungry, slaughtering a chicken, and frying it.

Finally, imagine starting some charcoal burning so you can do your ironing after lunch. The temperature is still 104 degrees. About that time, you would decide that you want to support the local economy and hire a servant.

Living in Africa

ACCUSED OF SMUGGLING

The Great Art of Africa

It is ironic that you do not go to Africa if you want to see great African art. You have to go to Europe.

The reason is that the colonial powers basically stripped Africa clean of antiquities and filled up the museums of London, Brussels, Paris, and Berlin. The Berlin Museum alone has over 500,000 African pieces in its collection.

When Nigeria gained independence in 1960, they knew it was time to protect their antiquities. They defined an antiquity as any object over fifty years old. No one was allowed to take an antiquity out of Nigeria without a permit from the Antiquities Commission.

Making Something New Look Old

While living in Nigeria, I never had the chance to purchase an antiquity. At one point, however, I did buy a little carving. It cost $1.40, and it was obviously new. It was so obviously new that I stuck it out in my garden in hopes that the tropical African sun and rain would give the carving a weathered look.

It came time to move back to the United States. I took the cheap little carving out of the garden and put it in my suitcase. I went to the airport and had to go through outgoing customs.

It was here that a customs official spotted the cheap carving in my suitcase and announced that I was trying to smuggle a Nigerian antiquity out of the country.

"But this is clearly a new carving that I tried to make look old." "No, it is clearly an old carving that you tried to make look new. You are a smuggler."

I was stunned --- the carving was not an antiquity, I was not a smuggler. Defending myself would mean talking to more customs officials. The plane back to the United States was leaving in an hour. The next plane to the United States wasn't until four days later.

To Bribe or Not to Bribe

I was in a dilemma and had to make a quick judgment. Was this customs official being vigilant and did he truly believe that I was an antiquity

9

Living in Africa

smuggler? Or was this customs official seeking a bribe to persuade him to overlook the carving in my suitcase?

I could certainly make a case that I was not guilty of being a smuggler. But if I offered a bribe, then I was definitely guilty of something.

Not only could a bribe backfire, but I had never bribed someone before. How should I bribe? How much money was enough? And what currency should I offer --- Nigerian or American? And what do you say when you bribe a customs official --- what are the exact words?

I startled to tremble as I made my decision. I fished around in my wallet and found a ten-dollar bill. I made sure no one was looking and furtively offered the customs official the ten dollars, saying, "I think we can end our discussion."

Bribe accepted. Discussion ended. Suitcase closed and placed on the conveyor belt.

I went to the waiting room and buried my face in a *Newsweek*. I was hoping no customs officials would come into the waiting room searching for the American who was a proven bribe giver and a suspected smuggler.

Got on the plane. Fastened seat belt. The plane took off.

When I heard the landing gear retract into the fuselage, I stopped trembling.

Living in Africa

TO SIT, PERCHANCE TO SQUAT

Like Seeing an Old Friend

On vacation in Italy in 2008, I left my five traveling companions in Verona and went on my own to Trieste.

When I got off the train in Trieste, I had to use the men's restroom, and I saw something I had not seen for a long time: a natural-position toilet.

A natural-position toilet is a large porcelain square that is embedded in the floor. There is no water in the toilet. You place your feet on the two porcelain foot pads, squat down, do your business, stand up, pull a chain --- and then water rushes through the porcelain square and cleans it out.

For me, seeing this toilet in Trieste was like seeing an old friend because I had a squat toilet in my house in Kano, Nigeria.

I knew the advantages of squatting: It puts pressure on your kidneys and pushes out toxic waste; it does not damage the prostate nerve; it means that your buttocks do not sit on a surface that some stranger's buttocks had sat on a few minutes before.

When I got back to Verona, I told my American traveling companions about using a squat toilet and told them how beneficial squat toilets are.

They were not impressed. In fact, they were horrified.

My Aim Is True

The squat toilet in my house in Kano, Nigeria, in the 1970's was not a nice porcelain model with convenient footpads that flushed into a sewer system.

Instead, I had a three-inch diameter hole in a cement floor. My waste matter fell through the hole into a catch basin that had been excavated in the ground. When you fill up the catch basin, a crew comes, breaks up your cement floor, cleans out the basin, re-cements your floor, and you are ready to go again.

Although squatting is a healthy way to move your bowels, you do need to have good aim. A three-inch hole is not very big, and even if it were big, you cannot see it because you are squatting over it.

Once I became proficient, my aim was a matter of pride. Every trip to the bathroom was an accomplishment.

Living in Africa

Turkey Was Hilarious

I enjoyed living in my adobe house on the outskirts of Kano.

One of my big dreams was that my parents would fly over from the United States and visit me. I pictured showing them the school where I taught and showing them how hospitable the students and staff are. I pictured my neighbors greeting them. I pictured my friends showing them around town.

When I went back to the United States on vacation in 1972, I had my parents invite their friends Ed and Mildred over for dinner. Ed and Mildred were the same age as my parents, and they had done a lot of world traveling. I figured that during dinner, I would suggest that my parents travel to Nigeria, and Ed and Mildred would encourage them to go.

To set the tone, I got Ed and Mildred talking about their travels, and somehow they started talking about their visit to Turkey and how hilarious it was. It turned out that Turkey was hilarious because there are squat toilets in Turkey. Ed, Mildred, Mom, and Dad were all laughing and laughing at the idea of a squat toilet.

I was not laughing. I was crushed. I did not bring up the idea of my parents traveling to Nigeria.

It did not matter that their dear sweet son was living in Nigeria; once Mom and Dad found out that there are squat toilets in Nigeria, they would never consider visiting me there.

Living in Africa

FREEZING IN AFRICA

Freezing in Africa

Africa is supposed to be the land of hot sun with sweltering days and torrid tropical nights.

When it came time to pack my suitcase and my foot locker for two years in Africa, I ignored a footnote in the Peace Corps' list of things to pack for living in Africa. The footnote said, "Perhaps you might want to take a light sweater with you since there may be a few chilly mornings in Nigeria." Pack a light sweater? Not me!

Turns out that I severely regretted not packing a light sweater --- I even regretted not packing a heavy sweater. There is such a thing as cold weather in Kano, Nigeria.

In northern Nigeria, the months of December and January are known as 'harmattan', the season when a dust-laden wind blows south from the Sahara.

The daytime temperatures don't go above eighty-five degrees Fahrenheit, and when the sun goes down, the nighttime temperatures plunge to fifty degrees. The giant drop in temperature makes you feel chilled to the bone. Everybody wraps up in blankets.

But a blanket was no help when I drove my motorcycle through the streets of Kano at nighttime. I was freezing; I didn't even have a light sweater.

Marrying an Older Woman

But there was someone in Kano who was all warm and cozy when he drove his motorcycle.

That was Fred Winch. Fred was a Peace Corps Volunteer from upstate New York. He had the foresight to bring a plaid wool jacket with him to Nigeria. The wool jacket was perfect for driving a motorcycle through the streets of Kano during harmattan.

One day Fred told me that he was moving back to the United States.

Fred said, "I am going back to upstate New York after I marry my girlfriend. I am worried about how my family will react because she is British, and she is eleven years older than me. I am very worried."

Living in Africa

I paid no attention to Fred's concern about earning his family's approval. Instead, I responded, "Really? Will you sell me your plaid wool jacket before you leave?"

Heading into the Army

I drove warm and cozy in Fred's plaid wool jacket until the Tet Offensive of January 1968 in Vietnam.

The war in Vietnam was not going well, and Uncle Sam had the largest monthly draft in history: 45,000 men. I was one of them.

I had tried a number of maneuvers to get out of being drafted, but to no avail. The Nigerian government even went through its ambassador in Washington to try to get me out of being drafted.

It was time to leave Kano. One by one, I told my friends the sad news. I said, "I am going back to the United States to serve in the army. The war is not going well, and I am worried that the army will send me to fight in Vietnam and I might get killed. I am very worried."

One by one, my friends paid no attention to my concern about getting killed in Vietnam. Instead, they responded, "Really? Will you sell me your plaid wool jacket before you leave?"

Living in Africa

LOVE AND CHOLERA

Living Through an Epidemic

This grudge goes back to 1988, and it was a comment by a book critic in the Boston Globe newspaper that got my goat. The book critic was reviewing *Love in the Time of Cholera* by the Colombian author, Gabriel Garcia Marquez.

The critic stated, "This is one of the best books of the year, but *Love in the Time of Cholera* is one of the stupidest titles of the year."

The critic obviously had never lived through a cholera epidemic, as I did.

You Vomit out Your Life

Cholera is frightening because it kills swiftly --- one moment, you are alive; the next moment you start to vomit; and when you have finished vomiting, you are dead.

Cholera is not so easy to avoid; it is spread via drinking water. Every time you lift a teacup to your lips, every time you lift a glass to your lips, every time you lift a coffee mug to your lips, every time you lift a thermos cup to your lips --- you wonder if it will be your last drink.

I lived through the cholera epidemic in Kano, Nigeria, in 1970.

The disease was raging throughout the city. Friends told me they saw people vomit and die right before their eyes. However, the Nigerian government was hushing it up because it was time for the pilgrimage to Mecca. If the Saudi Arabian government found out that Nigeria had a cholera epidemic, it would not allow Nigerian pilgrims to go to Mecca.

So the cholera epidemic had to be kept quiet, even when the garbage trucks in Kano no longer collected garbage --- they were too busy collecting corpses.

Love, in the Time of Cholera

At the end of 1988, that blasted Boston Globe book critic put *Love in the Time of Cholera* on his list of best books of the year and used that opportunity to reiterate his comment about how stupid the title was.

Living in Africa

But, Mr. Book Critic, I know that the time of cholera is an eerie time. The possibility of a swift death adds an edge to everything. When you say good night to your beloved, you do not know if they will be alive in the morning.

The time of cholera makes love important and precious.

Living in Africa

NEVER SQUISH IT; ALWAYS FLICK IT

Blistered by the Alarm Clock

When I arrived in Africa in 1965, I had to learn how to sleep inside a mosquito net.

There is a technique to unfurling a mosquito net so that nasty insects don't fly inside it. There is a technique to tucking it in so that no nasty insects can crawl inside it and a technique to slipping yourself inside so that no nasty insects take advantage of the brief opening.

It's a cozy world; cocooned from the abundant African insect life.

One morning, when I had been in Africa for about two weeks, my alarm clock blistered me. I had reached out of the mosquito net to turn off the alarm, and when I pulled my hand back inside the net, there was a large blister on the back of my hand.

The blister hurt. I popped it. The fluid inside the blister ran down my forearm and created more blisters. I was mystified. And I was concerned that the blisters would propagate themselves ad infinitum all over my body.

I was a schoolteacher, and when I got to work that morning, I described what had happened. Another teacher explained that a cantharides beetle must have been sitting on the clock when the alarm went off. The beetle excretes a fluid that causes blisters. I recognized cantharides as the beetle that is ground up to make Spanish fly, the aphrodisiac.

My fellow teacher gave me specific advice: Swab the area around the blisters with a thick layer of Vaseline, then pop the blisters so that the fluid does not touch any exposed skin. Only then will the vicious cycle end.

He added some good advice for living in Africa: never squish an insect that lands on you; always flick it off.

Ants in the Sugar Bowl; Geckos on the Wall

I realized that if I was going to live in Africa, I had to live in peace with insects.

When I found ants in the sugar bowl, I just took the bowl outside and placed it in a patch of sunlight. The ants crawled out of the bowl and headed for shade. I would then go back inside and sprinkle some sugar on my breakfast cereal.

Living in Africa

In the tropics, it seemed like there was an insect-of-the-week program. One week there would be swarms of flying insects with diaphanous wings; the next week there would be lots of dull brown crawling things. Each week would feature a different insect, and I enjoyed the show.

The geckos on the walls in my house also enjoyed the show. They spent most of their time motionless on the walls until an insect-of-the-week came within range. The gecko would gobble the insect and then go back to being motionless.

I did not enjoy mosquitoes. The mosquito net only protected me for eight hours, while I slept. The other sixteen hours of the day, I was exposed. It was inevitable that a female anopheles mosquito would bite me and malaria would enter my body. You cannot cure malaria, you can only suppress it. So every Sunday I took an antimalarial pill, so bitter that I shuddered violently when I swallowed it.

The pill kept the malaria at bay, and I learned to live in peace with the malaria parasites in my body, as well as the amoebas in my body that gave me chronic dysentery.

Insects, parasites, amoebas, geckos: I had come to terms with living in Africa

<u>Screaming Out Loud</u>

Then I moved to a different house, which had a pit latrine.

I never once saw a gecko in the pit latrine, probably because the pit latrine had giant African cockroaches. "Giant" was an appropriate description: The shiny brown roaches were from three to four inches in length. They were bigger than the geckos.

When I entered my latrine (which I did frequently because of dysentery), the roaches would scurry back into the pit or climb up the wall. The roaches were creepy, but as long as they acted afraid of me, I was OK.

Then came the day when I discovered that giant roaches could fly. When I entered the latrine, two of them did not scurry away, they flew right at me. I batted them away with my arm. It was the only time during my six years in Africa that I screamed out loud.

The giant cockroaches taught me a lesson: I could never make peace with them.

They never flew at me again, but from that time on, whenever I entered my latrine, I recognized that I was vulnerable. These African insects had taught me that I was not the master of my own house.

Living in Africa

A CRAZED HERD OF STAMPEDING GOATS

Days Made for Motorcycles

Certain days feel like they are made for motorcycles. The temperature, the air, the humidity, and the light are all perfect for riding.

A motorcycle was my only means of transportation for five years when I lived in Africa. There were many African days that felt like they were made for motorcycles. On those days I pitied the people who drove automobiles. They were all boxed up in their vehicles; they were disconnected from the feel of the African day.

On a motorcycle, I drove with no barrier between me and the African day; I was bathed in the ambient temperatures; enjoyed the clarity of the air, and felt the humidity while gliding through the ambient light.

Motorcyclists are in touch with their surroundings.

An Unexpected Clap of Thunder

But being in touch with your surroundings means you are also exposed to the consequences of your surroundings.

One afternoon I was driving past the main mosque in Kano, Nigeria, trying to get home before an impending rainstorm. There was a clap of thunder, which must have crazed a herd of goats gathered in an alley. The herd stampeded and came shooting out of the alley, knocking me off my motorcycle.

My face hit the street. The visor on my helmet kept my eye from getting gouged, but the visor did not cover my chin, and I had a gash in my chin. Passersby stored my motorcycle and got me to the hospital.

The doctor at the hospital took out a needle and thread. Without anesthesia, he started to sew my chin back together.

Then the doctor realized that sewing a chin back together is a two-person procedure. He turned to his right to ask a nurse to assist him. At this point, my chin was connected to the doctor by the thread, so my chin had to follow the doctor's hand. Unfortunately, I had arrived at the hospital at a change of shift. This nurse was heading home and would not stay to help the doctor.

Living in Africa

The doctor turned to his left, with my chin following him, to ask another nurse to help. Same story: this nurse was changing her shift and would not stay to help. The doctor could not find any nurse to assist him in sewing up my chin.

He did the best he could by himself.

The Twenty-Five-Year Beard

As soon as my chin healed, I grew a beard. I wanted to cover up the permanent gash on my chin resulting from the rough sewing effort in the hospital.

The beard lasted twenty-five years.

I finally got up the courage to shave and expose the gash on my chin. Without a beard, I felt like I was walking around with a big sign that said, "Look! I have a gash on my chin."

But nobody said anything.

In fact, nobody noticed. Even when I pointed to the badly sewn gash on my chin, people said it was no big deal.

This was disappointing. I thought people would notice my chin and ask me how I got the gash. Then I could tell them about how certain days are perfect for riding motorcycles, but you have to keep your eye out for crazed herds of stampeding goats.

Living in Africa

THE SACRED CROCODILES OF ZURU

At Sokoto Advanced Teachers College

In 1975-1976, I was on the faculty of Sokoto Advanced Teachers College. Sokoto is in the northwest corner of Nigeria. One of the nice features of working at the college was going out to observe our students during teaching practice.

We sent our students out to high schools all over Sokoto State to practice teach, and I was assigned to observe the practice teaching in Zuru. Zuru was a long drive: it was the southern-most town in the state.

I planned my time in Zuru so I could observe teaching practice and I would also have time to be a tourist. I had never been to Zuru before, and there were two things I wanted to see.

First, I wanted to see the sacred crocodiles of Zuru. The crocodiles were powerful: If you gave them an offering, they would grant wishes.

Second, I wanted to see some Dakakari grave sculptures. The sculptures, sprinkled about the countryside, dated back to the early twentieth century; they were made of clay and placed on the graves of important people, depicting events in their lives.

In the Sacred Grove

In Zuru, a British woman named Alison volunteered to show me around the town on her motorcycle. She drove me to see the sacred crocodiles, which lived in a sacred grove three miles out in the countryside.

She parked just outside the grove. We were the only people there, and we approached the crocodiles on foot. The crocodiles were lounging near a pool of water, and there were a number of chickens walking around.

Alison explained that the chickens were the sacrifices. Most of the people who went to the crocodiles were women, hoping to be granted fertility.

I was fascinated. The crocodiles were huge, probably from an abundant supply of live chickens. Then my mood changed from fascination to wariness when I noticed that there was no fence. There was nothing between us and the huge crocodiles except some trees and a few chickens.

Living in Africa

I took a quick photo and told Alison that I wanted to leave. I tried to hide the fact that I was worried about being eaten by a crocodile, sacred or not, three miles from the nearest town.

The Grave Sculptures by the Mud Hut

Alison knew where the sacred crocodiles were, but she had never seen any Dakakari grave sculptures.

I spotted a path leading through a valley and suggested she drive the motorcycle down the path to see if we came across any graves. The first set of graves we came to had no sculptures. Maybe the people in the graves weren't important, or maybe the graves used to have sculptures but someone sold them to a museum.

We drove a little further, and we came across a second set of graves near a mud hut. The graves had sculptures on top of them. We stopped the motorcycle, and I started to take photos of the graves.

At this point, a man came out of the mud hut and started walking toward us, holding a sheet of paper. I stopped taking photos.

Maybe the man was going to yell at me for taking photos of his ancestors' graves. Maybe he was going to accuse me of wanting to sell the grave sculptures to a museum. Maybe he was going to tell us to go away because we were trespassing.

The man spoke to us in English. Instead of yelling at me or accusing me or telling me to go away, he asked me if I thought Manchester United was going to beat Arsenal.

The piece of paper he was holding was a betting sheet. He wanted me to predict a British soccer match. I was dumbfounded. I knew more about sacred crocodiles than I knew about British soccer.

Alison then spoke up in a very confident British voice, "Manchester United." The man, happy to have gotten a prediction, went back to his mud hut.

I got on the back of Alison's motorcycle. Before she started to drive back to Zuru, Alison turned around and gave me a handy piece of advice. Here, in a little valley a few miles from the southernmost town in Sokoto State, she told me, "Always pick Manchester United."

22

Living in Africa

BURNING DOWN THE FIRE STATION

Am I the Only One?

I was teaching at a girls' boarding school in Kano, Nigeria, when the Ministry of Education announced that every school in the city had to send a staff member to a fire fighting course.

The principal told me, "Since Mr. Ogundeji is having eye surgery, you are the only one I can send. You will need to attend a two-day course at the main fire station to get certified."

I did not take this news lightly --- mainly because I was a believer in equality for women. Every day, in my teaching, I was striving to give the girls at the school a good education so that they would be the equal of the boys getting an education in Kano.

The school staff consisted of twenty-three women and two men. Why didn't the principal send one of the female teachers to the fire fighting course? Choosing between the two men on staff was not only sexist, it was impractical. Both Mr. Ogundeji and I lived miles away from the campus; we could not respond to a fire at night. Most of the women teachers lived in staff housing right there on campus.

I showed up at the main fire station, feeling grumbly. Eight schools (three girls' schools and five boys' schools) sent teachers for training, which consisted of a day of fire-fighting theory and a day of fire-fighting practice.

Wood, Cooking Oil, Old Boots

The fire chief dispensed a lot of fire-fighting theory. On day one, we learned about fire temperatures, types of fires, and types of fire extinguishers. We learned flash point, smoke point, and ignition point.

We even learned the water pressure in pounds per square inch in a fire hydrant. One teacher asked how many fire hydrants there were in Kano. Answer: only five --- and none of them was anywhere near a school.

When the teachers arrived for day two, the fire chief had lined up some different types of fire extinguishers in front of the fire station. He was getting ready for the three fires we were to fight: a wood fire, a cooking oil fire, and a fire of old boots.

23

Living in Africa

The first fire, a wood fire, made sense. Most of the people in Kano cooked with wood. The chief asked for a volunteer. A teacher stepped forward and picked out the proper type of fire extinguisher for a wood fire. The chief proceeded to set a pile of wood on fire; the teacher put out the fire. We cheered.

The second fire, a cooking oil fire, made sense. Most food in Kano was cooked in peanut oil in large pots that resembled woks. A teacher stepped forward, chose the proper extinguisher, and waited while the chief poured some peanut oil in a wok and set it on fire. The teacher put out the fire. We cheered.

The third fire, a fire of old boots, made no sense.

The Plastic Jerry Can

A volunteer teacher stood ready with a fire extinguisher as the fire chief lit a couple of matches and tried to get a pile of old boots to burn. He was having no luck, so he asked a fireman named James to go get a jerry can of gasoline. When the James brought the gasoline, the chief told him to pour some gasoline on the old boots.

All the teachers gasped. We knew there were a couple of matches lurking in the pile of old boots, and those matches were probably still glowing. We started backing away from the old boots.

Sure enough, as James poured gasoline on the boots, a river of flame worked its way up to the jerry can. When the flames reached James' hand, he let out a scream and tossed the flaming can high in the air. The can was made of plastic and burst open upon landing, sending a big wall of flame creeping across the ground right toward the fire station.

The fire siren went off, announcing that there was a fire in the city. All the on-duty firemen followed procedure by jumping in the fire engines, and starting up the motors. They did not go anywhere, because the fire was right there in front of them.

Eventually, the wall of flames was halted. We had almost burned down the fire station.

For me, the most important thing about the two-day course was the fact that one girls' school had sent a female teacher to the course, and one girls' school had sent a nun. My girls' school had sent a male teacher. I continued to feel grumbly.

PROUD MOMENTS

Proud Moments

PEANUT BUTTER STEW

The Dictator's Sister

The word "dictator" conjures up an image of ruthlessness. However, when I was living in Nigeria in the early 1970's, Nigeria had a very benevolent dictator. He was the supreme military commander, and I was once invited to his sister's house for dinner.

The dictator's sister served peanut butter stew.

Peanut butter stew shows off one of Nigeria's major exports: peanuts. The stew itself contains tomato, onion, ginger, chicken, and ground peanuts, but it is the toppings that make the dish special.

We dinner guests were given plates, and we had to assemble our dinner. First there was a big bowl of rice, and I put a pile of rice on my plate. Then came a big bowl of stew, and I spooned some stew over my rice. Then came the highlight of the meal: lots of little dishes of toppings. The dishes held banana slices, raw onion, orange segments, shaved coconut, mango pieces, peanuts, tomato chunks, raisins, chopped hard-boiled guinea fowl eggs, and cut-up papaya. The papaya came from a tree in the backyard.

I spooned lots of the toppings over my stew. My dinner plate looked like an ice cream sundae.

The peanut butter stew was tasty and colorful; the dictator's sister gave me her recipe.

The Connecticut Legislator

A couple of years later, I was visiting my parents and I made peanut butter stew for them --- even though they did not have a papaya tree in their backyard.

The stew was a hit with my parents, and my mother insisted that I make it for my cousin, who was coming to visit. My cousin was a former Connecticut legislator, and I think my mother wanted to dazzle her.

Peanut butter is an acceptor of flavors, and it allows you to go from the sweetness of oranges and raisins to the sharpness of raw onion to the crunchiness of peanuts to the mushiness of bananas. My cousin and her family were dazzled.

Proud Moments

So peanut butter stew became my signature dish. I have cooked it in the United States, in Britain, and in Belgium, where I stayed with a friend for three months in 1976.

The Star Ballerina

In the United States, most ballet companies put on *The Nutcracker* every year to raise money. In Brussels, the major ballet company was called The Ballet of the Twentieth Century. The company director had choreographed Beethoven's *Ninth Symphony*, and it was danced every year to raise money.

One night while I was in Brussels, my host and I went to see Beethoven's *Ninth Symphony*. It was a big production: a symphony orchestra, Congolese drummers, a large choir, and many dancers, including children. The production was so big that it was held in a sports arena. The arena was packed with dance enthusiasts --- everyone was dressed up in spite of the fact that they had to sit on bleachers.

The star ballerina was an American named Diane Gray-Cullert. They flew her to Brussels just to dance in this production. She danced brilliantly, and when she took her final bow, the audience went wild. They applauded, they cheered, and, because they were sitting on bleachers in a sports arena, they stomped their feet.

My host knew Diane and took me backstage to introduce me to her. What a thrill --- getting to meet the star ballerina.

"Diane, I would like you to meet my friend, Doug Schneider."

Her eyes opened wide. "Doug Schneider! Are you really Doug Schneider? I've wanted to meet you. Aren't you the person who makes peanut butter stew?"

I was flabbergasted. Instead of me telling the star ballerina that I admired her, she was telling me that she admired me.

I figured out how Diane Gray-Cullert knew about my stew. A few days before, I was in my host's kitchen cooking peanut butter stew while the Brussels Shakespeare Society was rehearsing in his living room. Diane was staying with one of the members of the society, who must have told Diane about the aromas that wafted through the Shakespearean rehearsal.

Peanut butter stew had made me a star in the eyes of a star.

Proud Moments

THERE GOES THE JUDGE

Loss of Dignity

After my open heart surgery in 2004, I was taken to the Intensive Care Unit.

The ICU room they put me in was a double, but I was by myself. I noticed that there was a television hanging from the ceiling. I was glad I had the room to myself because I could keep the television off. I needed peace and quiet for my recovery.

Also, I was glad to have the room to myself because I was wearing a hospital gown. These gowns are made of flimsy cloth; they are wide open at the back; they offer very little modesty; they impose a loss of dignity.

The hospital gown made me very reluctant to get out of bed and be seen by other people.

Here Comes the Judge

Suddenly there was a flurry of activity. A nurse told me that I was getting a roommate, and he was a judge for St. Louis County. They wheeled in the judge and I said hello. He said hello, and then he grabbed the remote.

To my dismay, the judge turned on the TV. He flipped through the channels and started to watch "Divorce Court."

I found it hard to believe that I had a roommate who was a county judge who was watching "Divorce Court." Maybe he was playing a practical joke on me.

However, the theme continued. When "Divorce Court" ended, my roommate started to watch "Judge Joe Brown." I realized I was stuck in a room watching a judge who was watching judges on TV.

I began to despair, thinking of all the Judge Judy shows and Judge Wapner re-runs that were going to be forced on me.

I wondered how to get rid of the judge. Then I remembered that I was wearing a hospital gown.

Saved by the Gown

I waited until the judge's wife came to visit him. She settled into a chair and started to watch television with her husband. They were watching "The Peoples Court."

Now was the time to wash my hands at the sink, which was located right below the television. I creaked out of bed. I used one hand to steady myself as I hobbled over to the sink, and I used the other hand to hold my hospital gown shut in the back.

Well, of course, you need two hands when washing your hands, so I had to let go of the gown, and it flew open. I slowly washed my hands as I mooned the judge and his wife.

Shortly after I finished, the judge's wife left the room, and shortly after that, the nurses wheeled her husband to another room.

The judge was gone, but the television was still showing "The Peoples Court." I grabbed the remote, clicked off Ed Koch, and reveled in the peace and quiet.

I was back on the road to recovery.

Proud Moments

THE MAN OF THE YEAR ASKS ME ONE QUESTION

Tony and His Pony

Although I had never taught reading before, my assignment at the Fort Lewis School Command was to teach army inductees how to read.

The teaching material I got from the School Command was a set of *Readers Digest* special editions. These contained regular *Readers Digest* articles that had been simplified down to the fifth-grade reading level. However, the covers looked just like a regular *Readers Digest*.

My first class of army inductees showed up; all of them were at third-grade reading level. I handed them each a copy of a special *Readers Digest*. One soldier took one look at the Reader's Digest cover and let out a sigh of relief: Thank God, we do not have to read *Tony Has a Pony*.

With that comment, a lightbulb went off in my head: I realized how I was going to teach these guys to read. They were grownups, and they needed grownup material. If I handed them a children's book, they would never make an effort to read.

So, I supplemented the *Readers Digests*. I typed out articles from *Time* magazine, simplifying as I went. I typed out short stories, simplifying as I went. I typed out an extract from Joan Baez' autobiography, simplifying.

The soldiers responded well. I decided that the best thing I could do for them was to get them to enjoy reading.

Big Cans of Brasso

I was teaching as part of an army program called McNamara's Hundred Thousand. The head of the army wanted to see how the program was doing, and, for some reason, he was scheduled to come visit my classroom.

Any visit by any army bigwig meant that the classroom had to be spic and span.

The School Command brought in a cleaning crew. They waxed and buffed the floors, washed the windows, and checked all the light bulbs to make sure the bulbs were all the same wattage. The classroom was in a wooden building and contained plenty of fire extinguishers; the cleaning crew had big cans of Brasso and made those fire extinguishers shine.

Proud Moments

The colonel from the School Command came and gave my classroom a thorough inspection. He approved of the floors, the windows, the light bulbs, and the gleaming fire extinguishers.

However, he stopped short in front of a large black-and-white poster of Muhammad Ali that was taped on the wall next to the blackboard. "You better take that down, Schneider."

I took the Muhammad Ali poster down. The classroom was ready for the head of the United States Army.

One and Only One Question

On the morning of the visit, the students and I did not have to wait long before William Westmoreland showed up in my classroom.

William Westmoreland, a five-star general, had been the commander of American military operations in Vietnam, but now he was on the Joint Chiefs of Staff. He was an advisor to the president of the United States.

Time magazine had named him Man of the Year.

And the Man of the Year was standing in my classroom with his entourage. William Westmoreland asked one and only one question:

"Are these soldiers learning to read?"

I knew I did not want to respond with a pointless "Yes, sir." Instead, I mustered enough composure to articulate my philosophy. "Sir, I am doing more than teaching these soldiers how to read. I am teaching them to enjoy reading."

The Man of the Year seemed satisfied with my answer. He swept out of the classroom, followed by his entourage.

I don't think William Westmoreland even noticed how shiny all the fire extinguishers were. And he certainly did not notice the blank spot on the wall where the poster of Muhammad Ali used to be.

Proud Moments

THE SCOURGE RAISES A RUCKUS

Proof He Has not Spent the Money

Years ago, Kevin Olmstead won a record-breaking $2,000,000 on the television show "Who Wants to Be a Millionaire." The ratings for the show had been sagging, so they were offering a million-dollar bonus at the time. Kevin got a million for answering the million-dollar question correctly, and he got a second million as a bonus.

In an interview, Kevin Olmstead said that he had not decided how to spend his two million, and it was sitting in his bank account. When the interviewer expressed some doubt, Kevin took an ATM receipt out of his wallet and held it up for the camera---account balance: $2,000,000.

The ATM receipt caught my attention because I used to earn my living supporting ATMs for BayBanks.

BayBanks was a medium-sized bank (nine billion dollars in assets) in New England that had figured out how to compete with big banks. BayBanks got into ATMs early, putting machines in the busiest locations in Boston. Their ATM location in Harvard Square had nine machines and was so busy that there was usually an ankle-deep layer of discarded ATM receipts on the floor.

I was in the IT department at BayBanks, responsible for the software that sent transactions from the machines to the main computer at the bank. The software was so reliable that our ATMs had earned the trust of the people in Massachusetts.

The only other bank in the United States that had a busier ATM network was Citibank (a whopping 310 billion dollars in assets). We were a David to Citibank's Goliath.

My Proposal Is Absurd

In 1989, the largest number a BayBanks' ATM receipt could show was $999,999.99. I was concerned.

I was at a meeting and proposed that BayBanks should expand the amount field on the receipt to display amounts in the millions. I even made an estimate of how many hours the project would take. The other people at the meeting went into a state of ridicule.

I was told that no one in their right mind would ever have a balance of a million dollars in a BayBanks account. I was told my proposal was absurd.

33

Proud Moments

I left BayBanks in 1991, and one year later there was a customer who had a balance of more than a million dollars in his BayBanks account. He had $1,026,000, and his ATM receipt truncated his balance, telling him that he only had $26,000 in the bank.

This was no ordinary customer; this man was an attorney.

The Scourge of the Criminal Justice System

This man was no ordinary attorney; he was O. J. Simpson's attorney.

Everyone in Massachusetts knows Alan Dershowitz's name. In addition to representing O. J. Simpson, he has represented Leona Helmsley, Jim Bakker, John DeLorean, Claus von Bulow, and Patty Hearst. *Life* magazine dubbed him "The Scourge of the Criminal Justice System."

And The Scourge raised a big stink about his BayBanks ATM receipt. His receipt made it look like a million dollars had vanished into thin air.

When Alan Dershowitz raises a ruckus, you have to listen. BayBanks immediately did a high-priority rush project to display amounts of a million dollars or more on ATM receipts. The project, ironically, took just as many hours as I had estimated back in 1989.

Of course, if BayBanks had listened to Doug Schneider back in 1989, they could have avoided a rush project and they could have avoided the wrath of Alan Dershowitz altogether.

It's so nice to feel vindicated.

Proud Moments

BIG ASS BEER

<u>Up the Mississippi from New Orleans</u>

St. Louis was founded in 1764 by French Catholic settlers who came up the Mississippi River from New Orleans, so it is natural that St. Louis celebrates Mardi Gras.

In February 2008, I helped St. Louis celebrate by volunteering for a beer booth. I got a 3 PM to 6 PM shift.

On the Saturday before Fat Tuesday, cars are banned from twenty-five city blocks in an area of the city with the fine French name of *Soulard*. This is where Mardi Gras is held; our beer booth was in Soulard.

I went down to Soulard in the morning and walked around the car-free zone. Soulard was built as a residential neighborhood in the mid-nineteenth century, and it was a treat to look at all these old houses without any cars parked in front of them.

The sky cleared; the sun came out; the revelers started showing up. The first goal of the revelers is to snag as many beads as possible. The beads are thrown from the 100 floats in the mid-day parade that is held on the largest street in Soulard.

After the Mardi Gras parade, the revelers then stormed into Soulard for their second goal: to consume as much alcohol as possible. In 2008, there were at least 100,000 people at Mardi Gras.

<u>Twenty-Four Ounces</u>

Our beer booth was competing with all the other beer booths. Soulard, in nineteenth-century fashion, has a bar on every corner, so we were also competing with the bars. Plus we were competing with the heated beer tents that had been erected for Mardi Gras.

When I started my shift, I quickly figured out that you do not sell a beer to someone who already has a beer. I looked for people walking by our booth with no drink in hand. I needed a hook to catch their attention.

I shouted at them: "Twenty-four ounce beer!" This got their interest. Then I shouted: "Big ass beer!!" This really got their interest, and many came over to our booth and bought a beer.

Proud Moments

This was a little odd, given that every other booth was also selling twenty-four ounce beers. But nobody at the other booths was pointing it out. Since a reveler wants to consume lots of alcohol, hearing "twenty four ounces" was a big draw.

Push Product

At our volunteer training, I learned that we were not selling beer, we were "pushing product." The more product you pushed, the more money your organization earned.

So I was pushing product as fast as I could when I realized that I had neglected to card people. At this point three policemen came up and surrounded me. They said they were there for the pick-up.

Pick-up? Had I sold a beer to a minor? Was I being arrested?? How would they get a paddy wagon through the streets of Soulard, which were jam-packed with 100,000 bead-wearing, beer-swilling revelers???

Actually, the police were there because the excess cash in our beer booth's money drawer was being picked up.

My shift ended; it was getting dark and windy. Most of the revelers had taken shelter in a bar or a heated beer tent for the evening.

I headed home on that February night. I was pleased that I had pushed product and pleased that I had found a hook to bring revelers to our booth. When I got home, out of curiosity, I looked up the word *Soulard* in a French-English dictionary.

I found out that it means "drunkard."

36

Proud Moments

HOGAN IS NOT A NAME

Making Friends with Scrabble

I always brought a Scrabble set along with me on my travels.

I threw away the Scrabble box, kept the Scrabble board, and put the tiles and the racks in a plastic bag. The board and plastic bag did not take up a lot of space in my suitcase.

I used my Scrabble set when I was on a passenger ship going to Sweden. I was in the lounge playing with a British fellow. Everything was going along fine until I played the word NIXED. He claimed it was not a word. I accused him of trying to rob me of a triple-letter score for the letter X. NIXED is the past tense of NIX, which means to veto something.

A woman strolled over and asked us what was going on. The British fellow said that NIXED was not a word. The woman said, "Yes, NIXED is a word. It is the past tense of NIX, which means to veto something."

Not only did I get the triple-letter score, I also found out that the woman was an American traveling solo to Stockholm. We spent a couple days of sightseeing in Stockholm.

Without my Scrabble set, I never would have made friends with a fellow traveler.

Creating Elation with Scrabble

I used my Scrabble set in Cambridge, England, where I had been invited to spend New Year's at the home of Leslie Barnett.

Leslie was a professor at Cambridge University, where she had researched DNA. Although Crick and Watson got the Nobel Prize for their work on DNA, it was really Leslie Barnett who had proven that DNA was a mathematical code.

Leslie's family and I played Scrabble in the living room. Everything was going along fine until I played the word BOCK. Leslie claimed that BOCK was not a word; I accused her of trying to rob me of a triple-word score. BOCK was strong dark beer brewed in the springtime.

I asked for a dictionary. BOCK was not in this dictionary. Then I noticed that the dictionary was printed in London; so, I asked for a dictionary printed in America.

37

Proud Moments

Leslie and her family had lived in New Jersey for a year, and her younger daughter did have an American dictionary, which she fetched from her bedroom. BOCK was in this dictionary, defined as a strong dark beer brewed in the springtime.

I was elated. Not only did I get the triple-word score, I had challenged one of the sharpest minds in twentieth-century science, and I had triumphed.

Enjoying Irony with Scrabble

I used my Scrabble set in Bida, Nigeria, where some British friends of mine lived.

One night we went out to a local bar and started playing Scrabble. Everything was going along fine until I played the word HOGAN. My British friends insisted that Hogan was a name; I accused them of trying to rob me of some points. Hogan was a word; it meant a Navajo Indian dwelling.

A man strolled over and asked us what was going on. My British friends claimed that HOGAN was a name and could not be used in Scrabble. The fellow said, "But, HOGAN is a word. It is a Navajo Indian dwelling."

My British friends asked the fellow if he was an American. He said that he was a Palestinian.

Not only did I get my points for HOGAN, I got to enjoy some sweet irony: A Palestinian telling some British people to let an American play a Navajo word in a Nigerian bar in the middle of Africa.

That is why I always brought a Scrabble set along with me on my travels.

RANDOM ACTS OF TACT

The Undisclosed Third Bathroom

I was young, around twelve years old, when some distant relatives from Maryland visited us one afternoon.

They had a couple of kids about my age and we were hanging out in our den when the two of them fell silent in awe. They had both spotted the bathroom that was right off our den. They spoke in unison, 'You have two bathrooms!"

Actually, we had three bathrooms, and I was about to brag about it, but I hesitated.

I realized that our relatives had only one bathroom and that two bathrooms must have been the height of luxury to them. Three bathrooms would be unspeakable luxury to them, so telling them about our third bathroom would not impress them --- it would be like rubbing salt in a wound.

Somehow, I knew not to disclose that we really had three bathrooms. I used some tact and said, "Yes, we have two bathrooms." Then I changed the subject by inviting them out into the backyard.

The Gardens of Oregon

It was my first visit to England, and I was in the town of Sevenoaks to visit a friend, her father, and her stepmother. The stepmother insisted that she take me on a tour of her garden.

I took one look at her garden and the word "Oregon" popped into my head. I had lived in the Pacific Northwest, and this garden in England looked just like the gardens in Oregon and Washington. I was very courteous as my friend's stepmother took me around and showed off various plants: I nodded my head, and I oohed and aahed at the appropriate moments.

When the tour was finished, the stepmother proudly asked me, "Do you have gardens like this in America?"

We have plenty of gardens like this one in America, but somehow I knew not to reveal that her garden was not unique. I would have taken the wind out of her sails and would have diminished her tour. So, I used some tact and said "No, we do not have gardens like this in America."

The Shiny Airport Limousine

I had landed at JFK Airport and was taking an airport limousine to my parents' house. The woman sitting in the seat in front of me on the limousine was bursting to tell someone about her recent trip. She turned around and spoke to me.

"I just went to Europe for the first time. I saw London, and Paris, and Amsterdam. It was wonderful." I could see the glow in her face as she remembered her trip.

Then, to be polite, she asked me where I had been.

Well, I had spent two weeks driving across the Sahara Desert from my home in Nigeria to the Mediterranean Sea. I had seen oases and ergs and the snow-capped Atlas Mountains and the casbah of Fez. I had visited the famous adobe minaret of the mosque in Agades; I had bartered ball-point pens for camel rides; I had camped at French Foreign Legion outposts; I met a guy who claimed to have been Mick Jagger's macrobiotic cook until Mick grew tired of macrobiotic food. After Africa, I went to Spain, tried tapas for the first time, saw a bullfight, and visited the Prado Museum. Then I flew to London for a few days before catching a plane to JFK Airport.

Somehow I knew not to reveal where I had been. I knew that my trans-Saharan trek would burst this woman's bubble. I used some tact and replied, "I visited London."

But I am not proud that I remember these three moments of great sensitivity: "two bathrooms," "no gardens like this," and "London." I am not proud; I am actually disturbed. I am disturbed that these moments when I used tact stand out in my mind because it means they must be few and far between.

Proud Moments

I USED TO BE CLEVER IN MATHEMATICS

As Encouraging as Possible

1971: I was returning to Nigeria to teach for the second time. The first time, I had taught mathematics at a boys' school. This time I was going to be teaching mathematics at a girls' school.

I was given the first-year class at Women's Teachers College, Kano, Nigeria. The class of 1975 would spend five years at the College training to be elementary school teachers. At the end of five years, they would take a big qualifying exam for their teaching certificates.

I knew there is a general perception that girls are no good at mathematics. I vowed that I would never let this perception infiltrate my classroom. I would try to make my students believe that girls are good at mathematics.

In my teaching, I was as encouraging as possible. I acted as if mathematics was simple and easy. I was never upset by a wrong answer. For me, a wrong answer was an opportunity to learn; wrong answers let me know what the girls were thinking and helped me keep the class on track.

As an American, I had to buck the Nigerian grading system, which said you only needed 40 percent to pass a test. Hence, no Nigerian teacher ever gave out 100 percent as a grade because 100 percent meant perfection to them.

I had no problem giving out 100 percent as a grade. To me, '100 percent' meant that the student got all the answers right. To my Nigerian students, '100 percent" meant that they were perfect.

Can't Set Foot in the Dormitory

I think I did a good job of fighting the perception that girls are no good at mathematics. But I could not fight the fact that girls will be girls.

There was a lot of chatter in the classroom, which I learned to suppress.

There were also fits of pique, which I never learned to suppress. For example, the classroom had a portable blackboard. One day, Dije got upset at Halima and picked up the blackboard and threw it at her, right while I was teaching. This sort of stuff never happened when I was teaching at the boys' school.

Whenever things got out of hand at the boys' school, I simply stopped teaching, left the classroom and walked back to the staff room. In a few

41

Proud Moments

minutes, one of the boys would come to beg me to return to the class and resume teaching.

In the girls' school, only once did I leave the classroom and walk back to the staff room. I wound up sitting in the staff room for a long time; no girl came to beg me to return to class. In fact, I don't think the girls even noticed that I was gone.

Women's Teachers College was a boarding school; all staff members were on the roster to do dormitory inspections. However, it was impossible for me to do an inspection; being a man, I was not allowed to set foot in the dormitory. Luckily, one female teacher liked doing inspections but hated supervising study hall. I was constantly trading my inspections for her study halls.

Annoyances added up. After two terms at the girls' school, I asked for a transfer back to the boys' school where I taught from 1965 to 1967. When the transfer was granted, I visited my old school. When the principal announced that I would be returning, the students stood up and cheered.

I had a hard time keeping my eyes dry.

Big Qualifying Exam

After leaving Women's Teachers College, I heard a quote through the grapevine. One girl had said, "I used to be clever in mathematics when Mr. Schneider was teaching."

Clever was the Nigerian word for "smart." I felt good that a former student thought she was good at math. Hopefully, they all did.

In 1975, the girls that I had once taught took their big teacher-qualifying exam. For the first time in the history of the school, the entire class passed their final exam in mathematics.

This was a remarkable achievement. People credited the man who taught the girls mathematics in their final year.

But some credit should have gone to the man who taught the girls in their first year at Women's Teachers College.

By being encouraging, by acting as if mathematics was easy, by dealing nicely with wrong answers, by handing out grades of 100 percent, I gave the girls a foundation. I gave them self-confidence and the belief that they were clever in mathematics.

CHILDHOOD

Childhood

Childhood

THE TWINKLING LIGHTS OF PLAYLAND

The Sweltering Night

On sweltering summer nights, when I was a teenager, I would wait until I was certain that my parents were asleep. Then I would slip out of the house undetected. My goal was to cool myself off with a late night swim in the harbor.

It was an easy walk down our road to the top of the wooden stairs that went down a steep hillside to the Beacon Hill Association beach. There were about 100 stairs, and I would pick my way down them in the dark to reach the beach. I could not go to the beach in the daytime because we were not members of the Beacon Hill Association.

Once I reached the bottom of the stairs and took off my shoes, the night sand always felt cool and moist beneath my feet. I would wind my way past the piles of dead seaweed giving off a mildly pungent odor to reach the edge of the harbor, where small waves made muffled lapping sounds.

I stripped off my clothes and entered the water: My goal was to reach a large wooden float that was anchored about forty yards off shore.

The Phosphorescence

I always liked to do the breast stroke during my night swims because of the phosphorescence.

The movement of my arms through the water would agitate the tiny creatures that lit up and blinked in the water as I swam in the night sea. It was like gliding through a meteor shower.

When I reached the float, I would climb up, squeeze the stinging salt water out of my eyes, and look north. The harbor opened to the north and you could see the mainland about eight miles away.

Playland was on the mainland. It was an amusement park all lit up with red and white lights that twinkled as I looked north. The Ferris wheel was so large that, even so far away, I could clearly make out its shape on the horizon.

Playland was the stuff of dreams, unreachable. I knew my parents would never take me there. It was a short distance by water, but it was a long journey by car that involved taking a bridge to the mainland.

Childhood

I stood on the float, looking at the twinkling lights and listening to the lapping of the waves. It was peaceful.

The Blinding Searchlight

Some nights the peacefulness was shattered by a man-made sound. The sound of the engine of a tugboat churning up the harbor as it searched in the night for the barges it was going to take out in the morning.

In order to find barges in the darkness, the tugboats had searchlights --- big searchlights, the kind that you see in prison escape movies.

Sometimes, instead of sweeping the waters of the harbor with its searchlight, the tugboat would sweep the shore and sweep across the float, where the bright light would dazzle me; I had to raise my forearm in front of my face to shield my eyes.

I wondered if the tugboat crew was going to report me. They could tell my parents that I had snuck out of the house; they could tell the Beacon Hill Association that a nonmember was using their beach; they could tell the police that there was a naked teenager standing on a float forty yards from shore.

Then it was time to breast stroke back to shore through the phosphorescence, find my clothes, navigate 100 wooden stairs in the dark, and sneak back into our house.

The late night swim had cooled me off, and no matter how sweltering the night, I fell asleep as soon as I crawled into bed. And no tugboat ever reported me to my parents, the Beacon Hill Association, or the police.

Childhood

WEST EGG VS. EAST EGG

In *The Great Gatsby*

They are two peninsulas on the north shore of Long Island. In his novel, *The Great Gatsby*, F. Scott Fitzgerald looked at the shape of these peninsulas on a map and called them West Egg and East Egg. Daisy lived in West Egg; Gatsby in East Egg.

On the map, they are called Great Neck and Port Washington. I was born in Great Neck (West Egg), but I grew up in Port Washington (East Egg), the same place where Gatsby lived.

I learned a lot about the difference between these towns when two of my high school friends became newspaper editors --- one for the Great Neck paper and one for the Port Washington paper --- and they had different experiences.

My friend who edited the Great Neck newspaper found that she was the target of people's ire. At local meetings, people would yell at her for things she wrote in her editorials. My friend who edited the Port Washington newspaper, in all her career only got yelled at once, and the person who did the yelling called up and apologized to her the next day.

What made the difference between the two towns? Why was Port Washington a peaceful peninsula?

Nowhere to Go But South

I used to tell people that my town was peaceful because it was on a peninsula. You can't go east, you can't go west, you can't go north --- you can only go south.

Back in the 1700s, the colonists built a fence across the bottom of the peninsula, and turned it into a giant pasture for their cows, calling it Cow Neck. When I learned this fact in history class, I was disappointed to hear that the town did not keep the catchy name of Cow Neck. The town got renamed in honor of George Washington. Washington never actually set foot in Cow Neck, but he did have lunch in the next town south.

Port Washington had a spectrum of homes: modest homes, middle-class homes, and mansions worthy of an F. Scott Fitzgerald novel. It had the same percentage of African-Americans as New York City. It had plenty of churches and a couple of synagogues.

And everyone in town got along.

Childhood

But being on a peninsula did not guarantee harmony. Great Neck is also on a peninsula, and my friend who edited the Great Neck newspaper found that town to be tumultuous.

I have another explanation for the peacefulness: the railroad.

Living at the Start of the Railroad Line

Most of the men in Port Washington commuted to work in New York City by train. The Long Island Rail Road has a line that starts at Port Washington, goes through Great Neck, and ends at Penn Station in Manhattan.

When you commute from Port Washington in the morning, you find a train sitting at the station. When you get on, everybody you see is from your town. The train is quiet and uncrowded; you can sit with anyone you want. When you commute back home in the evening, as the train approaches the end of its journey, once again everybody you see is from your town.

Living at the start of the line creates a bond.

In F. Scott Fitzgerald's novel, Gatsby used to go down to the harbor in East Egg and gaze across the water at West Egg. He was gazing at the green light at the end of Daisy's dock. The green light was Fitzgerald's symbol for all the elusive things that Gatsby was striving for in life.

If I could have stood next to Gatsby, I would have told him to stop gazing at West Egg. East Egg is the place to be: a peaceful peninsula at the start of the railroad line.

Childhood

NEW JERSEY PASTORAL

Connected to The Boss

Bruce Springsteen is also known as The Boss. I used to be indifferent to his music --- until I went to his concert here in St. Louis in 2002.

The concert was promoting a newly released CD: Bruce Springsteen's reaction to September 11, 2001. I had never heard these songs before, and I became absorbed. I became a fan. I felt a connection to New Jersey's Bruce Springsteen.

The guy sitting next to me at the concert had come all the way down from Rock Island. I was impressed.

But not as impressed as I was when I met a guy who had flown from Cleveland to St. Louis for the Springsteen concert. In fact, he had been at twenty of the last twenty-three Springsteen concerts.

I am not a fan the way the guy from Rock Island and the guy from Cleveland were, but I now view Bruce Springsteen as someone to listen to. Not just listen to his music, but listen to his ideas.

When I heard that Bruce Springsteen recommended Philip Roth's *American Pastoral*, I went out and bought the book.

Connected to Philip Roth

American Pastoral is quite a book.

The main character is a blue-eyed, blond-haired Jew who looks so non-Jewish that he is called the Swede. The world is this guy's oyster: He is a New Jersey high school football hero, he marries a former Miss New Jersey, he buys a classic home in the New Jersey countryside, and he takes over his father's factory in Newark.

But the Swede's life is not all roses. The factory he owns is a glove factory, and Americans have stopped wearing gloves. Newark is sliding deeper into the economic doldrums. Since this is a Philip Roth novel, The Swede has a painful secret: A daughter hiding from the FBI.

I zoomed through page after page of *American Pastoral*, glad that I had taken Springsteen's advice.

49

Childhood

But on one of those pages, my reading came to a screeching halt. I found a phrase I had not heard in years: "melted cheese sandwich."

This phrase transported me back to childhood.

Connected to Melted Cheese Sandwiches

About one Sunday per month, my mother would make melted cheese sandwiches. A slice of bread, a slice of cheese, two tomato slices, all topped with a strip of bacon. This was cooked under the broiler. You ate the sandwiches with a knife and fork, and the cheese glistened with all the bacon drippings it had absorbed.

When I left home, I seemed to have left melted cheese sandwiches behind.

I vividly remember that evening in 1965 when my housemate fried a cheese sandwich. I had no idea that you could fry a sandwich. My housemate called it "grilled cheese" even though it had not been cooked on a grill; it had been cooked in a frying pan. This guy was from the West Coast, so I put down the frying of sandwiches as some West Coast eccentricity.

Now, years later, "grilled cheese" has prevailed, and the only place I have come across my childhood's melted cheese sandwiches is in a Philip Roth novel.

My childhood is connected to melted cheese sandwiches, which are connected to Philip Roth, who is connected to New Jersey's Bruce Springsteen, aka The Boss.

Childhood

TRACING INDELIBLE JOURNEYS

All the Railroads in the World

When I asked Santa Claus for a world atlas in 1951, I was eight years old. Santa brought me an atlas full of delight.

The atlas had maps of countries and continents at a time when the world was divided between pink (British possessions) and green (French possessions). There were maps of all forty-eight states, as well as imposing facts, e.g., Arkansas has bauxite; Georgia has naval stores.

Somehow, at age eight, I knew that 'naval stores' meant turpentine.

Best of all, the atlas showed all the railroads in the world. The railroads were red lines, and I would spend hours mentally tracing rail journeys in the atlas.

Atlases cost money, but road maps were free back then. I decided to start a roadmap collection. I set about building my collection with great fervor.

The Texaco Man Wearing a Bow Tie

In the 1950s, every gas station had a rack of free roadmaps. Whenever we stopped for gas on a family trip, I would check out the rack in each gas station.

The problem was that most of our family trips were to New Jersey, only one state away. I had to figure out a way to get maps of states that were far away.

Then I noticed an ad in the travel section of the newspaper.

The state government of Virginia wanted people to come visit and offered a free travel pack, which included a map of Virginia. I sat down and wrote a letter to Richmond. I knew that if the state government discovered I was just a kid, they probably wouldn't send me anything. So I used a little flattery, "Hello, we are planning to drive to your beautiful state of Virginia, and would like a free travel pack."

Flattery helped my collection grow. I had maps from state governments with pretty pictures of scenery. I also had maps from gas stations with pictures of a Texaco man in a bow tie happily cleaning a customer's windshield or pictures of a Sinclair station with the motto, "At Sinclair, We Care for You."

Childhood

My collection came close to getting all forty-eight states. I would pick a state map at random, unfold it, and daydream about traveling by car.

But then Hawaii and Alaska joined the Union. You couldn't drive to Hawaii, and Alaska had hardly any roads to speak of. These two new states were discouraging. My days of collecting roadmaps for the sake of collecting roadmaps came to an end.

In the Middle of Lunch

But maps continued to play a role in my life, especially wall maps.

When I lived in Nigeria, I bought a big map of the country, the kind used in a schoolroom.

The map took up an entire wall of my dining room. I would stand in front of the map looking at Nigerian towns ---- if I had visited that town, memories came swirling into my mind; if I had never set foot in that town, I yearned to visit. My eyes would follow roads, checking to see if they were all-season roads or if they were closed during the rainy season.

Sometimes I would even get up in the middle of lunch to look at the map.

Right after I moved to London, an English friend sent me a wall map of England. I put the map up on my bedroom wall. Every time I looked at the map, English towns would beckon to me. It was the stuff of dreams.

Maps have power. Whether it is an atlas showing all the railroads in the world or a roadmap that a state government sent for free or a giant wall map that interrupts lunch --- maps grab my attention.

Once a map has my attention, it makes me begin to trace journeys, indelible journeys.

Childhood

KETCHUP AND SALTINE SANDWICHES

With Dad in the Shiny Automat

When I was a little kid, my mother and I would take the train from our suburb into Manhattan to meet Dad for lunch.

Dad would take us to the Automat. The Automat was a restaurant that was like no other place to eat in the world. Founded in 1902, it was a giant walk-in vending machine. It was very hygienic --- full of shiny stainless steel.

At the Automat, we each grabbed a tray, while Dad estimated how much our lunch would cost and asked a lady sitting in a glass booth to convert paper money into coins. Dad would give me a pile of coins, and I would slide my tray along, looking at rows of little glass windows. Each window held an individual food item, along with a sign telling you what it was and how much it cost.

I would hunt for the window with the best-looking tuna salad sandwich. I would insert the correct number of coins in the slot, turn a porcelain knob, and the window would pop open. The window hinged from the top; I would lift up the window, take out the tuna sandwich, and put it on my tray.

I would then finish assembling my meal, hunting for the window with the best looking Jell-O behind it, and then get a glass of milk.

Lunch with Dad at the Automat was a big treat.

Salt Shaker Trick

As a young teenager I would sometimes go to the Automat with other young teenagers, and we would act like young teenagers.

The salt and pepper shakers at the Automat were made of clear glass with shiny chrome screw-off tops. While no one was looking, I would take the top off a salt shaker, place a small piece of white paper napkin across the opening, and put a little pile of pepper on the napkin. The top got screwed back on. If there were traces of napkin sticking out, I would tear them off.

I sat back and imagined, with glee, when the next person to sit at the table wanted to salt their food. That person would pick up a salt shaker, and be very puzzled when pepper --- instead of salt --- came out of the shaker.

Childhood

Although I was young teenager and liked to play tricks on people, I knew that there were people at the Automat who could not afford tuna salad sandwiches and Jell-O.

These people could only afford a cup of coffee; back then they were called bums. The Automat had free saltines at each table, and I would watch a bum buy a cup of coffee, sit down at a table, unwrap some saltines, add some ketchup, and eat little ketchup and saltine sandwiches.

I felt sorry for the bums, who survived on ketchup and saltines. But I also noticed that they never needed to use a salt shaker. So I felt good that these poor people would never fall prey to my little trick and find pepper coming out of a salt shaker.

On My Own in the Shiny Automat

As an older teenager, I worked summers at JFK International Airport.

Usually, I would drive from our suburb to JFK. However, for one week each summer, I would stay with my brother at his apartment in Manhattan. Then I would take public transportation to work --- a subway ride followed by a bus ride.

There was an Automat near the subway station.

Every morning during my week in Manhattan, I would eat breakfast in that Automat. I would get a tray, estimate how much my breakfast would cost, and ask a lady sitting in the glass booth to convert some paper money into coins. I would hunt for the best-looking cantaloupe half and the best-looking Danish pastry, and then get a glass of milk. I would use coins that I had earned myself to assemble my breakfast.

Eating breakfast at the Automat on the way to work made me feel very grown up; it was the early 1960s.

The Automats are all gone now; there are fast-food restaurants instead. No more peering through little glass windows for the best-looking food; no more coin ladies in glass booths. Bums are now called homeless people, and there are no more free ketchup and saltine sandwiches for them to survive on.

Childhood

DO YOU REALLY MEAN THAT I WAS REALLY MEAN?

No More Cliques

If you were at the country club that night and you were not from our high school class, you would have said that we looked kind of old. You would have noticed bald heads and double chins.

But if you were from our high school class, you would have said that we looked terrific.

Our fortieth High School Reunion consisted of cocktails, dinner, and dancing in a country club in our hometown of Port Washington, Long Island. With each old classmate I met, I felt a bond. This person and I had managed to navigate a journey of forty years.

I did not see my classmates as grownups in their mid-50s; I saw the teenagers they had once been. I did not notice the bald heads or the double chins. I just noticed the camaraderie.

The camaraderie made the old cliques and dividing lines disappear. At the reunion, a woman who never said a word to me in high school invited me to come visit her home in Tennessee. A man whose path never crossed mine in high school bought me a drink.

And I felt like a teenager again.

A Musical Farce

At least, I felt like a teenager until the DJ started playing "Come Along and Be My Party Doll" and I asked a friend to dance. Back in high school, she could have danced all night; at the reunion, all it took was one dance before she needed to sit down and catch her breath.

Then I went to find Sally. Back in junior high, Sally applied to take shop. In 1956, girls were supposed to take home economics; only boys were supposed to take shop. So Sally was denied shop class because she was not a boy. This was based purely on gender lines.

I found Sally and said, "I wanted to let you know how much I admired you for trying to break the gender barrier when you applied to take shop class."

Sally replied: "I never applied to take shop class."

Childhood

What? How could she have forgotten all that?

But Sally was not the only person who did not remember things about themselves. Anne asked me if I remembered how I was not very nice to our teachers.

"Do you really mean that I was really mean? To our teachers?"

Anne reminded me, "Yes, Doug. For example, in U.S. history class, our teacher liked to call the Civil War a 'musical farce.' One day you got everyone to bring in toy musical instruments and hide them in their desks. Then, when the teacher said 'musical farce', out came the instruments and we all blasted the teacher with music."

What? How could I have forgotten all that?

Chasing the Cloud from My Mind

I looked around the room at the country club. Everyone at the fortieth high school reunion was cheerful and confident.

Then a cloud came over my mind. Maybe this group was self-selecting. Maybe only cheerful and confident people come to reunions.

I chased the cloud away. Yes, some of us got winded after just one dance. Yes, some of us forgot the pranks we pulled on the teachers. Yes, some of us had lost their hair. However, we had all navigated forty years of life as adults. We were doing fine.

And we really did look terrific.

56

Childhood

WITH A TOWEL OVER MY HEAD

Jumping off the Refrigerator Meant Death

When I was a little kid, my older brothers figured out that I was afraid of heights. When Mom was out of the house, they would sweep me up and sit me on top of the refrigerator. I would stay there begging to be let down. I was stuck; I was convinced that jumping from the top of the refrigerator to the floor meant certain death.

Acrophobia has stuck with me, even now that I am grown up.

Sometimes I am brave: At age 30, I climbed up the open-air staircase that led to the first stage of the Eiffel Tower. Climbing up, I knew that my fear of heights would take over if I looked up or down or around. I fixed my stare on the heels of my friend who was climbing the stairs ahead of me. I made it.

Sometimes I try to be brave: At age 42, I optimistically started to go up the inside of the Statue of Liberty. There is a pair of staircases inside the Statue of Liberty --- one staircase is for going up to the top, and the other is for going down. I started up the staircase and made the mistake of looking up. Fear set in, and I did not want to go any further. But I could not turn around because there were hordes of tourists climbing up behind me. I spotted a nearby door: it said "Emergency Exit for National Park Service employees only."

I announced "I am a National Park Service employee" and quickly disappeared out the door to wind up on solid ground, where my fear dissipated.

An Approaching Locomotive Meant Death

When I lived in Minneapolis, I decided I would confront my fear of heights head on. I would do the scariest thing possible, and then my fear would be defeated.

I chose to walk a railroad bridge over the Mississippi River. The railroad bridge is parallel to the Interstate-35W bridge that collapsed in the year 2007. The railroad bridge is high. It was not a solid surface; walking across it meant stepping from tie to tie; in the space between the ties I would have a clear view of the river below.

I walked the bridge on a Saturday morning. I did not tell anyone I was going to do it because they would have pointed out that if a locomotive came across the bridge while I was on it, I would be dead.

Childhood

The thought of a locomotive was only a motivator to me. A high bridge was full of gaps, with an icy cold river below and the possibility of getting squashed by a train - surely, if I made it across, my fear of heights would be cured forever.

No Ordinary Bridge

I made it across the Minneapolis railroad bridge, one tie at a time. But it did not cure my fear of heights.

Uncured, at age 55, I had to go across the Chesapeake Bay Bridge. This is no ordinary bridge. It is a monstrous structure that soars high in the air and feels like it is in the stratosphere --- an acrophobe's nightmare. The bridge is so bad that the Maryland State Police have set up stations at both ends, and you can ask a state trooper to drive your car over the bridge for you.

In this case, I was not driving. My buddy Randy was driving, and his daughter Shannon was in the back seat. I knew it would be hard for me to go across the bridge, even though I was just a passenger.

I found a solution: As we approached the bridge, I grabbed a towel from the back seat and put it over my head, saying, "Tell me when we get to the other side."

So, looking back over my life, heights have held power over me --- paralyzing me on the top of Mom's refrigerator, making me pretend to be a National Park Service employee, and being thankful that there was a towel in the car when we drove over the Chesapeake Bay Bridge.

Childhood

THE WRONG ISLAND SNAIL ROAD

Guaranteed to be Electrocuted

We called it "The Wrong Island Snail Road," a smart-alecky play on words for "The Long Island Rail Road," which was the lifeblood of our town. The train ran from our town into New York City, and every morning it took my father and thousands of other fathers into the city to work. Every evening, it returned our fathers home.

As a kid, the train was a thing of awe. In our town, the train tracks ran past houses, but if we rode our bicycles to the next stop, Plandome, the tracks ran through a golf course. Here you could stand by the side of the tracks and no one could see you from their houses.

Here you could experience fear. First was the fear of being hit by a train.

Second was the fear of being hit by a flying penny. It would be your own penny that hit you. Before the train came, we would put pennies on the tracks. The train would pass by, sending the pennies flying. If you could find the pennies, you would be rewarded with a flattened disc with an elongated Abraham Lincoln running through the center.

But the biggest fear was fear of the third rail. There were two running rails, and next to one of the running rails was a third rail that carried enough electricity to run a train, which was also enough electricity to fry a human.

There was a wooden cover over the top of the rail, but the side was exposed, ready to deal death. I was always afraid that a friend would touch the third rail (or worse, pee on the third rail). Then I would have to ride my bike home, explain what we were doing on a golf course in Plandome in the first place, and describe how my friend had turned into a crispy heap of charcoal.

Teenagers on a Train

But there was no fear of riding on the train. Starting at age eleven, I was allowed to travel into New York City without my parents.

As a teenager, I organized groups of friends to go into the city for concerts, for Yankee games, for cheap ethnic restaurants, for buying books, for five-cent rides on the Staten Island Ferry, for frequenting beatnik coffeehouses, and for Broadway shows. In those days, you could get a seat in the back two rows of a Broadway theater for seven bucks.

For these excursions, I always hoped that there would be a double-decker car

Childhood

on the train. The double-decker had a series of open compartments, alternating up and down; each compartment was designed to seat four people. We teenagers, of course, would try to fit five into the compartment, maybe six, maybe eight. We had a blast.

But, no matter how youthful we acted on the train, we always observed the sign in the restroom: "Passengers will please refrain from flushing toilet while the train is standing in station." This was before the days of chemical toilets, and the contents of the railroad toilet flushed right onto the tracks, which is why you were supposed to wait until the train was traveling between towns.

One of my teenage friends used to cringe whenever an airplane flew overhead. She thought there must be signs in airplane restrooms that say, "Please refrain from flushing toilet while the airplane is standing at the airport."

Because of the Long Island Rail Road, she imagined the contents of the airplane toilet raining down on her as a plane flew overhead.

Mr. Blue Moves His Foot

The Long Island Railroad formed me. On the bright side, it gave me access to New York City. On the dark side, it gave me a healthy fear of the third rail.

Just recently I saw my fear justified --- I watched the original version of *The Taking of Pelham One Two Three*. In this movie, a New York City subway train and its passengers are taken hostage, and the hijackers demand a ransom. New York City subways have a third rail.

Robert Shaw plays a hijacker named Mr. Blue --- an insurance salesman turned renegade. At one point, Mr. Blue comes face-to-face with a transit policeman and is about to be arrested. The camera gives a quick glimpse of Mr. Blue's foot, only inches away from the third rail.

I went tense. Can it be? Mr. Blue is too proud to be arrested. He moves his foot and makes contact with the third rail. The camera then lingers on Mr. Blue's arm as it shakes and turns to charcoal.

There, on the screen, my childhood nightmare came true. Good thing that I am an adult; if I had seen that scene when I was a kid, I would have spent many sleepless nights thinking of little wisps of smoke rising from Mr. Blue's fingertips.

CALL IT COURAGE

Buying a Yellow Teapot in London

When I picked up the phone, I heard a voice that I had not heard since I graduated from high school.

Diana was reconnecting with me because our fiftieth high school reunion was coming up. She was my high school classmate, but, to Diana, it is more important that we were sixth grade classmates, back when we were twelve years old.

On the phone, Diana told me that she remembered what I did on the first day of sixth grade. And she remembered what I did on the last day of sixth grade.

On the first day of sixth grade, our teacher, Miss Ohanian, made each of us get up in front of the room and tell everyone what we had done over the summer. I told the class that my parents and I went to London, where we stayed long enough to look at the Thames River, eat lunch, and buy a teapot before going back to the United States.

This was all true. I explained to the class that we drove from Detroit, Michigan, to London, Ontario, where the river is called the Thames. After we ate lunch, my mother bought a yellow teapot, and then we drove eastward to Niagara Falls, New York.

Cannot Restrain the Tears

What I remember most about sixth grade was that Miss Ohanian showed us that nothing is impossible.

Miss Ohanian had us produce a monthly magazine; our class sold copies for a nickel each. I wanted to be the gossip columnist, but I was gently guided into the position of current events editor

Miss Ohanian had us dance. Once a week she taught us dances from all over the world; she taught as if we would have no problem learning them. And because of her attitude, we had no problem learning them. We put on a recital at the end of the year, and Miss Ohanian acted as if we would have no problem with the recital; so, we didn't.

Miss Ohanian had us listen to a book named *Call It Courage*; she read it aloud to the class.

Childhood

Mafatu, a young boy, left his island in disgrace because he was afraid of the ocean. He sailed until his canoe crashed on the coral reef of a deserted island. Mafatu had scraped his knee on the coral. To prevent infection, he found a lime tree and squeezed lime juice in his wound. I mentally filed that remedy away in my mind, in case I grew up to live on an island in the Pacific where my main means of transportation was an outrigger canoe.

On the deserted island, Mafatu overcame obstacles, overcame the dangers on the island, overcame his childishness. He became a young man and rebuilt his canoe to sail back to his home island.

Once back on his home island, Mafatu went to see his...wait, are Miss Ohanian's eyes glistening?...Mafatu went to see his father and ask for...wait, are those tears in Miss Ohanian's eyes?...to ask for his acceptance...those really are tears!

I was stunned. I knew that Miss Ohanian read this book every year to every class. Surely the ending could not be a surprise to her. Surely she could restrain her tears.

But the ending was sad, and it was powerful. When Miss Ohanian closed the book, her entire sixth grade class was silent, honoring her tears and her sadness.

The Leopard-Skin Bathing Suit

Miss Ohanian taught us that we could write and other people would read our writing. Miss Ohanian taught us that we could dance and other people would watch us dance. The book she read aloud taught us that we could persevere and we could gain acceptance.

These lessons made a great impression on my twelve-year-old self.

On the phone, Diana told me what I had done on the last day of sixth grade. Miss Ohanian took us to the town beach to go swimming in the harbor. On that day, Diana was wearing a leopard-skin bathing suit. I took one look at her and nicknamed her "Bongo."

Her last name was Beers. "Bongo Beers." It sounded catchy.

Before hanging up the phone, Diana had one more thing to tell me. In 2008, she was in the Lord & Taylor department store on Fifth Avenue in New York. The women's department had leopard-skin bathing suits for sale.

Diana bought a leopard-skin bathing suit. However, she did not wear it to our fiftieth high school reunion.

THE MILITARY

The Military

The Military

ITALY ON $6.81 A DAY

Resembles Romy Schneider

It was 1968, and my local draft board on Long Island wanted me to take my draft physical.

The draft board was not deterred by the fact that I was not living on Long Island; I was living in Kano, Nigeria. The board simply told me to show up at the nearest U.S. Army base, which was in Pisa, Italy --- a long air journey of over 2,000 miles each way.

I used Nigerian money to buy a round-trip plane ticket from Kano to Rome and on to Pisa. There is only one plane a week between Kano and Rome. It leaves on a Saturday and comes back on a Friday. I took all my American money with me: $47 --- this was to last me for seven days in Italy --- which comes out to $6.81 per day.

I was in for a frugal time: five days in Rome, two days in Pisa.

In Rome I chose a really cheap pensione because a guidebook said that the Italian owner resembled Romy Schneider. Romy Schneider was a hot French actress at the time, who definitely added some glamour to the Schneider name.

There was only one other guest in the pensione: a guy from Saskatoon, who was a Baha'i. The Baha'i religion teaches obedience to government, and he was very supportive of my long journey to take my draft physical.

Salt Stains on My Shoes

A lot of sights in Rome were free: the Trevi Fountain, the Pantheon, the Villa Borghese, and the Spanish Steps. The Coliseum sat by the roadside; in those days you could wander through it at will. I strolled along the banks of the Arno River and watched the locals play bocce.

To avoid paying for public transportation, I walked everywhere, including a very long walk to Vatican City to see St. Peter's Basilica and the Sistine Chapel. The basilica was free, but I was willing to pay to see the Sistine Chapel. However, I found a sign on the chapel door: Closed at 3:00 PM --- I was a half-hour late.

I looked down at my shoes. All this walking in Rome made my feet sweat, and the sweat had dried on my shoe leather, leaving salt stains. But I resolved to walk back to Vatican City the next morning.

The Military

When I returned to the Sistine Chapel, I found a sign on the chapel door: Closed on Tuesdays.

I gave up on the Sistine Chapel; I was flying to Pisa on Wednesday.

A Celebrity in the Barracks

While I was on the plane to Pisa, I checked out all the passengers who were in U.S. Army uniforms.

I figured out who was the highest ranking person on the plane, the person most likely to have his own car. When the plane landed in Pisa, I asked the officer for a ride to the army base.

He not only took me to the base, he also took me to the quartermaster, who got me some bedding and put me in a barracks for free.

The army guys in the barracks swarmed around me; they all wanted to talk to me. I felt like a celebrity.

Then I realized I was not a celebrity; I was just a fresh pair of ears. The guys were tired of talking to each other and wanted to complain to me about the army or talk to me about their girlfriends at home. They bought me hot dogs and beer and took me bowling, and the next morning, they showed me where to catch the shuttle bus to the base hospital for my draft physical.

The physical went smoothly. When it was finished, the U.S. Army doctor sat down with me and apologized. He was sorry that he could not find anything wrong with me, and he would be telling my draft board on Long Island that I was fit for military duty.

I got on the plane back to Rome and transferred to the plane for Nigeria. When I arrived back in Kano, I still had $2 in my wallet. I was proud that I had managed to live for a week in Italy on $45.

And I wondered how long I would have to wait for what now seemed inevitable: a draft notice.

The Military

PROTECTING SOUTH CAROLINA FROM THE ENEMY

I Will Guard Everything within the Limits of My Post

Part of army basic training at Fort Jackson, South Carolina, in February 1968 was learning how to perform guard duty. Guard duty training had two parts: daytime training, followed by manning a guard post during the night.

The daytime guard duty training covered a lot: how to shoulder your rifle, how to walk a perimeter, how to spot an approaching person, how to challenge an approaching person. Our instructors stressed how important it was to stand guard duty and protect vital American military installations from the enemy.

We finished daytime training by shouting our general orders in unison until the orders were committed to memory: "I will guard everything within the limits of my post; I will perform my duties in a military manner; I will quit my post only when properly relieved."

The second part of guard duty training awaited us: We would be taken to our guard posts at night, and the commander of the guard would come around to test us.

I Will Perform My Duties in a Military Manner

Nighttime came. I was issued a rifle and was told to get on a truck that would take me to my guard post.

I was eager to find out what vital American military installation I would be guarding. I was trained; I was armed; if the Enemy should launch an attack in South Carolina tonight, I would be ready.

The truck stopped, and I was told to dismount. There was my guard post: a vital American military installation known as "Fort Jackson Laundromat Number 7."

The building was locked and dark. I shouldered my rifle, and started walking the perimeter.

The Military

It was winter in South Carolina, and I soon noticed how chilly the wind was. I stopped patrolling around the building and started huddling next to the laundromat chimney in order to get out of the wind. I figured it was too dark for anyone to notice that I was no longer patrolling.

Then I heard someone approaching. It was the commander of the guard, coming to test me.

I Will Quit My Post Only When Properly Relieved

I sprang into guard duty mode, and confronted the approaching person.

"Who goes there?" "It is Captain Belton."

"Friend or foe?" "Friend."

"Place your ID on the ground, Sir, and take ten paces back."

The commander of the guard placed his military ID on the ground and took ten paces back. I took ten paces forward to the spot where I thought his ID was. I quickly realized that I had been issued a rifle, but I had not been issued a flashlight.

No one had mentioned this situation during daytime training. I held my rifle and spoke with authority:

"Do you have a flashlight, Sir?"

The commander of the guard did not have a flashlight either.

Somewhere on the ground, in the middle of a chilly South Carolina night, lay his military ID. I dropped my rifle, and both the commander of the guard and I got down on our hands and knees and started fishing around in the dark for his military ID.

This would have been the ideal time for the Enemy to invade South Carolina and launch an attack on "Fort Jackson Laundromat Number 7."

The Military

NOT A HELICOPTER IN SIGHT

Being Stockpiled by the Army

The army spent a lot of time and money training me to be a UH-1 jet helicopter crew chief. After helicopter training, I was stationed at Fort Lewis, where there was not a helicopter in sight. Clearly, the army was stockpiling me at Fort Lewis, waiting until it was time to ship me to Vietnam.

In the meantime, I was assigned to the army security office, working under Sgt. Dessauer. My job was to issue security clearances.

The army had strict guidelines for who could do what, based on their civilian criminal record. The guidelines weren't always logical. For example, if I found out that someone had been convicted of statutory rape in civilian life, I had to deny them clearance for driving jeeps in the army.

Holding Back the Flood

Spec-4 Sekunda and I were the two new clerks in Sgt. Dessauer's office. We quickly discovered that the sergeant despised Communists and despised hippies. He acted as if he were protecting the U.S. from these two vile forces. He was keeping his finger in the dyke to hold back the flood.

Sekunda and I understood the Communist part. The sergeant had grown up in Germany and knew about oppression behind the Iron Curtain. Sekunda and I did not understand the hippie part; but it became clear that, for some reason, the sergeant suspected the two of us of being closet hippies. We could not shake his suspicions, so we decided to fuel them instead.

Sekunda and I would spend our weekends at Fort Lewis, doing laundry, drinking 3.2 beer, and going to the movies for fifty cents. On Mondays we would tell the sergeant that we had spent the weekend in Seattle, which had a large hippie population. And, specifically, we had spent the weekend hanging out in the U District --- the epicenter of hippiedom in Seattle. We also hinted to the sergeant that in our foot lockers were long-hair wigs, which we wore to cover up our army haircuts while hanging out in the U District.

Sgt. Dessauer seemed thrilled to have closet hippies working right there in his office, and he kept a watchful eye on Spec-4 Sekunda and Spec-4 Schneider.

The Military

My Past Caught Up with Me

One day, my past caught up with me. Another clerk in the army security office found out that I had been in the Peace Corps.

There is a long-standing federal policy that no ex-Peace Corps Volunteer shall work in any intelligence agency, including army security. The policy is due to a concern that foreign nationals often associate the Peace Corps with spying.

I had to leave Army Security --- I was actually sad to go. Sgt. Dessauer had been great to work for and showed his appreciation for my efforts. He had even invited Spec-4 Sekunda and me over to his house where we watched him boss his kids around and make them call him "Sir" to compensate for the way officers boss him around and make him call them "Sir."

I think the sergeant was sad to see me leave.

I also think he was probably afraid that when I was no longer under his watchful eye, I would turn from a closet hippie to a full-blown hippie. But I do know that he appreciated my vigilance in issuing or denying security clearances, making sure that statutory rapists don't drive jeeps while they are in the army.

The Military

MUHAMMED ALI WILL FEEL WELCOME

McNamara's Hundred Thousand

I was an army clerk-typist in the orderly room of the 109th Aviation Division at Fort Lewis when I got a phone call out of the blue.

The phone call was from a lieutenant who said he was transferring me to the Fort Lewis School Command, where I would help with McNamara's Hundred Thousand.

"McNamara" referred to Robert McNamara, the Secretary of Defense under President Nixon, and "Hundred Thousand" referred to the number of people McNamara estimated had been cheated by the civilian school system.

These were people of normal intelligence who had gone through twelve years of the civilian school system, and had never learned to read beyond the third-grade level. They were given a high school diploma anyway and were sent out into the world, unprepared. Worse yet, because of their poor reading skills, they were ineligible to be drafted by the army --- and the Secretary Of Defense thought these people surely would benefit from serving in the army.

McNamara's Hundred Thousand worked this way: The army would draft people who had third-grade reading skills, teach them to read, put them through basic training, and turn them into soldiers.

At the Fort Lewis School Command, I was to teach remedial reading, even though I had never taught remedial reading before. It sounded a lot better than being an army clerk-typist.

McNamara's Personal Vendetta

When I arrived at my new posting, I asked how the army determines who would be drafted as part of McNamara's Hundred Thousand.

The answer: The army induction examination had 100 questions. If you get less than 20 correct, you fail the test and become ineligible for the draft. Under this new program, if you get between 16 and 19 correct, you become eligible for McNamara's Hundred Thousand.

Then I remembered the most famous person who had failed the army induction examination: Muhammad Ali.   I remembered that the government was furious that he had slipped out of their net. I did a little research and found out that Muhammad Ali had scored 18 on the exam.

The Military

Because of this new program, Muhammad Ali's draft status was upped to 1A, and he was now eligible to be drafted. I realized that the McNamara had set up an elaborate scheme not to help a hundred thousand people, but to nail one person.

McNamara was on a personal vendetta against Muhammad Ali.

Off to the Poster Shop

My first group of inductees showed up in my classroom. The group included a soul singer from Los Angeles, a tugboat worker from Portland, and a groundskeeper from Little Big Horn National Monument in Montana. There was no world heavyweight boxing champion, however

The inductees were around nineteen years old, and were reading at the third-grade level. My job was to get them up to fifth-grade reading level in six weeks. This was not as difficult as it sounded. These guys knew they could not read, and they knew they needed to know how to read.

As the weeks went by, I still wondered if the Secretary of Defense would finally win his vendetta and get Muhammad Ali into the army. Since there was a possibility that Muhammad Ali could show up in my classroom, I went off to a poster shop and bought a three-foot-by-four-foot black-and-white poster of him.

I taped the poster up next to the blackboard. I wanted Muhammad Ali to feel welcome in case he became one of McNamara's Hundred Thousand.

The Military

ONE ESKIMO WEEPING

No Firewood

I was drafted into the U.S. Army in 1968. Within a few months, the army had me teaching remedial reading to new army recruits.

These recruits had been drafted in spite of their low reading scores. The army gave me a group of ten recruits, and I had six weeks to get the group up to fifth-grade reading level (the federal definition of literacy).

The first group showed up, and I taught the first hour. For break time, nine of them went outside and one of them chose to sit at his desk and weep.

Homesick? Trying to shirk work? I decided to ignore him. But he wept during the second break. When he was weeping during the third break, I approached him. I heard him mutter, "No firewood. No firewood."

An explanation was forthcoming: He was a Yup'ik Eskimo from the village of Negeqliq in Alaska. He was the only adult male in the village, and he had been drafted into the army. Cold weather was approaching, and there was no one in his village to transport firewood to keep people warm in the winter.

Catch and Release

The only adult male in an Alaskan village got drafted? That did not sound right to me. I sent him to the chaplain, who managed to get him discharged and flown back to Negeqliq.

Then a new class arrived. One recruit had trouble seeing the words on the book we were reading. This guy had only one eye, and he got drafted. I sent him off to the chaplain.

Six weeks later, another new class arrived. One recruit coughed a lot. A tuberculosis survivor. Another one for the chaplain.

By now a pattern had emerged.

The local draft boards all across America were given quotas to fill, and the draft boards were worried more about filling quotas than the suitability of the people they were sending to the army. So what if the army sent a few back home; the quotas had been met. It was like a catch-and-release program.

73

The Military

The Yup'ik Eskimo, the one-eyed guy, the tuberculosis survivor, and I had all grown up under the shadow of the U.S. Selective Service. We were a generation that lived in apprehension, facing the possibility of being drafted into the military.

Congratulations on Your Ulna

There were ways to get exempted from the draft.

At one point, all students were exempt, and people flocked to colleges. Then married people were exempt, and people flocked to wedding chapels. Then people with children were exempt, and people flocked to maternity wards.

A friend from my hometown was exempt because of his ulna, which had limited rotation. The ulna is a bone in the forearm; you need a good ulna to operate a rifle.

I congratulated my friend on his bad ulna. I was glad for him, but I knew it meant one less person in the draft pool, and it increased my chances of being drafted.

I thought I was exempt because I was serving in the Peace Corps. That was true for two years, but then I got a draft notice. My local draft board used me to fill its quota.

I served two years in the Army as a draftee. During those years I helped rectify a few rough edges of our draft system.

My list: I helped a one-eyed guy go home. I helped a tuberculosis survivor go home. And I helped a Yup'ik Eskimo stop weeping and go home.

I hope that a little village in Alaska wound up with enough firewood for the winter of 1968.

The Military

MY GROIN IS ON FILE IN LITTLE ROCK

A Rash in the Shape of a Ring

The army stationed me at Fort Rucker during a typical hot and semitropical summer in Alabama.

In Alabama, I noticed that I had a rash in the shape of a ring, and the rash was in my groin. The ring kept growing so I went to the post dispensary.

When I saw the army doctor, I told him that I had a rash in the shape of a ring and it was in my groin. He did not tell me what I had; he just prescribed some cream to smear on my rash. The cream did not work, and the ring got bigger.

I went back to the post dispensary and saw a second army doctor. I told him that I had a rash in the shape of a ring and the rash was in my groin. "Why, that is ringworm. I am prescribing a different cream to smear on your rash."

Ringworm! I was mortified that the first army doctor did not put two and two together. The cream prescribed by the second army doctor did work, and the rash went away.

But I noticed that there were stretch marks in my groin where the ringworm had been, and the stretch marks did not go away.

We Want a Photo for Our Files

Eventually, the stretch marks started to bother me so much that I went to see an army dermatologist.

I told the dermatologist that I used to have a rash in the shape of a ring, and the rash was in my groin, and now I have stretch marks there. The army dermatologist looked at my medical records, looked at the stretch marks in my groin, and said, "Wow, you were prescribed an improper medication for ringworm and that is what caused the stretch marks."

The dermatologist then whipped open his desk drawer and pulled out a camera. "Can I take a photo of your groin for our files?"

I was thrown off guard. I hadn't expected to be a medical oddity; I hadn't expected my groin to be put on file. But I figured it was best to agree to the photograph, since I was hoping that the dermatologist would agree to do something about my stretch marks.

The Military

The dermatologist used a special camera: It had a rectangular metal frame projecting from the front of it. The metal frame was for pressing against an area of skin and flattening it out for a photo.

As the army dermatologist pressed the metal frame up against my groin, I read the certificate hanging on his wall: the University of Arkansas Medical School. The photograph of my groin was going to be put on file in Little Rock.

After he put the special camera away in his desk drawer, the army dermatologist told me there was nothing he could do about my stretch marks.

Disfigured by the United States Army

My last day of active duty in the United States Army was February 5, 1970. The Army used the term "ETS" for leaving the army.

The army gave us a choice: Stay up late on February 4 and ETS at 12 midnight, or get a good night's sleep and ETS at 8 in the morning. If I chose the good night's sleep, it meant I would be in the army eight hours longer than I needed to be. I chose to skip the sleep and ETS at midnight.

The night of February 4, I stood in various lines. When I saw the medical desk clerk, he asked me if I had any permanent medical condition resulting from active duty. I told the clerk about the stretch marks in my groin resulting from an improper medication prescribed for ringworm.

"Do you want to sue the United States Army for disfigurement?"

I first thought the clerk was joking. Then I contemplated the impact of his question: If I sued the army, I may get a bunch of money, but by doing that I would have to admit I was disfigured.

I asked the medical desk clerk what would be involved in suing the army. "You must stop your ETS processing tonight and come back at 8 in the morning."

So I had to choose between ignoring my disfiguration or staying in the army for another eight hours. Staying in the Army for another eight hours was not worth any amount of money. I skipped the lawsuit and became a civilian on February 5, 1970, at 12 midnight.

76

The Military

I WOULD NEVER SAY HELLO TO HER

My Shoes Are Not Highly Polished

My commanding officer, Captain Marjorie Johnson, said that she was recommending me for promotion to sergeant. All I needed to do, she said, was be examined by the Fort Lewis promotion board.

I said, "Thank you, Ma'am," and started worrying about facing the promotion board.

On the day I was to go before the promotion board, I polished my shoes, put on a highly starched uniform, and walked over to the building where the board was, avoiding stepping in any dust that would undo my polishing job.

The board was meeting on the second floor of a wooden barracks, one of hundreds of barracks that have dotted Fort Lewis since World War II. The second floor consisted of a large room with a small cadre room at one end. All the promotion candidates were squeezed into the cadre room; they called us out one by one to be examined by the three-person promotion board.

The tension was high in that cadre room as we waited. Finally one soldier cracked, looked at my shoes, and berated me, "Your shoes are not highly polished!"

I had read the army manual on personal appearance, and the manual says that shoes must be polished, not highly polished. I think that "highly polished" must have come from some MGM movie about army life.

The outburst about my shoes made me worry even more about facing the board.

Facing the Three-Person Board

My name was called. I left the cadre room and stood at attention in front of the promotion board.

I scoped out the board members; there were two men and one woman. I waited to answer their questions; I wanted to get things right.

One of the men was a sergeant, who sported eight stripes on his sleeve --- obviously a career military man. He asked me military questions, such as, "What is the maximum effective range of an M-14 rifle?" It had been a year since I had touched a rifle back when I qualified as a sharpshooter in South Carolina. However, I knew the answer: 505 yards.

The Military

The other man was a lieutenant. He asked me some general questions about my past Army training, and then he threw out a bombshell question.

"What do you think of the Vietnam War?"

I swallowed hard; if these three people knew what I thought of the Vietnam War, I would never get a promotion. President Nixon came to my rescue. Two days previously, he had announced that the United States was implementing a policy of de-escalation.

My response to the lieutenant: "Sir, I agree with the Commander-in-Chief, and think we should de-escalate."

A Trick Question

Then it was the woman's turn to ask me questions. She was a captain. She asked me some general questions about my current army duties. Then she asked me a trick question.

"I see that your commanding officer is Captain Marjorie Johnson. Would you say hello to her?"

Women in the military were very sensitive about being treated differently from men in the military. I knew that I needed to show equal respect in greeting an officer no matter if male or female. My promotion hung on getting the answer right.

My answer: "I would never say hello."

The captain looked startled, perhaps because I had not been tricked by her question. She asked it again:

"Would you say hello to her?"

"Oh, no, I would never say hello to her. I would say 'Good morning, Ma'am' or 'Good evening, Ma'am.'"

The captain switched tactics and re-worded her question.

"Captain Johnson and I were in Officer Candidate School together in Alabama. Would you say hello to her for me?"

"Yes, Ma'am, I will say hello to her for you."

I got my promotion to sergeant.

The Military

THANK YOU, RICHARD MILHOUS NIXON

Swarms of Cyclists

I was on vacation in West Africa in 1971 with an American friend who had an American car. Our vacation destination was Ghana, which meant we had to drive westward through the country of Togo to get there.

As we drove westward through the capital city of Togo, it was like a gauntlet; our car was surrounded by swarms of motorcycles.

The motorcyclists would adjust their speed to match our speed, and they yelled "Exchange!" at us. Sometimes bicyclists would pedal furiously to keep pace with the car and yell "Exchange!" at us.

We were in an American car. The motorcyclists and the bicyclists were moneychangers, and they desperately wanted our dollars.

We disappointed them. We did not change any money in Togo. We went into Ghana, spent a few days, and then headed east back to Nigeria. As we drove eastward through the capital city of Togo, not a single motorcycle or bicycle approached our car.

While we were in Ghana, President Nixon had announced that the U.S. dollar was no longer a fixed currency --- the dollar would float. On hearing this news, the moneychangers in Togo had lost all interest in the dollar.

Living in British Pounds on the GI Bill

In 1973, I moved to London to attend the University of London. I planned to use my GI Bill to support myself for the two years it would take to get a master's degree.

The GI Bill was set up so that you got a fixed amount of money for every month you were on active duty in the military. I had done twenty-four months of active duty; I could attend school for twenty-four months.

Then Nixon announced one-and-a-half months of schooling for every month of active duty. Half a year later, he announced two months of schooling for every month of active duty. I was jubilant thinking about how I could finish up my master's in London and go on for two more years of school somewhere else.

The Military

Now that the dollar was a floating currency, the exchange rates fluctuated. The pound started dropping against the dollar. The number of dollars I got from the GI Bill stayed the same, but the number of British pounds I got at the bank kept on increasing.

It was like hitting a jackpot every month.

Chicks and Ducks and Geese Better Scurry

During summer break at the University of London in 1974, I went back to the U.S. for a visit. A friend and I did a little tour around New England. Stopping in Boston on August 9, 1974, we ate lunch at Joyce Chen's Chinese restaurant.

At lunch, we heard the news on the radio: President Nixon would be resigning at 9:00 PM that night. After lunch, we headed for Cape Cod. We found a motel in an idyllic little town with a park overlooking the harbor. The gazebo in the park had a sign: community concert tonight.

We went to the concert. At 8:30 PM, the conductor turned to the audience and said, "If you want to watch the president resign on television, you should leave now. Otherwise, you can stay here and we will play a medley of tunes from Rodgers and Hammerstein's *Oklahoma*."

What a choice: A unique moment in American history versus "The Surrey with the Fringe on Top." But we had made our choice. We went back to the motel where we had stashed a six-pack of beer and some pretzels for watching the president resign.

In 1984, I moved to Boston. On August 9, 1984, I ate lunch at Joyce Chen's Chinese restaurant. During lunch, I heard the news on the radio: Exactly ten years ago today, President Nixon resigned.

The news made me think about how I wanted to thank Richard Milhous Nixon. I wanted to thank him for upping the number of months I could use the GI Bill. And I wanted to thank him for floating the dollar so that I could hit a jackpot every month that I lived in London.

FATHER

Father

BUYING A FATHER'S DAY CARD

Hallmark's Image of a Father

When I was a kid, buying a Father's Day card really made me notice how my Dad did not live up to Hallmark Cards' image of a father.

Year after year, Hallmark printed Father's Day cards that had drawings of duck decoys on the cover or else golf clubs or a pipe rack or a pair of slippers.

Hallmark never once printed a Father's Day card for fathers like mine who did not spend time outdoors hunting ducks or playing golf. My father spent his time outdoors in a shabby coat doing yard work.

Hallmark never once printed a Father's Day card for fathers like mine who did not spend time indoors smoking pipes or wearing slippers. My father spent his time indoors doing other people's income taxes, hunched over huge columnar pads with a pile of freshly sharpened number 2 pencils next to him.

Year after year, Father's Day after Father's Day, I would buy a Hallmark card, and I would wish that my Dad hunted ducks or played golf or smoked a pipe or put on slippers when he got home from work.

Father-and-Son Sports Activities

Mr. Wade lived down the street. Although he had given his son the unconventional name of "Torlen", I thought Mr. Wade was a great father. The proof was in all the time he spent with Torlen.

In warm weather, Mr. Wade and his son would be out in the street playing catch with a baseball. In cool weather, they would toss a football. In chilly weather, Mr. Wade and Torlen would shoot baskets, and when the weather got really cold, father and son would play Ping-Pong in their basement.

For Torlen, life was an unending stream of father-and-son sports activities. My father never once played catch with me, never once shot baskets with me.

I wished my father could be like Mr. Wade.

Father

Lunch with Torlen's Sister

My view of my father changed as I grew older.

A revelation happened when two girls from my high school called up Dad one day, and invited him to the movies.

I convinced myself that they had invited him because he could drive to the movies and they couldn't. But somehow I could not totally ignore the possibility that they actually liked my dad. They liked my non-duck-hunting, non-golf-playing, non-pipe-smoking father.

A bigger revelation came when I was on leave from the army and visited San Francisco for the first time. Torlen's sister lived there, and I arranged to have lunch with her.

Over lunch, I talked about how I had been so jealous of her brother when I was a kid, how Torlen got to do all those father-and-son sports activities, and I never did.

Torlen's sister dropped her fork in amazement.

She spoke, "Doug, my brother hated playing catch with our father. He hated tossing footballs with our father. Torlen hated shooting baskets and hated playing Ping-Pong in our basement. Torlen used to tell me that he felt stuck having to do all those father-and-son sports activities."

"My brother was jealous of you. He wished that our father could be like your father."

Father

THE EVER-TALKING HENRY SCHNEIDER

Talking at New York City's Main Post Office

My father, Henry Schneider, never hesitated to talk to anyone anywhere at any time.

His granddaughter sums it up by saying that whenever she went to the grocery store with him, she had to add twenty minutes to the trip because of all the time her grandfather spent talking to everybody in the store.

My father worked for a printing company in New York City. Dad once gave a tour of the company to a printer who was visiting from Japan. When the visitor went back to Japan, he wanted to thank Dad for the tour, but he had lost the name and address of Dad's printing company. So, he sent a thank you letter anyway, addressed simply:

>Henry Schneider
>New York City
>USA

New York City's main post office delivered the letter to Dad.

My father worked in New York City, but he did not live in New York City, so the post office could not have looked him up in the phone book. However, Dad was a customer at the main post office, and most likely at one time or another he had talked to everyone who worked there.

Talking at Heathrow Airport

Mom, Dad, and I were flying to Budapest from London.

London had been the scene of numerous IRA bombings at the time, and there was heightened security at Heathrow Airport. You had to be frisked by the police before you could leave the terminal and board your plane. The Budapest-bound passengers formed up two lines: male passengers to be frisked by a policeman, female passengers to be frisked by a policewoman.

I got frisked, left the terminal, and walked across the tarmac toward the airplane. My mother got frisked, left the terminal, and walked across the tarmac toward the airplane. We both noticed that behind us, only female passengers were leaving the terminal. Something was keeping the male passengers in the terminal.

Father

I recognized the problem and sprinted back into the terminal to tell Dad that he had to stop talking to the policeman --- the other male passengers needed to be frisked so they could get on the plane to Budapest.

<u>Talking on the Train in Romania</u>

Once we were in Budapest, Mom, Dad, and I boarded a train to travel to Romania. Our goal was to visit the city where my father was born.

After we changed trains, Mom and I wound up sitting together, and my father wound up sitting next to a teenage Romanian boy. Dad immediately turned to the teenager and started to talk.

My father: "Do you speak English?"
Romanian teenager: "Nici." (Nici is the Romanian word for "no.")
My father: "Sprechen Sie Deutsch?"
Romanian teenager: "Nici."
My father: "Well, that is my wife over there, and that is my son sitting next to her..."

The boy sat there politely as my father talked to him in English all the way to our destination. The boy must have been a little bewildered, because he made it clear that the two of them did not have any language in common.

Yes, my father never hesitated to talk to anyone anywhere at any time. It is no wonder that New York City's main post office did not need a street address to find Henry Schneider.

Father

I PLAYED BASEBALL AGAINST LOU GEHRIG

At Food Town in 1974

My parents retired to Hampton Bays, Long Island. The town had two supermarkets, but Mom and Dad always shopped at Food Town. Sometimes Dad walked up and down the supermarket aisles with Mom, and sometimes Dad sat on the window ledge at the front of Food Town and waited for Mom to finish.

One day in 1974, Dad was sitting on the window ledge at the front of Food Town when a stranger, about Dad's age, sat down next to Dad and said, "Hi. I played baseball against Lou Gehrig."

Dad was astonished. Dad had never missed an opportunity to tell people that when he was in high school, he had been manager of the High School of Commerce baseball team, and his friend, Lou Gehrig, was the first baseman on that team.

Here, instead of Dad initiating a conversation about Lou Gehrig, a stranger was initiating a conversation about Lou Gehrig.

The Best Batter in New York City

My Dad was off and running; he started regaling the stranger sitting next to him on the window ledge. Dad told him that when he was in high school, he had been manager of the High School of Commerce baseball team, and his friend, Lou Gehrig, was the first baseman on that team.

Dad said, "We were the team that was invited out to Chicago in 1920 to play the Chicago city champions, and Lou Gehrig, who had just turned seventeen, hit a grand slam home run over the right field fence at Wrigley Field. Everybody talks about that game in Chicago, but, as the manager, I was not worried about that game because I knew we would win it. The game I was really worried about was when we represented Manhattan and played Brooklyn for the New York City championship."

"You see, the Brooklyn team had the best batter in New York City high school baseball. This batter was amazing, and I got really really worried in the ninth inning of that game. We were ahead of Brooklyn by only one run, and Brooklyn had two men on base when that batter came up to bat. The count became one ball and two strikes. I was holding my breath."

87

Father

"The Brooklyn batter happened to be very ostentatious. After every pitch, that guy would show off by taking his bat and knocking the dirt off his cleats. Our catcher noticed this and walked out to the pitcher's mound to talk to our pitcher:"

'Look, this batter is a show-off. I want you to throw a pitch that is so far from the strike zone that he won't even think of swinging at it. Then, I will quick get the ball back to you, and while the Brooklyn guy is knocking the dirt off his cleats, I want you to throw a strike.'

Dad continued. "And that is exactly what happened. The Brooklyn batter did not swing at the first pitch, and while he was ostentatiously knocking the dirt off his cleats, our pitcher threw the second pitch --- right in the strike zone. The best batter in New York high school baseball was out; the High School of Commerce won the game; we were New York City champions and got invited to Chicago; and Lou Gehrig got to hit a home run out of Wrigley Field."

That Fateful Baseball Game

The year 1974 was more than fifty years after that fateful baseball game when the High School of Commerce played Brooklyn for the New York City championship. The stranger sitting on the window ledge at the front of Food Town slowly turned to Dad and said,

"I was that batter."

Father

SQUIRRELS RULING THE BIRD FEEDER

<u>Dad and Squirrels in the Bird Feeder</u>

Our Missouri squirrels have a lot to learn from the squirrels in Hampton Bays, Long Island, where my parents retired.

Out in Hampton Bays, Dad used to fill up the bird feeder every morning before breakfast.

Dad had hung the feeder on a wire from a large branch on a tree in the backyard so that he and Mom could watch the birds from the breakfast table. Instead of watching birds, they got to watch squirrels. The squirrels would slide down the wire into the bird feeder and feast on bird seed.

Dad hoped to outwit the squirrels and replaced the wire with a string. Surely, squirrels could not slide down a string. However, the next morning, the string proved no obstacle.

Instead of sliding down to the feeder, the squirrels stood on the branch above and grabbed the string. Then, paw-over-paw, they pulled the feeder up until it was at branch level, and proceeded to eat the bird seed.

These squirrels were proactive. On the mornings when they pulled up the feeder and found it empty, they swung into action. They climbed down the tree and then jumped up on the air conditioner in my parents' bedroom window. The squirrels would then bang on the window to wake up slacker Dad, letting him know that the bird feeder was empty.

<u>Martha Stewart and Squirrels in the Bird Feeder</u>

I swear I am not making this up; I read it in the *St. Louis Post-Dispatch*.

Someone wrote to "Ask Martha Stewart" and asked Martha Stewart what he could do about the squirrels that were eating all the food in his bird feeders.

Martha responded, "Do you own a shotgun? Squirrels are not an endangered species."

Father

<u>Sydney and Squirrels in the Bird Feeder</u>

One day in 1999, I got home from work and saw that dinner was ready to go on the table. But first my buddy Randy wanted to show me something. There on the kitchen counter alongside the serving bowls was a piece of an animal.

I was overcome with pride: It was the tip of a squirrel's tail. It meant that Sydney, our Australian shepherd, was finally getting the hang of how to terrorize the squirrels in our bird feeder.

Whenever we spotted a squirrel in our bird feeder, we let Sydney out the door. To escape, the squirrels used to rely on speed, but Sydney learned to run faster. The squirrels used to rely on zigzagging, but Sydney learned to anticipate their movements. The squirrels used to run up the maple tree, but Sydney learned to get between the feeder and the tree.

The dog had actually caught a squirrel and took a bite out of its tail. However, a mouthful of squirrel tail startled Sydney. The dog lost focus as she tried to spit out the fur. This was the piece of fur that got displayed on the kitchen counter.

Martha Stewart, we do not need a shotgun; we have Sydney.

Father

IT RAINS PENNIES FROM HEAVEN

At the Drop of a Hat

In my father's generation, everybody sang.

Back then, people were not shy about singing. Sing-a-longs were popular. People had booklets with printed lyrics, and people had records that were specifically designed for singing along. Dad was the proud owner of a record called "Music to Break a Lease By."

My father's favorite song was "Pennies from Heaven." It was a comforting song, full of optimism: --- Every time it rains, it rains pennies from heaven. Don't you know each cloud contains pennies from heaven?

Dad would sing that song at the drop of a hat: in the car, in the supermarket, at the dining table, while visiting people --- it was Dad's signature song, and he used it to spread cheer.

At the Big Duck

The Big Duck was a cement building in the shape of a duck in the town where Mom and Dad had retired.

The Big Duck was thirty feet long, twenty feet high (with car headlights as its eyes) and had a large door in its breast. It had been built by a local farmer, who used it for selling eggs to the public.

Dad and I had gone to the Big Duck a couple of times to buy eggs.

Eventually, the farmer got out of the egg business, and the Duck sat empty. Dad was worried that this quirky landmark would be torn down.

After Mom and Dad died, I went back to the town where they had retired; I had arranged a ceremony to spread their ashes in the ocean near the town. The day before the ceremony, I decided to go see if the Big Duck was still standing.

It was not only standing, it was sporting a sign that said Long Island Heritage Society Gift Shop. I was relieved to see that the Big Duck had been saved.

I pulled into the parking lot, opened the car door, and heard Bing Crosby singing. The Long Island Heritage Society had put speakers in the parking lot so that people coming to the gift shop would be greeted by music.

Father

Bing was singing "Pennies from Heaven." How did I wind up being greeted by my father's signature song on the day before his ashes were scattered in the ocean? Was that my father continuing to spread cheer?

At the Cajun Restaurant

It was ten years later when I next heard "Pennies from Heaven."

We were having dinner at a Cajun restaurant in St. Louis that featured a strolling guitarist playing Cajun music. The guitarist stopped at our table. Instead of playing a Cajun song, he played "Pennies from Heaven."

I took it as a sign.

The next day, my brother called me up and announced that my niece had given birth. The child, a girl, would be the seventh and final great-grandchild of my father.

So, as far as I was concerned, this great-grandchild had come into the world greeted by "Pennies from Heaven." My father was continuing to spread cheer.

CULTURES

Cultures

Cultures

I AM A STUPID AMERICAN

Bad Disk, Good Disk

Brussels is a popular place for international corporations. Maybe this is because Belgium never made war on anybody in Europe and never conquered anybody in Europe. So there is not much animosity towards Belgium. It is a country with a nice bland image.

This is why the European Union is headquartered there.

And this is probably why SWIFT is headquartered in Brussels. SWIFT is the Society for Worldwide Interbank Financial Transmission, whose goal is to facilitate the movement of money from banks in one country to banks in another country. They handle 10 million transmissions a day.

When I worked at U.S. Bank in Minneapolis, one of my responsibilities was to install new versions of SWIFT software on our computers. The software came to us on a disk every few months.

Things went smoothly until the time SWIFT sent us a bad software disk. I planned to tell SWIFT about the bad disk so they would send us a good disk.

You Are a Stupid American

I calculated the Minneapolis/Belgium time difference and went into work really early. I phoned up SWIFT in Brussels and got a technician. I told the technician that SWIFT had sent a bad disk to the U.S. Bank in Minneapolis.

I was totally unprepared for the tirade that ensued. I thought I was simply reporting a fact, while the Belgian treated my report as a direct accusation of Belgian incompetence, which had been delivered with the utmost arrogance.

I was stunned when I heard him say, "No, no, no! We would never send you a bad disk. You are a stupid American. Try the disk again, and you will see it is a good disk. SWIFT does not send out bad disks."

Well, it sure looked like SWIFT had sent out a bad disk. I did try the disk again, and I still got a message on my screen reading, "Error D10 - Bad Disk."

Cultures

I was at an impasse, uncertain how I would ever get a good disk. Then I realized this was not a matter of good disk vs. bad disk. It was a matter of presentation. What Americans saw as fact, Belgians saw as arrogance.

I needed to replace my arrogance with humility.

Error D10 — Bad Disk

I prepared to humble myself and talk to Brussels as if I were a stupid American. The next morning I called and got the same Belgian technician again.

"Hello, I have loaded a SWIFT software disk at First National Bank of Minneapolis, and I am very puzzled. I must have made a mistake, because I get an unexpected message when I load the disk."

"Really, what message do you get?"

"It says 'Error D10 - Bad Disk'. I wonder how I could ever have received a message like that."

"Alors! We sent you a bad disk. We will mail a good disk immediately."

Humility paid off; the stupid American got the disk he needed.

Cultures

IT'S NO USE MEIN GETALKING

<u>Language as a Weapon</u>

Grandma Schneider, my father's mother, died before I was born. She was born in Europe, grew up speaking German, and learned English when the family immigrated to the United States in 1906. I was told that her strudel was wonderful, and she could roll out dough on her kitchen table until it became paper-thin.

I was also told that Grandma Schneider could get in a snit if she felt like she wasn't being listened to. She would use her pet phrase, a mixture of English and her first language, German, "It's no use mein getalking, when ich bin nicht gepreciated."

Grandpa, Grandma, and Grandma's sister all lived together. All three of them spoke German and English, but only Grandma and her sister knew how to speak Hungarian. I was told that they had sisterly conversations right in front of Grandpa without him knowing what they were saying.

From that story, I learned that language could be a weapon.

Hmm... My father spoke German. My mother did not. If I learned German in high school, my father and I could have father-and-son conversations right in front of my mother without her knowing what we were saying.

I was not sure what my father and I needed to keep secret from my mother, but I dreamed of using language as a weapon. I could not wait to get to high school to take German from the legendary Mr. Schoenborn.

<u>Listing and Sinking</u>

I started taking German in Mr. Schoenborn's class in 1958. He wore the most ornate wristwatch I had ever seen. And he heaped praise on his students; he once told me that my pronunciation was so good that I could walk the streets of Hamburg and no one could tell I was from the United States.

But his wristwatch and his praise did not make him legendary; he was legendary because he was on the *Andrea Doria* on the night it sank.

Mr. Schoenborn and his mother had visited Germany in 1956, and they returned to the United States as passengers on the *Andrea Doria*. On July 16, 1956, the *Andrea Doria* collided with another ship off the coast of Massachusetts and started to list to one side. The captain gathered

Cultures

the passengers on deck and told them that the ship was sinking, and they should get in the lifeboats.

Mr. Schoenborn did not get in a lifeboat right away; he ran back below decks to get a suitcase. He realized that he could only manage one suitcase since the ship was listing badly; he had to choose between his mother's suitcase and his suitcase, which contained all the slides he took in Germany. He fetched his mother's suitcase.

Alas, all the slides that Mr. Schoenborn took in Germany are now at the bottom of the sea. He would sometimes grow wistful in front of the German class, thinking of his loss.

Forty-six people died on that night in 1956. The fact that Mr. Schoenborn was willing to risk his life on a listing and sinking ship made him legendary in my estimation.

<u>Unser! Unser!</u>

It was six years after high school when I got to walk the streets of Hamburg.

In spite of Mr. Schoenborn's praise, no one in Hamburg mistook me for a native speaker of German. In fact, they could spot me as an English speaker a mile away, and everyone spoke to me in English.

Except for one woman, who spoke to me in French. Considering what time of night it was, and which street in Hamburg I was walking down, she was sounding romantic and offering some short-term companionship.

The German I learned from Mr. Schoenborn was not much of a weapon. I could hold conversations with my father in front of my mother, but my father and I never had any real secrets to keep hidden from my mother.

I know my mother picked up a few words of German by osmosis. When the three of us traveled in Europe, my father often talked to people in German. He would point to me and identify me as "mein Sohn" --- my son.

My mother would then hit my father on the shoulder and say "unser Sohn" --- our son.

The German I learned from Mr. Schoenborn was, however, a good connector. I never knew my grandmother; I never saw her roll out paper-thin strudel dough; I never heard her complain, "It's no use mein getalking, when ich bin nicht gepreciated."

But, because I learned German, I feel connected to her.

Cultures

LIFE ACCORDING TO BOLLYWOOD

Hindi with Subtitles

When I lived in Kano, Nigeria, there were four movie theaters in the city. The theaters only showed a few movies in English each week. Mostly, they showed black-and-white movies from India, in Hindi with subtitles.

These Bollywood movies were very popular with Nigerians, and I went to one to find out what the appeal was. It only took me one movie to figure out the Bollywood formula.

The movie opened with a woman giving up her baby boy to a local villager to raise. Because the baby was born out of wedlock, she could not raise him herself. She draped a locket around the baby's neck as a final farewell.

The woman went on to be the hard-as-nails boss of a timber company. She was a Corrupt Old Person. She personified Evil. Her baby, however, grew up to be a Kind Young Man. He personified Good.

The timber company wanted to destroy the nearby village to harvest more timber. Good vs. Evil. Then a fire broke out, and the Kind Young Man saved the life of the Corrupt Old Person. She recognized the locket he wore around his neck. The village was saved from destruction.

Throughout the movie, actors broke out into song and dance at the drop of a hat.

The African audience did not need to understand a word of Hindi; they did not even need to be able to read the subtitles in English. Spectacle, recognizable Evil, recognizable Good, and fate winning the day. The story was clear; it was life according to Bollywood.

Born into Brothels

It was forty years before I went to see another movie made in India. I knew this movie would be different: It won the 2005 Academy Award for Best Documentary: *Born into Brothels*.

The film told the story of an American woman who went to India to photograph prostitutes. The American saw that the children growing up in the red-light district faced a dismal future; they would grow up to work in the red-light district, just like their mothers.

Cultures

The American wanted to break the cycle. She gave cameras to some kids, and their inner creativity sprang forth. She managed to get Sotheby's to auction the children's photos. The proceeds financed boarding school for the kids. Photography broke the red-light cycle.

I was impressed. I had seen a film made in India that had no Kind Young Man, had no Corrupt Old Person, and no actors bursting into song and dance at the drop of a hat. This was not life according to Bollywood.

After seeing this movie about photography saving Indians from a life in brothels, I stopped at Starbucks. I settled in, thumbing through magazines and sipping my latte. A bunch of Indians came into Starbucks, sat at the table next to mine, and started sipping their drinks. Then they pulled cameras out of their pockets and started taking photographs.

Life was imitating art right in front of my eyes. I did a quick check to see if my latte was making me hallucinate.

A Millionaire in Rupees

In 2009 I went to see *Slumdog Millionaire,* which won the Academy Award for Best Picture. I wanted to check out how far films from India have come since the day I sat in an African movie theater.

In the movie, a fellow, who grew up in the slums, winds up as a contestant on "Who Wants to Be a Millionaire" on Indian television. As he managed to answer one question after another, I noticed that he was a Kind Young Man. His childhood sweetheart meanwhile had fallen into the clutches of a gangster kingpin. The gangster was clearly a Corrupt Old Person. Good vs. Evil.

The film has flashbacks recounting the slumdweller's life; the flashbacks are threaded through questions on "Who Wants to Be a Millionaire." After two hours of *Slumdog Millionaire*, fate wins the day.

There was no singing and no dancing. I knew that the poor actors must have been aching to burst into song and dance. Yes, they finally got to perform a big dance number while the closing credits rolled on the screen.

This was a movie showing us life according to Bollywood, only in color and English this time.

Needless to say, I did not visit Starbucks after this film. I was afraid that a bunch of Indians would sit down at the table next to me and, as I was sipping my latte, they would start asking each other questions from "Who Wants to Be a Millionaire."

Cultures

TOO MUCH TIME ON YOUR HANDS

The Book from Canada

Friends who live in British Columbia used to work at the same school I did in Nigeria, and they enjoy reading about Africa. Somebody loaned them a book called *Shadow of the Sun*. This is a collection of observations on politics and life in Africa by Polish journalist Ryszard Kapuscinski, who has reported on Africa since 1960.

My Canadian friends decided that they wanted to buy a copy of *Shadow of the Sun* for themselves. But when they went to amazon.com, they found they could get a copy cheaply if it was mailed to a U.S. address, but it was prohibitively expensive if it was mailed to a Canadian address.

They decided to buy the book and ship it as a gift to me in Missouri rather than pay lots of money to have a copy shipped to their Canadian address.

They announced this gift via an e-mail.

A phrase in their e-mail caught my eye. Years ago, when people gave you a book, they would have said, "We hope you enjoy the book." In 2003, my Canadian friends said, "We hope you find time to read the book."

The E-mail Link from Canada

Yes, free time has become a shrinking commodity. Nearly everyone feels perpetually pressed for time --- pressed for time to do the things we would like to do and even pressed for time to do the things we need to do.

A friend who lives in Manitoba sent me an e-mail with a link to a little animation created by a Japanese programmer. I clicked on the link, ran my cursor over the drawing, and was delighted:

But a phrase in my friend's email caught my eye. Years ago, when people were delighted by something clever, they would have said, "That Japanese programmer is very clever." In 2003, this Canadian friend did not say that the programmer is very clever; he said that the Japanese programmer has too much time on his hands.

The ultimate 2003 putdown, implying, of course, that you yourself have lots of worthwhile things to do, while that Japanese programmer has nothing better to do.

Cultures

A coworker named Leslie baked a coffee cake and brought it in to share at work. While I was admiring the coffee cake's aroma, another coworker walked by, took a glance at the home-baked coffee cake, and said in a loud voice, "Leslie has too much time on her hands."

This putdown sounded like an act of jealousy. Maybe the second coworker was wishing he had time to be creative.

Starting a Campaign against the Putdown

What's next? Someone announcing that they found a cure for lung cancer, only to be told that they must have too much time on their hands?

I feel that I should start a campaign --- appearing on television, writing to newspapers, and lecturing people that we must eschew the phrase "too much time on your hands."

Of course, to have an effective campaign, I need to find the time to start it. And once I got that campaign rolling, people would probably respond by telling me that I have too much time on my hands.

Cultures

JEWISH PEOPLE ALWAYS SHOW UP FOR FUNERALS

Not Picking Up My Messages

I started my East Coast vacation in Boston. That was where I heard a little voice in my head talk to me. The little voice told me to call up my answering machine at home in Minneapolis and pick up my messages.

I replied to the little voice: I was on vacation, and it seemed extravagant to pick up my messages long distance. I would handle whatever messages were on my answering machine when I got back home.

My vacation plans were for a leisurely drive down the East Coast from Boston, stopping first in Poughkeepsie, then visiting in New Jersey, and finally going on to Maryland.

The New Jersey visit would be with Claire, who is related to me on my father's side of the family. She was 87 years old then, and had been a longtime volunteer at St. Barnabas Hospital in Livingston. I planned to meet Claire for lunch at the hospital.

On Such Short Notice

It was 11:30 when Claire and I went through the St. Barnabas Hospital lunch line, and we settled in at a table. I expected Claire to tell me about the hospital, or talk about her grandchildren, or ask me how I was doing.

Instead, Claire said, "Did you know, Doug, that Jewish people always show up for funerals?"

She said this in an admiring tone. "Jewish funerals are held two days after the death, often sooner." Claire's tone grew more admiring. "It's amazing: On such short notice, people manage to show up for the funeral."

I was puzzled why Claire wanted to talk about Jewish funerals when we had a lot of other things we could have talked about. I simply assumed that in her volunteer work, Claire had recently dealt with a Jewish patient at St. Barnabas who had died, and she attended the funeral.

Cultures

The Message on My Answering Machine

When I got back home from my East Coast vacation, I listened to my answering machine.

Someone from my mother's side of the family had left a message in Minneapolis while I was in Boston. Jeoji, my cousin's wife, had been killed in a car crash. The phone message went on to list details about the funeral.

The town where Jeoji's funeral service was held was seventy miles away from St. Barnabas Hospital where Claire was a volunteer. The day of the funeral was the same day that Claire and I had lunch. The time of the funeral was 11:30, the exact time when Claire was speaking admiringly about people who showed up at funerals on short notice.

Claire, who is from my father's side of the family, could not have known about Jeoji, who was from my mother's side of the family.

Because I did not listen to the little voice when it spoke to me back in Boston, the little voice must have gotten so angry with me that it decided to go inside Claire's head so it could subtly berate me.

There are people who make great efforts to be at funerals. I had not even made the effort to pick up my phone messages long distance.

104

Cultures

SECONDS COUNT

Time in Kano

To announce the beginning and the end of class, my high school used a buzzer. When I went to university, they rang bells that were located in a number of bell towers on campus.

When I was teaching in Kano, Nigeria, the school used a two-foot long piece of rail that they got from the Nigerian Railway Corporation. The rail hung from a tree in our school's central courtyard. When hit with a metal mallet, it made a rather loud sound, announcing the beginning and end of class.

Because Kano was close to the Equator, the sun rose and set pretty much at the same time all year round. My neighbor had a rooster that crowed at daybreak. My body grew used to the rhythm of the day; my day started when my neighbor's rooster crowed at daybreak.

Plus, Nigerians were very forgiving if you did not show up for an event on time. So I never bothered to wear a wristwatch.

Occasionally, I needed to ask a Nigerian with a wristwatch what time it was. They would not say "two thirty." They would tell me "two twenty-nine and seventeen seconds."

I thought it odd that a society that was rather casual about time would be concerned with announcing the exact time down to the second. Then it dawned on me that the radio always gave the precise time, so Nigerians did the same.

Time at Fort Jackson

From a tropical life, where time was fluid, I went directly into an army life. In 1968, I was at Fort Jackson for basic training. During basic, I no longer had any time.

The army had my day tightly scheduled. The army told me when to get up; the army gave me just enough time to wash up and put on a uniform; the army had a full day of training. Even the time while waiting for a meal was spent exercising, not relaxing.

Nighttime in the army was unstructured, but there were boots to polish. At mandatory lights out, I would crawl into my bunk, where exhaustion would plunge me directly into a deep dreamless sleep.

Cultures

I only had flashes of free time, mainly because I do not smoke. When the army gave us trainees a five-minute smoke break, instead of whipping a pack of cigarettes out of my pocket, I would whip a piece of paper and a pen out of my pocket. I became adept at writing an entire letter in 300 seconds.

Sometimes, I thought back to my pre-army life, back to the days when I had lots of unstructured time --- and I never appreciated it.

Time in Seattle

In 1977 I attended Seattle Community College to start my career in information technology. We had to use punched cards.

For my computer programming classes, I would write out a program by hand, then go to a keypunch machine and produce a wad of punched cards. I would rubber band the cards together and place them in the outgoing tray.

At 2 PM, a courier would take all the programs in the tray over to the other side of the city, where the school's mainframe computer was. At 8 AM the next day, a courier would bring the output back. That was an eighteen-hour turnaround. Nobody complained.

After a few months, punched cards were replaced by terminals. All the information technology students were connected to the mainframe. You typed your program into the computer, submitted it, and within two minutes, you had your output.

Now, however, I heard people complain. If they had to wait three or four minutes, rather than two minutes, they would be upset. People, who had once been content with an eighteen-hour wait, were not content with a four-minute wait. The additional 120 seconds seemed like an eternity.

When I was in Nigeria, the radio made people think that seconds were important. When I was in the army, I learned that seconds were precious. Now, living with computers, I am reminded constantly that seconds count.

Cultures

URANIUM-CRAZED ZOMBIES

A Gun is Wholesome Fun

Funny things have been happening across the road from our subdivision in Valley Park, Missouri.

First, we were surprised to see a cellphone tower being constructed over there. So many people complained that the mayor decided to camouflage the tower. It was painted brown, the same color as a tree trunk --- in hopes that passers-by will mistake the new cellphone tower for a sequoia.

Then Valley Park announced a hearing: Someone wanted to construct an indoor firing range across the road. This range will be nestled next to a veterinarian's office, across the parking lot from a restaurant with patio dining, and close to a condominium complex.

I went to the hearing, expecting to find kindred souls there: people who did not think our neighborhood was an ideal location for an indoor firing range. Only three other people objected to the firing range. Dozens of people eagerly testified that a firing range was a big plus. They testified that guns are wholesome. One person testified that he has been shooting guns since he was four years old.

An Underbelly Tour

Then I won an item in an auction run by the St. Louis Poetry Works. The auction was to finance a film they are making about uranium-crazed zombies. They had found the perfect location to film it: Valley Park, Missouri.

Of course! Cellphone towers disguised as sequoias. Firing ranges where four-year-olds could have wholesome fun. And now, uranium-crazed zombies.

I offered to take the film crew on an underbelly tour of Valley Park. I would talk about murder and thugs and ambushes and corrupt mayors and cowardly mayors.

Mainly I planned to show them how Valley Park was once an idyllic nineteenth century town, a resort with European-style spa hotels and boating clubs and rustic cabins. Part of it was a company town, built by a benevolent company that wanted its employees to have decent housing.

Then John Buckner was lynched from a bridge over the Meramec River in 1894. In the nineteenth century, lynchings were not racially motivated; they

107

Cultures

were a form of vigilante justice. More white men than black men have been lynched in Missouri.

A flood came along in 1915 and wiped out the bridge and the benevolent factory. Valley Park has never regained its prosperity. Some folks blame the spirit of John Buckner for all the misfortunes the city has undergone in the twentieth and twenty-first centuries.

Buy Your Liquor Barefoot

The movie director, a cameraman, and a notetaker showed up at my door.

The first underbelly tour stop was to be Dawn's Liquor Is Quicker. This liquor store has a drive-up window where people don't need to get out of their cars; they can be barefoot as they drive up, roll down their window, push a buzzer, and buy liquor.

We did not get as far as Dawn's. The film crew was shouting: "Look at that doorway! Tell us about it!!"

The doorway was pretty shabby. I explained, "That is the entrance to a bank that was turned into a car wash many years ago."

As we drove on, the crew listened politely as I showed them our railroad hotel, our grain elevator, our levee; I even showed them the site of the old wagon bridge where the lynching took place.

They didn't get excited until we passed a plain rectangular building. They shouted, "Look, glassblock windows! We want to get inside!! We want to film a scene inside a building with glassblock windows!!!"

The crew turned to me and asked me who owned the building and how could they get permission to film inside it. The building did not have a sign on it. In fact, it didn't even have a street number on it. I had no idea who owned it.

Then I realized we had a disconnect. I thought I was dealing with poets; actually, I was dealing with a film crew made up of poets. They were far more interested in finding film locations than in understanding the history of Valley Park.

I cut my well-prepared tour short. When they dropped me off at my home, the three filmmaker-poets said, "Bye! See you on the set!"

See me on the set? It sounded like they expected me to be in their movie. Maybe this really hadn't been a tour of Valley Park. Maybe the crew was secretly auditioning me for a role in their movie.

Maybe they thought I would make a great uranium-crazed zombie.

EATING

Eating

Eating

THE ALLURE OF SUSHI

Hungry on Fifth Avenue

We met in Manhattan at Christmastime.

My friends came down from Poughkeepsie with their kids; I came down from Boston. Our goal was to join the holiday crowds wandering along Fifth Avenue --- admiring skaters at Rockefeller Center, doing some window shopping, watching street performers, and absorbing the excitement of being on this special street in this special city at this special time of year.

The highlight was exploring the flagship store of FAO Schwarz. The store had two floors bursting with toys. We walked every aisle, and then we asked the kids what they wanted for lunch.

My friends' ten-year-old son enthusiastically said, "Let's have sushi!"

I was stunned. Manhattan offers every possible cuisine in the world. Why would a kid choose sushi? In fact, how did a ten-year-old from Poughkeepsie even know about sushi?

Sandwich after Sandwich

Kids are notoriously conservative about their food choices.

Kids break out in tears if a pea rolls across the plate and touches their mashed potatoes. Kids expect parents to make peanut-butter-and-jelly sandwiches using the exact same peanut butter and the exact same jelly and the exact same bread, sandwich after sandwich.

In spite of these barriers, sushi makes a connection with the younger generation.

Sushi is party food; it is colorful, it has fun names, and it is always freshly made. When the waitress brings your sushi order to the table, it is similar to being presented with a Thanksgiving turkey or a birthday cake; your eyes admire the food while your mind sets up a plan on what you will eat first.

A coworker sent his daughter away to college, fearing that she would pick up bad habits while away from home. She did; she picked up a sushi habit. Sushi is not a cheap meal, and now my coworker can't afford to take his daughter out to dinner.

111

Eating

Friends at the dogpark took their kids to a sushi restaurant for fun. Much to their regret, sushi has become the kids' favorite meal out. Their budget is being strained.

When I moved to St. Louis and my buddy Randy's teen-aged daughter lived with us, the best way to get her to straighten up her room was to promise her sushi. It was a costly promise, but the room did get straightened up.

Sushi on Our Yacht

Sushi first made a connection with me when I saw it for sale in a supermarket one day. I realized that all you have to do is buy a packet, unwrap it, and, presto, there was dinner. You don't even have to heat it up.

Sushi made a connection with Randy when we rented a yacht during a vacation in Costa Rica. The crew of the yacht consisted of a helmsman, a host, and a chef. The chef made sushi while we were sailing on the Pacific Ocean. (No, he did not catch a fish and turn it into lunch --- the ingredients were already onboard.)

Nowadays, it is unusual for a month to go by without us having sushi.

But when I mention the word "sushi", many people start to shudder. They tell me that they could never eat raw fish.

I tell them that sushi can be made with cooked ingredients and that the shrimp and crab in sushi are usually cooked. And there is vegetable sushi as well.

And they tell me back that I am wrong. These people, who would never set foot in a sushi restaurant, tell me that sushi is always made with raw fish.

I realize that I cannot convince these people otherwise, so I just bide my time. Some day they will find out the truth about sushi --- probably on the day when they ask their kids what they want for dinner and their kids enthusiastically say, "Let's have sushi!"

Eating

TEMPTATION ON THE COB

Heavenly Paintbrush

My mother knew how easily I gave in to temptation. If she put some corn-on-the-cob on my dinner plate, I would fill up on the corn and neglect the rest of my dinner.

My mother's solution: She declared that corn was a dessert and, therefore, had to be eaten last. I could not have any corn until I finished the rest of my dinner. Her solution worked.

Since corn-on-the-cob was a huge favorite of mine, I looked forward to being old enough to go to Boy Scout camp.

My older brother had told me about the way they served corn-on-the-cob at the camp. There was a big kettle of corn and a little kettle of melted butter. One guy fished an ear of corn out of the big kettle and put it on your plate. Then another guy dipped a paintbrush in the little kettle and swabbed your corn with melted butter. It sounded heavenly to me.

When I got to go to Boy Scout camp, I would wake up every morning in my tent, wondering if it was corn-on-the-cob day. But times had changed. The camp never had a big kettle of corn or a small kettle of melted butter.

I never even saw a paintbrush anywhere in camp. I had missed out on corn heaven.

A Residue of Ash

When I moved to West Africa, I was surprised to find corn-on-the-cob there. It was sold by street vendors, who strip off the husks and roast the corn on a small charcoal fire. Not over the charcoal, but directly on the charcoal.

Since the fire burns unevenly, it means that some of the kernels get charred black, some kernels pop, some are underdone, and some are just right. There is always a residue of ash on the corn, which means you do not need to salt it. You ate this without butter.

Where I lived in Africa, corn was a snack, and it fit in my mother's category of dessert.

113

Eating

After leaving Africa, I wound up living in Minnesota. Agriculture is a big business there, and you cannot use the word "corn" because it is too general. You have to specify if you are talking about corn for livestock (field corn) or corn for humans (sweet corn).

It was in Plainview, Minnesota, that I found corn heaven.

Star Wars on the Main Street

Plainview has a harvest festival called Corn-on-the-Cob Days.

At the festival, I watched a parade of farm machinery going down the main street. These days farm machinery is enormous and monstrous, with the farmer sitting way up top in an air-conditioned cab that remains level as the machine rolls over hill and dale. As the alien-looking farm machinery paraded by me, it made me feel like I was on a *Star Wars* set.

After the parade, they served free corn-on-the-cob. A guy fished ears of sweet corn out of a big kettle and put them on plates.

There was no little kettle of melted butter and no paintbrush. Instead, they placed one-pound blocks of butter out in the sun, and you rolled your sweet corn in the slowly-melting block. The butter quickly acquired a groove where people had rolled their corn; eventually, the groove grew so deep that the walls collapsed, and it got replaced with a new block of butter.

I feasted. In Plainview, sweet corn was appetizer, entree, and dessert.

Everywhere else, however, corn is still dessert.

It is over sixty years since my mother established her dinner table rule, and the rule is deeply ingrained in me. People tell me that I am an adult and I can eat my corn anytime. But I do not give in to temptation; I clean my plate before I touch my corn-on-the-cob.

I would be wracked with guilt if I ate my corn first.

Eating

LUNCH WITH THE DUKE OF ATHOLL

The Most Visited Castle in Scotland

When I was living in Boston, I told a friend that I was planning a trip to Scotland. My friend was a member of the Scottish clan headed by the Duke of Atholl.

She told me to arrange my trip to Scotland during the Atholl Gathering, which was held once a year on the grounds of the duke's castle. Not only would I get to see the gathering, but my friend would get me an invitation to have lunch with the duke and would get me on the guest list for a big party at the local pub.

The Duke of Atholl is the only person in Europe who is allowed to have his own private army. So the Atholl Gathering consists of Scottish piping, dancing, and athletic events, with the added attraction of displays of military formations.

I arrived at Blair Atholl Castle on a typical Scottish morning, when there was a lot of dew on the grass. I was wearing a kilt but decided not to wear my good shoes because of the dew. I wore my army boots instead. The duke was walking by me; he stopped and pointed at my boots. I expected him to haughtily tell me that U.S. Army combat boots were not proper attire with a kilt. Instead, the duke told me that he thought my boots were very practical.

Ah, I was off on the right foot with the duke.

I looked forward to talking with him at the lunch. He had invited about three dozen Americans to dine with him in his castle --- in recognition of how far we had traveled to come to the Atholl Gathering.

Cold Cuts for Lunch

I was wondering how he would manage to speak to all three dozen of us, when the duke entered the room and made a beeline for a chair that was wedged between a sideboard and the wall.

The duke was a bachelor and was used to dining by himself. Apparently he had no intention of talking to three dozen Americans. So he sequestered himself in the most inaccessible spot in the room and watched us go through a buffet line of cold cuts, potato salad, and drinks at room temperature.

I guess it was his castle and he could do whatever he wanted

Eating

In the evening, at the big party in the local pub, the duke was the host but never got on the dance floor. I, of course, was out on the dance floor for every dance.

During the dancing, I figured out that the people who really knew how to do Scottish dancing were the visiting Americans. Once, I wound up in a square of eight people: seven Scots and me. The seven Scots did not know how to dance, and most of those seven Scots were too plastered to care whether they knew how to dance or not.

I spent the evening being an American in Scotland teaching the Scots how to dance their own dances.

Frustrated in Boston

I was all excited when I got back to Boston from my trip to Scotland. I wanted my friends to know that I had met a duke.

I told the first friend that I had lunch with the Duke of Atholl. My friend's response: If he was such an atholl, why did you have lunch with him?

I told the second friend that the Duke of Atholl had praised my army boots. My friend's response: Why would you listen to an atholl?

I told the third friend that I went to a pub party hosted by the Duke of Atholl. My friend's response: I hope he wasn't a really big atholl.

I got frustrated and stopped talking about my trip to Scotland.

Next time I have lunch with a duke in his Scottish castle, I'll make sure it is the Duke of Montrose or the Duke of Hamilton --- someone whose title does not remind people of a vulgar word.

116

Eating

BECAUSE WE EAT OUR HAMBURGER RAW

Raw Hamburger as a Snack

When I was a kid in the 1940s, it was hard to find snack food at the supermarket.

You didn't buy popcorn, you popped it yourself. If you wanted a hot dog, you went to a ball game. And the cookies at the supermarket were not for snacking, they all had health implications --- graham crackers to help adults maintain good health, or zwieback crackers to help infants develop good teeth.

But our mother had a tradition; she always brought snack food back from the supermarket for us --- a pound of raw hamburger sitting on a cardboard tray.

Us Schneider kids were expected to take care of the afternoon munchies by opening the refrigerator door, scooping some raw hamburger out of the package, rolling it into a ball, and popping it in our mouths.

Raw Hamburger as a Delicacy

Twice a year, the Schneider family would head to Newark, New Jersey, where Uncle John conducted the Mandolin Club, a group that had elevated raw hamburger to a snack art form.

Down in the basement, the Mandolin Club would sell you a beer or a soda and some "roh hack". Roh hack was raw hamburger spread on untoasted rye bread, garnished with squares of raw onion, and sprinkled with black pepper. I liked my roh hack with cream soda.

Aunt Edna Schneider also viewed raw hamburger as a delicacy, and that is what she fixed when she heard that her future daughter-in-law was coming to meet her.

Aunt Edna fed her future daughter-in-law steak tartare, a family favorite consisting of raw hamburger mixed with raw egg. No one is certain whether Aunt Edna was trying to impress her future daughter-in-law or trying to discourage her.

The future daughter-in-law, who had grown up in a Greek household and who had spent her entire life eating only cooked meat, declared Aunt Edna's steak tartare delicious. Daughter-in-law and mother-in-law were forever bonded.

Eating

Raw Hamburger as Lethal

There is a Kurt Weill song in *The Threepenny Opera* with the chorus: "because we eat our hamburger raw." The song is sung with great swagger, as if eating hamburger raw was a macho act, something ruthless pirates would do.

It is now the twenty-first century, and eating raw hamburger can be lethal.

Dozens of ground up cows wind up in the same pound of raw hamburger from the supermarket. The uncooked meat can contain beef trichinosis, which leads to fatal breathing disorders, and can contain mad cow disease, which leads to fatal brain disorders.

Frito-Lay now safely takes care of most Americans' snacking needs. Maybe if you looked in the fridge of a ruthless pirate, you would find some raw hamburger. But no one in the Schneider family snacks on raw hamburger any more.

A tradition has died.

Eating

YOU CAN'T LIVE WITH US IF YOU SHOP AT HARROD'S

Yams in the Great Hall

When I moved to London in 1973, I shared a flat with three British women --- Diane, Yvonne, and Elizabeth.

My British flatmates had read about Thanksgiving dinner but had never eaten one. Since they assumed that all American citizens are perfectly capable of cooking a Thanksgiving dinner with ease, they announced that I would be cooking them their first Thanksgiving dinner. And they would be inviting some friends over to help them eat it.

I had no idea how to cook a Thanksgiving dinner, but I did not want to disappoint my three flatmates, so I agreed to do it.

The butcher shop in our part of London sold me a turkey. However, our local greengrocer did not carry cranberries, pumpkin, or yams. I tried the local supermarket but came up empty-handed.

Then I realized that London has the number one gourmet shop in the world --- the Great Hall at Harrod's. Harrod's is London's premiere department store, catering to the wealthy and the superwealthy. I went to Harrod's and found cranberries, pumpkin, and yams in the Great Hall.

I carried my groceries back to the flat and set them on the kitchen table. My three flatmates took one look at the Harrod's shopping bag and were horrified. They had budget-busting visions of my buying all our groceries at Harrod's every week.

I was admonished: "You can't live with us if you shop at Harrod's."

The Californian, the Idahoan, and James Beard

A friend of mine from California was living in London at the time. A friend from Idaho was living there as well. Since I had never cooked a Thanksgiving dinner before in my life, I recruited them to help me cook.

The Californian came over with the book that every American needs to survive in a foreign country --- James Beard's *American Cookery*. He used the book to make creamed onions. The Idahoan came over and used James Beard to make a pumpkin pie, while the Californian and I struggled with a British turkey.

119

Eating

British turkeys in 1973 were sold hand-plucked, with little pinfeather stubs sticking out all over them. James Beard told us to turn on the gas burner and hold the turkey carcass over the flame to burn off the pinfeather stubs. James Beard then told us how to prepare and stuff the turkey.

The Idahoan's pie was ready to bake. Unfortunately, James Beard's recipes were in degrees Fahrenheit, and the knob on the British oven was not calibrated in degrees --- it was calibrated in regulo gas marks. We had to guess: the pie was baked at regulo gas mark 5; the turkey was roasted at regulo 3.

Your Thanksgiving Dinner is Served

Once the cooking was under control, my friends from California and Idaho left, and I set the table.

When Diane, Yvonne, Elizabeth, and their guests sat down, I served them Harrod's yams, James Beard's stuffing, mashed potatoes, creamed onions, cranberry sauce, and a turkey that got cooked in spite of having to guess at which British regulo gas mark to use.

The British diners were ecstatic; they enjoyed every bite. They loved the pumpkin pie that was served for dessert. I exhaled, satisfied.

I thought back over all the work that was involved. Three Americans --- from California, Idaho, and New York --- had put in twenty-six man-hours of labor to make the dinner.

Glancing at the kitchen clock, I realized that it had taken the British less than an hour to devour the dinner.

Eating

A LIFETIME IN A LUNCHTIME

<u>Pulled Pork</u>

When I moved to St. Louis in 1997, the city heightened my interest in architecture. It is a city of brick and stone because of an ordinance that was passed after a huge waterfront fire in 1849. The ordinance forbade building in wood. In the twentieth century, St. Louis did not grow as much as other cities, so many old buildings and homes remain. The city is an architectural delight.

I keep my eye out for interesting neighborhoods, and Cherokee Street caught my architectural eye. The ground beneath the street is limestone. Limestone leaches easily, and a giant cave runs for blocks underneath Cherokee. The cave is so gigantic that brewers used to chill their beer in the cave, and railroads ran into the cave to pick up the beer for shipping.

When the streetcars came through in the late nineteenth century, commerce began to sprout up, and Cherokee Street became a shopping destination. But Prohibition closed the breweries, suburban flight closed the stores, and the neighborhood stood empty at the end of the twentieth century, waiting to be reborn.

And reborn it was. It was re-settled by antique dealers at one end, and by anarchists and Mexican-Americans at the other end.

Now it is urban and vibrant, and I went down to Cherokee Street for lunch one Saturday. The restaurant I chose has a tripartite menu.

The first of the three parts is St. Louis barbeque, featuring pulled pork.

<u>Stuffed Cabbage</u>

But the second part of the menu intrigued me the most. The restaurant had recently been purchased by a Romanian immigrant, who had come from the same area of Romania where my father was born in 1903. And, like my father, the restaurant owner was a German speaker.

The owner was waiting tables at lunchtime, and I got to ask him a couple of questions about Romania. But he was too busy for me to find out if there was some kind of connection between his family history and mine.

The menu, however, did have a connection. The second of the three parts featured Romanian cabbage rolls.

121

Eating

When I was a kid, we would drive from our home on Long Island to New Jersey to visit my father's sister. Aunt Margaret would greet us at the door wearing an apron, and often she served us cabbage rolls for lunch. Cabbage rolls were ground meat rolled up in a cabbage leaf and baked in tomato sauce.

But Aunt Margaret would tease me, saying that the rolls were called "mice". I would look at those pale green lumps sitting in pool of red tomato sauce in the baking pan. I could not get over the idea of "mice". My appetite was severely diminished.

I am an adult now, and my appetite is not affected by teasing. I would have ordered the cabbage rolls from the Romanian section of the menu, except that I am a vegetarian.

Instead, I ordered vegetable fajitas, from the third part of the menu, the Mexican part.

Jamaica Water

I told the owner that I wanted a nonalcoholic Mexican drink to go with my fajitas. He asked me if I had ever had jamaica water before, and I said I would try it. Actually, I had misheard him and thought he said "jicama", the crunchy root that sometimes shows up in salads. I wondered how you could make a drink out of crunchy roots, but I was going to try it anyway.

The drink turned out to be red with a nice flavor reminiscent of cranberry juice. And it turned out to be very familiar. It tasted just like soborado, my favorite drink in Nigeria. Every couple of months, dried flowers would appear in the market of the Nigerian city where I lived. My cook would boil up the dried flowers to make soborado.

When I left Africa to move back to the United States, I thought I would never taste soborado again.

But here I was drinking soborado again. It turns out that soborado was made from dried hyacinth flowers, and "jamaica" is the Spanish word for hyacinth.

The jamaica water was a direct connection to the years I spent in Africa. The cabbage rolls on the menu were a direct connection to my Aunt Margaret. The background of the restaurant's owner was a direct connection to my father's background.

All of this in one Romanian-Mexican-barbeque restaurant on a street in St. Louis that caught my architectural eye. A lifetime was summarized in one lunchtime.

122

PEOPLE IN AFRICA

People in Africa

People in Africa

THE HOUSE FACED EAST

On My Sitting Stoop

My mud house in Kano, Nigeria, had a long sitting stoop in front, and the house faced east. Because the house faced east, my stoop was in the shade when the African sun was blazing hot in the afternoon. It was a popular gathering spot for the neighborhood.

Every afternoon, a bloodletter set up shop on my stoop. Nigerians have a theory that you stay healthy by generating new blood cells. The bloodletter makes small incisions in the skin, heats up the air in a hollow cow horn, and places the horn over the incision. As the air cools in the horn, the old blood cells are gently drawn out, forcing you to generate new blood cells.

The theory must have some truth because all of the bloodletter's customers looked robust.

My next-door neighbor, Mallam Yau, did not have a sitting stoop, so he often sat on mine in the afternoon. He was a very old man and had two surprisingly young sons, aged 5 and 7. Mallam Yau and I would chat in Hausa. I was not fluent, and Mallam Yau would graciously finish my sentences for me.

It was another neighbor who told me how Mallam Yau had kept trouble away.

Shortly after I moved into my mud house in 1968, the Nigerian National Police wanted to investigate a rumor that there was a white man living in a black neighborhood. Six policemen arrived in a police van. I was not at home. They walked up to Mallam Yau and asked him if a white man was living there.

Mallam Yau, while sitting on my stoop, said to the policemen: "A white man? Living here? I have no idea what you are talking about." The police never came back.

The Red-and-White Kiosk

Coca-Cola kiosks are plywood sheds about six feet by eight feet, with a roof. The kiosks have refrigerators and sell both chilled Coke and chilled water.

My neighbors, without consulting me, decided to put a Coca-Cola kiosk in front of my house. They decided it was a good location for a kiosk because my house was the only one on the block with electricity and running water.

One day I came home from work and found a red-and-white kiosk in front of my house. I did not say a word, even though I could see an extension cord

125

running from the kiosk's refrigerator into an electrical outlet in my house. Inside my house, I found Mallam Yau's two sons at my water tap, filling up empty bottles with water to be sold in the kiosk.

Clearly, this was a neighborhood endeavor. My role was to foot the bill for the kiosk's electricity and the bill for the kiosk's water. I gave my unspoken consent to the arrangement.

A Small Charcoal Brazier

Years later, when I was living in a different part of Nigeria, I went back to visit the old neighborhood in Kano. The bloodletter was there on the sitting stoop. The Coca-Cola kiosk was doing a brisk business.

I asked about Mallam Yau and was escorted inside his home. He was quite ill, lying on a mat on the floor in one of his mud rooms. There was a small charcoal fire in a brazier sitting next to him.

I crouched down. Mallam Yau told me about his aches, about how he constantly felt cold, and about how he wondered if he would ever recover. I told him about my life in a different part of Nigeria. We spoke in Hausa. Mallam Yau graciously completed my sentences for me.

Nowadays, when people ask me why I liked living in Africa, I tell them about how exotic and exciting it was. I don't always tell people another reason I liked living in Africa: It was a place where people finished your sentences for you, even when they were on their deathbed.

People in Africa

THE MAN IN THE BLUE VEIL SITTING ON MY PORCH

I Get a Government House

The Nigerian government treats its teachers very well, calling them "education officers".

When I first went to teach in Nigeria in 1965, the government put me in a fully furnished two-bedroom ranch house with electricity, running water, and a circular driveway.

I also was paid a salary that enabled me to afford two servants. Musa was my cook; he had learned to cook while in the British Army during World War II. Musa was a Nigerian; he was congenial, and it was pleasant having him working in the house.

The other servant was Yusuf, a night watchman. All the government houses had night watchmen, and none of the night watchmen were from Nigeria.

The night watchmen were from a group called the Tuareg that lived in an area deep in the Sahara. These men had left their wives, children, and camels behind to take up night security jobs in Nigeria. They had no sentimental attachment to anyone in town and were considered quite fearsome.

Yusuf was rather quiet, and would sit on my porch all night, keeping me safe.

Graffiti in the Desert

All day and all night, Yusuf would wear a blue veil.

In the Sahara, women did not wear veils; men did. The veil really was an extra loop of blue turban cloth that covered the mouth so that only the eyes were visible. Tuareg men didn't take the veil off to eat; they just lifted it up with one hand while eating with the other hand. The mouth must not be seen.

The Tuareg were exotic. Not only did these men wear blue veils, but they always carried large swords.

The Tuareg had their own language and their own writing system, which was also exotic.

Our writing system is constrained compared to theirs. In English, a capital E has to be vertical with three lines pointing to the right. Turn the E on its side,

127

People in Africa

and people get confused. But the Tuareg can recognize their letters from any angle: upside-down, backward, or sideways. The English language can only be written left-to-right, but the Tuareg can write from left-to-right, or right-to-left, or up-to-down, or down-to-up, or in spirals.

The Tuareg like to write graffiti on rocks in the Sahara, and I am told that the graffiti is usually about the hot babes at the next oasis.

Tomatoes on the Doorstep

One day a Tuareg got into a bicycle accident near my house.

I went out and found his thigh gashed open with his flesh just hanging there. I surprised myself; without a hint of squeamishness, I sprang into action.

I grabbed a towel to cover the wound, and calmly explained to him that I would store his large sword in my house for safekeeping because the hospital did not allow swords. I drove the guy to the hospital, and he was sewn up.

Then my life changed.

Tuareg whom I had never seen before would greet me on the street. I would find tomatoes carefully placed on my doorstep as gifts. I had become known as the man who had helped a Tuareg.

I was really glad to be on the good side of these blue-veiled men from the Sahara who carry large swords with them everywhere and make a living off their fearsomeness.

People in Africa

A WHITE MAN IN A BLACK NEIGHBORHOOD

Twelve Gates into the City

The people of Kano, Nigeria, built a massive mud wall around their city in the twelfth century. The wall had twelve gates and secured an area large enough to grow crops to support the population in case of siege.

When I moved to Kano to teach school in 1965, the wall was still standing. There were still only twelve gates to get into the city. Over 100,000 people lived inside the city, all of them in mud houses. The city was ruled, as it had been for many centuries, by an emir.

In the way that Oz was an emerald city, Kano was an adobe city. Kano was exotic, intriguing, and forbidden --- forbidden to me because foreigners were not allowed to live inside the wall.

My school provided me with a nice house; it was made of cement with electricity, running water, and good cross-ventilation. But the house was outside the city wall, surrounded by other cement houses where white people lived. It was almost like living in a California subdivision. This was not what I envisioned when I decided to go to Africa.

In the entire history of Kano, the emir had only allowed one white person to live inside the wall. I decided that I was going to be the second white person to live inside the wall.

We Have No Objection

I always bought my Lipton tea from a shop run by a man named Aliyu.

Aliyu invited me to visit his home inside the wall. Aliyu's house was made of mud. I met his wife and young child, and I confided in him that I wanted to live in a mud house inside the wall.

Aliyu said the first step was to get the emir's permission.

My school principal contacted the palace and set up an audience for me. It was the first time I had talked to royalty. I tried buttering up the emir by telling him how beautiful his city was and how wonderful it would be to live inside the wall.

His response was brief and royal, "We have no objection."

129

People in Africa

I zoomed over to Aliyu's shop and told him that the emir had no objection. Aliyu started to look for mud houses for rent in his neighborhood.

As Aliyu searched, a pattern emerged: He would find a house for rent and then I would look at it. The landlord would realize that I was a white man. The house would suddenly be no longer for rent. We were given excuses: One landlord's brother was moving to Kano and needed the house; another landlord's son would be finishing school soon and needed that house.

I told Aliyu that I wanted to end the house search. Apparently, the emir had no objection to my living inside the wall, but other people did. However, Aliyu was determined; he started searching for a mud house for rent outside the wall.

Let's Call the Whole Thing Off

Aliyu did find a house outside the wall. I looked at the house; the landlord realized that I was a white man. The house was suddenly not for rent. The landlord said he needed money and had to sell the house instead of renting it.

I wanted to call off the house search. Aliyu had been so gracious, spending many hours trying to help me, without any gain for himself. He had made himself unpopular with his neighbors as he tried to break a centuries-old tradition and bring a white person into the city.

I felt that I had imposed on Aliyu's graciousness enough. I saw the future as just a long string of landlord excuses. I said, "Let's call it off."

"No," said Aliyu, "Let's call the landlord's bluff. Let's buy the house."

I scraped up $300; Aliyu put in $300; the six-room mud house was purchased in his name. Legally, it was not my house, but it sure felt like it was my house.

I was twenty-two years old, and I was thrilled. I was thrilled to be living in a mud house, even if it was outside the wall. And I was certainly thrilled to have a friend who spent so much effort to arrange for a white man to live in a black neighborhood.

130

DAY TRIPPING WITH THE PUBKEEPER'S DAUGHTER

Eileen, the Pubkeeper's Daughter

Tom and Eileen Horton were friends of mine when I lived in Sokoto, Nigeria. Tom was a civil engineer, and they had come from England on a two-year contract with the highway department in Sokoto State.

Tom and Eileen told me that they loved Africa. They said that they woke up every morning excited with the prospect of learning something new each day. Eileen was the more sociable of the two. She was a pubkeeper's daughter; that must be where she got her sociability.

No one had ever written a travel guide to Sokoto State, so I decided that I would write one.

This would mean making lots of day trips around the state to check out the local markets and various points of interest. I invited Eileen along on a number of these trips; she proved to be a fine traveling companion.

Day Tripping to Villages and Markets

Eileen and I would go to small villages, where we would meet the village chief, and Eileen would be very sociable. We would go to rural markets, where Eileen would chat with the merchants and never once complain about how the dust in the market messed up her shoes.

Then it was time for us to visit the holiest site in Sokoto State: the tomb of Usman dan Fodio. Usman dan Fodio was an Islamic reformer who lived in the early nineteenth century. He is still held in great respect, and his tomb is an Islamic pilgrimage site.

Because it was a holy site, I carefully told Eileen how to prepare for our visit: early morning, lots of coins, long sleeves, covered head.

First, we needed to go early in the morning. You have to take your shoes off at the entrance to the courtyard and walk barefoot along a cement path to enter the tomb itself. If we went later in the day, the blazing African sun would make the cement unbearably hot for bare feet.

Second, we must take lots of coins. Holy sites attract lots of beggars, and we would need to give alms as we walked along the cement path.

People in Africa

Third, since Eileen was a woman, she should follow Islamic dress code. The Koran does not say that women should wear a veil, but it does say that women should cover their heads and arms.

Visiting the Holy Tomb

On the morning of our visit, Eileen came out of her house and proudly showed me how carefully she had prepared.

She had on a long-sleeved dress with a matching cap. The outfit was black, a nice touch for visiting a tomb. She had a black purse, which she shook so I would know that she had lots of coins to give to the beggars.

Early morning, lots of coins, long sleeves, covered head. She met all the requirements I listed for her. But I had never mentioned that the dress should be modest; her black dress had a sexy plunging neckline that exposed most of her upper chest.

Because she had gone to so much effort, I decided not to mention her bosom.

We went off to the tomb of Usman dan Fodio. We took off our shoes as a sign of respect. As Eileen walked down the cement path to enter the tomb with her feet bare and a lot of her chest bare, the beggars were so awestruck that they forgot to ask us for alms.

I wondered if I needed to put a comment in the travel guide I was writing: If you wear a plunging neckline when visiting Islamic holy pilgrimage sites, you do not need to bring lots of coins with you.

People in Africa

A FISH THAT LIVES IN A WELL

The Ferry to N'Djamena

There were four of us on vacation in Cameroon in West Africa, and we thought that as long as we were visiting Cameroon, we might as well visit the Republic of Chad. All we had to do was cross a river. We planned to arrive in Chad in the late afternoon, spend the night, and come back the next day.

So the four of us drove our Volkswagen beetle onto a ferry and headed toward the ferry dock in N'Djamena, the capital of Chad. As we approached the dock, we saw a large sign that said "Welcome to Chad" in French.

When the dockworkers spotted us and our Volkswagen, they started waving us away. They were shouting at us in French. They were not saying "Welcome to Chad"; they were saying "Stop!" "Do not land!" "Go back across the river!" This did not sound very hopeful.

When the ferry docked, we found out that we were on the last ferry of the day, and the immigration office had already closed. The authorities could not process us, so we had to remain on the ferry and return to Cameroon.

On the ferry back to Cameroon, I talked to a Nigerian merchant. He listened to our story about how immigration had closed even though the last ferry of the day had not arrived. The merchant had visited Chad many times and was not surprised.

He told me, "Everyone in Chad is like a fish that lives in a well. All they know of the world is their own little circle of sky."

Standoff at the Immigration Office

When the ferry took us the four of us back to Cameroon that evening, we looked back across the river at N'Djamena. It was the first time any of us had ever been expelled from a country.

We vowed that we would set foot in Chad.

We spent the night in a hotel in Cameroon, and early the next morning we were back at the ferry. Although we would only have enough time for lunch in N'Djamena, we were determined that we would get authorities to let us into Chad.

This time the dockworkers did not wave us away or shout at us. We got to go into the immigration office. Because I spoke a little French, it was my job to

133

People in Africa

show our passports to the immigration officer, who immediately asked us where our visas were. I said we expected his office to issue visas on the spot; he told us that we needed to go to a Chadian embassy. I pointed out that the nearest Chadian embassy was hundreds of miles away. We were at a standoff.

I decided to use flattery on the clerk. I told the clerk over and over that we had heard how good-hearted the people of Chad were and what a beautiful country Chad was. I also made it clear that I was going to stand there praising his country until I wore him down and he issued visas to the four of us.

Finally, the clerk budged. He consulted his supervisor and said that they would issue us visas. The clerk then asked me how long we planned to stay in the beautiful country of Chad with all its good-hearted people.

My answer, "Six hours." The clerk gasped --- all that bickering over such a short visit --- but he still issued each of us a six-hour visa.

In the Beautiful Land of Good-Hearted People

Six hours was just enough time to finish checking in through immigration, import the car through Chadian customs, find a nice place to eat lunch, export the car through Chadian customs, check out through immigration, and catch the ferry back to Cameroon.

The six-hour visit was a lot of effort, but we had a strong sense of satisfaction. We could now say that we had been in Chad. In the process, we met a good-hearted immigration clerk and had lunch in a beautiful restaurant.

Plus, we had managed to overcome the bureaucracy of a country where everyone is like a fish that lives in a well.

People in Africa

STRANDED IN MY LIVING ROOM

No Ticket to the United States

In 2009, I heard the song "Twin Rocks, Oregon" for the first time.

Written by Shawn Mullins, the song is filled with nice images: "It's been years since I've smelled this salty sea" --- and nice thoughts --- "ain't it a blessing to do what you wanna do." The song is almost a counterculture anthem, and it mentions the book *The Tokyo-Montana Express* by Richard Brautigan, a man who personified the counterculture movement in the 1970s. In fact, the last line of 'Twin Rocks, Oregon' is "Sitting on his bedroll looking just like Richard Brautigan."

And whenever I hear the name Richard Brautigan, I think of the day in 1972 when Phillip Shea came to my house with his brother Edmund in tow.

I was living in Kano, Nigeria. Phillip Shea was a historian doing research in Kano. His brother had flown out from California to visit him and to see Nigeria before Phillip wrapped up his research and went back to the United States.

Phillip was about to leave Nigeria, but his brother was not going with him. Edmund had bought a one-way ticket from California to Kano and did not have a ticket back to the USA.

Since I had a guest room, could Edmund stay with me? I was told that it wouldn't be for long. Edmund was Richard Brautigan's favorite photographer, and Brautigan owed Edmund money for a cover photo he took for his latest book. Brautigan would be sending the money to Africa any day now.

Trout Fishing in America

Phillip left Kano, and Edmund moved in with me for what I thought would be a couple of days.

I would come home from work each day, and Edmund would be sitting in my living room. He would ask me how my day was. He would listen attentively, and then he would report that he had trekked down to the bank, and Richard Brautigan's money still had not arrived.

This happened for one week, which stretched into two weeks. I fed Edmund; I took him along with me on my evening jaunts, buying him beers and paying his admission to the movies.

135

People in Africa

And then I started to wonder if I had been duped. Brautigan, whose book *Trout Fishing in America* was a big best seller, was probably too busy to worry about somebody being stranded in my living room in Africa. I had no proof that Edmund really was Richard Brautigan's favorite photographer. In fact, I had no proof that Richard Brautigan even knew Edmund.

I started to dread coming home to hear the same story about trekking to the bank and finding no money.

<u>Revenge of the Lawn</u>

Finally, Richard Brautigan really did send Edmund money, and Edmund bought a ticket back to the United States. Before he left for the airport, Edmund gave me a thank-you present, an advance copy of Brautigan's latest book: *Revenge of the Lawn*.

The photo on the cover really was Edmund's ticket home.

In 2010, I entered Edmund Shea's name into Google and found out that Edmund had died in 2004. Reading his obituary, I discovered some things about Edmund.

I discovered that I was not the first person to have Edmund as a houseguest. He had been Lenny Bruce's houseguest in the 1960s. Yes, the very same Lenny Bruce who is rated one of the top American comics of the twentieth century. The obituary said that Edmund used to give Lenny advice on how to deal with federal drug charges.

I was stunned. Edmund never mentioned to me that he had stayed in Lenny Bruce's house.

I discovered that Edmund was also friends with Fleetwood Mac and photographed them for their album covers. Edmund was friends with Herbie Hancock. And with Keith Jarrett.

Edmund Shea never mentioned that he knew these icons of American culture. All he did was ask me how my day was and thank me for the beers I bought him.

Now I realize that I had a bit of a celebrity staying in my house who was very quiet about his celebrity. In fact, he treated me like I was a bit of a celebrity myself.

People in Africa

A LEPER IN MY HOUSEHOLD

Puffy and Sweaty

When I first went to Kano to teach in 1965, the Nigerian government provided a house for me.

Behind the house were servant quarters. The quarters had two separate rooms and a common latrine. The cook, Musa, lived in one room with his wife and son. The night watchman, Yusuf, lived in the other room, and they all shared the latrine.

This became a problem.

Musa came to me and told me that Yusuf was puffy and sweaty, and he did not want Yusuf using the same latrine as his family. I must have had a blank look on my face because I did not see what puffiness had to do with sharing a latrine.

Musa had to explain, "Puffiness and excess sweating are signs of leprosy."

Leprosy! Before I left America, I was told that I did not have to worry about leprosy in Africa because the only way to catch it was to live in close proximity to someone with the disease. But now I did need to worry because there was a leper in my household, living in close proximity with my cook's family.

Dank and Foreboding

I started to wonder about Yusuf. Once leprosy was confirmed, would he become a pariah, living a life of exile? Would he become fingerless? Blind?

Lepers lose their fingers because their nerves atrophy and they cannot feel. They cannot feel the heat of a cooking fire, and sometimes their fingers burn down to stubs.

Lepers become blind because their facial muscles atrophy and they cannot blink. Without the sweep of their eyelids, their eyes become infected and they become blind.

I wondered how to break the news to Yusuf that he may have leprosy, but it turned out to be easier than I thought. He knew that something was wrong with him. I took him to a doctor, who confirmed our suspicions.

Yusuf then packed his few belongings (some clothes, a teapot, and a giant sword), and I moved him to the Kano Leprosarium on the outskirts of town.

People in Africa

I had seen dank and foreboding leper colonies in Hollywood movies, and I had read about dank and foreboding leper colonies in novels about Hawaii. I was prepared for the worst.

Hopeful and Clever

But the Kano Leprosarium was a sunny and cheerful place; it was run by American Protestant missionaries. I was glad to see that Yusuf would be in such a pleasant institution.

The missionaries offered hope. There was a drug that would keep leprosy from progressing. It came in the form of a small pill, way too powerful to be taken whole; it had to be cut into nine pieces and was carefully dispensed at the leprosarium.

For the lepers who had lost fingers, there was nothing the American missionaries could do. For the lepers whose facial muscles had atrophied, there was something they could do.

American missionary eye surgeons had cleverly invented a procedure in Kano where they would take ligaments out of a leper's leg and implant them in the leper's face. The ligaments would connect the jaw to the eyelids. Every time the mouth opened, the eyelids would sweep the eye, keeping it moist.

I knew that I left Yusuf in good hands. The leprosy drug would keep him stable. He would not become a pariah; he would not get to the point where he needed a ligament implanted in his face.

I had left Yusuf in the hands of hopeful American missionaries, who invented an important leprosy procedure in the middle of Africa.

It made me proud to be an American.

138

CAREER

Career

Career

I HAD A HAND IN BUILDING IT

Keal and Spray Paint

The merchants were understandably angry. There were plans to build a skyscraper, which meant their Manhattan neighborhood was going to be demolished. Their neighborhood, consisting of two-story shops lining narrow streets, had not changed much since the end of the nineteenth century.

The merchants decided to fight back.

They knew the first step for planning a skyscraper was surveying the area. They watched how the survey crews operated. The surveyors document their work with yellow spray paint and a yellow chalk, called keal. The spray paint marked turning points where rodmen placed their rods, and the keal was used to write measurements on the street or sidewalk.

The merchants went out and bought their own yellow spray paint and their own keal. They waited for the surveyors to take a coffee break, a lunch break, or to pack up shop at the end of the day. The merchants proceeded to spray false turning points. They used their keal to change the measurements written on the sidewalks.

The merchants were determined to stop the surveyors.

But they were devout Jews.

Eager to Get Overtime

Devout Jews do not do business on their Sabbath. Therefore, their shops are shuttered on Saturdays. The neighborhood is quiet then.

The organization building the skyscraper realized that the only way to survey the area was to do it on Saturdays. They told all their survey crews, spread around New York City, to come and earn some overtime working on Saturday.

That's where I come in. I was working as a surveyor for the organization. My crew volunteered to survey on Saturdays.

I was eighteen years old. I didn't have any concerns about a historic low-rise neighborhood being wiped out for a skyscraper. I eagerly accepted the assignment because it meant getting paid overtime.

The organization I worked for was the Port of New York Authority.

141

Career

The skyscraper that they planned to build would come to be known as the World Trade Center.

Intertwined in Our Grief

When the World Trade Center was attacked on September 11, 2001, it became clear how intertwined Americans are.

One of the first responders at the site was my cousin's son. One of my dear friends worked a block away from the site and witnessed too many upsetting things. One of the firemen at the site grew up across the street from the house where my mother and father retired.

My employer in St. Louis had a small office in the World Trade Center; they announced that all of our employees were accounted for. My buddy Randy works for a company in St. Louis that made the window frames for the World Trade Center. I realized that I once worked in an office building in Minneapolis designed by Minoru Yamasaki, the architect of the World Trade Center.

When flights were grounded on 9/11, we opened our home to a fellow who was stuck at the St. Louis airport

Americans were intertwined in the event. And intertwined in our grief.

As a surveyor, I grieve the loss of something I had a hand in building. As someone who grew up in the New York area, I grieve the loss of life and the loss of a landmark. As an American, I grieve because our borders did not keep us safe.

Career

OVERCOMING THE WRATH OF MY TEAM LEAD

My Favor Backfires

I had been working as a programmer at U.S. Bank for a few months when I got a new team lead; her name was Evelyn.

Under my old team lead, I made a vacation request and it was denied due to the priority of the project I was working on. To make up for the denial, the vice-president of the bank had told me that whenever my next vacation request would be, I was guaranteed to get it approved.

Once the high-priority project was complete, I handed my new team lead, Evelyn, a vacation request. I decided to fill Evelyn in on what had happened to my previous vacation request. I explained that the vice-president had said that my vacation request would get approved no matter what.

I thought I was doing Evelyn a favor --- no point in her denying my request if the vice-president was just going to overrule her.

Suddenly, I was the subject of my team lead's wrath. I was stunned. Evelyn viewed my statement as a threat to go over her head; she was furious. She raked me over the coals at that time and raked me over the coals again when it came time for my annual performance review.

She did approve the request, but I wondered if I could ever get on her good side.

Doughnuts on Saturday

This was during the 1980s, the decade when the tail began to wag the dog. Banks used to view information technology as a just another department in the bank. Then banks started to realize that information technology was vital to their business.

The 1980s were also the time when information technology started to act more business-like. Evelyn was in the forefront at U.S. Bank. She introduced timelines, project plans, and monitoring. Up to this point, projects had been haphazard, kind of running on their own.

Whenever a project was falling behind, Evelyn would ask the programmers on her team to come in on Saturday. But whenever we came in on Saturday,

Career

Evelyn would also come in. She didn't need to be there, but she was. She brought along doughnuts, adding a festive note.

Nowadays, I look back on those Saturdays and realize that Evelyn shaped my definition of a good team lead --- someone who would not ask people to do extra effort that they were not willing to do themselves.

The Finest Tribute

Evelyn left the bank and went to use her team lead skills at Target Stores.

By now I was on her good side. We kept in touch, especially when Evelyn and her husband joined the recipe-of-the-week club and asked people over to their house to try out the latest dish.

Then breast cancer struck Evelyn. I was still invited me to dinner, even though Evelyn was undergoing chemotherapy. She was cheerful and sociable, and I made sure to compliment her on her choice of wigs to cover up her hair loss.

Then came hospitalization for Evelyn. I talked to her on the phone: I was getting ready to move from Minneapolis to St. Louis, and I wanted to see her before I left. But Evelyn said she was not up for visitors.

Shortly after I moved to St. Louis I got a phone call saying that Evelyn had died. In her will, she had listed her choices for pallbearers, and I was one of them.

Being named as a pallbearer was the finest tribute Evelyn could have paid me. That rocky time when I was the object of her wrath was far behind.

I realized how I had benefited from knowing her: She had definitely taught me never to go over my supervisor's head; but she also showed me how to run projects, how to be a good team lead, and how to go through chemotherapy with grace.

By naming me as a pallbearer, Evelyn put me at peace. And I, of course, hope that Evelyn is now at peace as well.

Career

LARRY, MOE, AND CURLY AT THE BANK OF AMERICA

Getting Bopped with a Giant Mailing Tube

I moved to Boston in 1984 to work as a computer programmer for the Bank of America.

The bank's programmers worked in the same building as the computer. The two-story building was windowless, except for an eighteen-inch-square piece of glass in the door. For security reasons, the building had no signage except for a number on the front. There was a historical marker next to the building: George Washington passed this spot in 1776, bringing cannon from Fort Ticonderoga to dislodge the British troops occupying Boston.

Our cubicles were in groups of four. On my first day on the job, I noticed that the other three programmers in my grouping kept giant six-foot long mailing tubes in their cubicles. I quickly found out why.

Every morning, my cubicle neighbors would sneak around and bop each other over the head with a giant mailing tube. They would yell "Nyuk, nyuk." They got into heated discussions about Larry, Moe, and Curly. I would spend the morning programming, while my three neighbors re-created Three Stooges episodes.

After lunch, they started working. At 5 PM, as I was getting ready to go home, they phoned their wives and said they would be working into the night. One of them lived in New Hampshire and kept a sleeping bag under his desk.

It never occurred to my coworkers that if they spent the morning working, instead of wasting it being knuckleheads, they could go home for dinner.

Phone a Friend for the Weather

Every morning the Three Stooges came to life, until the Bank of America said that the programmers were moving out of the computer building into the bank's nearby office building.

Our team leader pointed out the advantages of moving: Our group would no longer be isolated, and there would plenty of natural light in the office building, which had lots of windows.

The team didn't want to move; they claimed that we didn't need windows. If you want natural light, just walk to the door and look out the eighteen-inch-

Career

square piece of glass. If you want to know what the weather is, just phone up a friend and ask.

The argument was about windows, but the real reason to stay was to re-enact the Three Stooges. Once our team was integrated into the bank's office building, there would be no more bopping each other with giant mailing tubes, no more nyuks, no more sleeping bags under desks.

Everyone Has One

Our programming team moved to the Bank of America office building in 1986. While we were changing buildings, the world of computer programming was changing.

When I started working with computers in 1977, programmers were a rare breed. We used punched cards, which were nasty. Drop a tray of cards, and you had to spend an hour putting them back in order.

Punched cards got replaced by computer terminals. Suddenly, lots of people were accessing computers. Soon computers started appearing in people's homes. Now everyone has one.

Programmers stopped being a rare breed. Our move to a building with windows in 1986 was a physical indication that programming had become mainstream.

Once in the new building, I discovered a memo that had been sent out two years previously, announcing that I had been hired. The memo said, "Doug Schneider will be joining our team. He brings a wealth of computer and banking experience. Unfortunately, he is not a fan of the Three Stooges."

I was thunderstruck by the memo. The Bank of America had hesitated to hire me because I did not admire Larry, Moe, and Curly.

The memo also explained why no one ever offered me a giant mailing tube. I was glad that computer programming had gone mainstream.

Career

THE STANDOFF AT THE JEWISH DELICATESSEN

A Perfectly Good Refrigerator

Growing up, I knew that Jewish people did not eat pork, but I did not learn what kosher meant until a high school friend announced that his family was going to start keeping kosher.

Keeping kosher meant separating meat items from dairy items. They had to throw out a perfectly good refrigerator because it had been used to hold both meat and dairy items. The family bought two new refrigerators, one just for meat and one just for dairy.

They could not serve meat and dairy items at the same meal, so they had to throw out all their old dinnerware. From that point on, one set of dinnerware would be used for meat items and one set of dinnerware would be used for dairy items; likewise: pots, pans, and silverware.

I was dazzled by the amount of money all of this must have cost, just to separate meat items from dairy items.

At the Bar Mitzvah

My father suffered most of his adult life from a stomach ulcer, and his doctor instructed him to have a glass of warm milk with his meals. When Mom was cooking, she always put a glass of milk in the middle of the stovetop so that Dad's milk would be nice and warm for him.

Milk became Dad's standard drink; he had it with every meal.

One day Dad was invited to a bar mitzvah at the Jewish Community Center. The guests were treated to a nice roast beef dinner, and once he was seated, Dad beckoned to the waiter.

"Please bring me a glass of warm milk to go with my roast beef."

The Jewish Community Center waiter whispered back to Dad, "Sir, if I bring you a glass of milk, I will lose my job."

That was one of Dad's few milk-less meals.

Career

<u>At Goldie Locks Deli</u>

I spent three summers working as a surveyor for LaGuardia and Kennedy airports in New York.

Nobody on our survey crew brought a lunch from home. Instead, right before lunchtime, we would go to a delicatessen near the airport, get sandwiches and sodas, and head back to the office to eat lunch.

I usually ordered a cold corned beef sandwich for my lunch; it was my favorite.

For a change, the survey crew decided to go to a Jewish delicatessen called "Goldie Locks." At the Goldie Locks Deli, I hit an obstacle when I asked the sandwich maker for a cold corned beef sandwich.

"We only serve hot corned beef sandwiches."

"But, look, your corned beef is sitting in a cooler case and you need to heat it up for a hot corned beef sandwich; so, just skip the heating step, and make me a cold corned beef sandwich."

"Sir, we only serve hot corned beef sandwiches." The Jewish delicatessen sandwich maker and I were at a standoff.

Then I remembered what happened to my father at the bar mitzvah, and I knew how to win the battle. "If I can't have a cold corned beef sandwich, then I will have a hot corned beef and cheese sandwich."

"One cold corned beef sandwich coming up. Would you like mustard on that, sir?"

Career

THE ROOM WHERE JOHN F. KENNEDY DIED

Facing Squeamishness Head On

I moved to Dallas in 1969 and needed a job that would tide me over for four months. I decided that this was an opportunity to face my lifelong squeamishness head on. I applied for a job at Parkland Memorial Hospital, working as an orderly in the emergency room --- or "triage", as Parkland preferred to call it.

Parkland hired me; there are always openings for orderlies in triage. I showed up for day one of training.

Parkland is the public hospital that covers all of Dallas County, and triage gets very busy. So besides teaching medical terminology and teaching how to put on rubber gloves on Day One, the hospital also teaches how to deal discreetly with patients who are often left lying on gurneys in crowded hallways.

On day one, they taught me how to discreetly take the rectal temperature of a patient left lying on a gurney in a crowded hallway. The procedure involves turning the gurney so the patient's back is to the wall, inserting the thermometer, and draping with a towel --- draping gently so you do not knock the thermometer out.

They also gave me a tour of the triage area. We went into each of the operating rooms. The rooms were identical, but we lingered in the last one: It was the room where John F. Kennedy had died six years before.

Amidst Blood and Gristle

At the end of day one, the trainer made a comment that Parkland's triage gets extremely busy on Saturday night, the night when people in Dallas County drank lots of Lone Star Beer and made use of their handguns.

I realized that my squeamishness was not the problem. I had not been uncomfortable in triage on day one. My imagination was my problem. I had visions of working on a Saturday night, dealing with blood and gristle amidst the reek of Lone Star Beer.

I decided there would be no day two. I phoned up Parkland Memorial Hospital and resigned.

I still needed a job for four months, so I went down to the Dallas City Library and got hired in their mailroom. Surely I would not have to face blood and gristle in the library.

149

Career

Dallas Is Dallas

Day one of my new job at the Dallas City Library went smoothly. But on day two, an armed robber, being pursued by the Dallas Police, ran into the library, through the reference room, and into the main stairwell. A gunbattle ensued.

I avoided the library's main stairwell until all evidence of blood and gristle had been cleaned up.

The library had an art gallery on the top floor. Its official name was "The Meditation Room". On day four at the Dallas Public Library, someone went into the Meditation Room, and blew their brains out with a handgun.

I avoided the library's Meditation Room until all evidence of blood and gristle had been cleaned up.

Finally, I got the message. Dallas is Dallas. County hospital or city library --- you are never far from blood and gristle.

Career

CHUCK WOKE UP AND COULD NOT FIND A WHITE SHIRT

Dressing like a 1927 Insurance Salesman

My first programming job was with Safeco Insurance in its home office.

Safeco was known in Seattle as the company that had not changed its dress code for fifty years. All male employees, including the programmers in the home office, had to dress like a 1927 insurance salesman.

The dress code stated that beards were forbidden, and moustaches could not extend beyond the corners of the mouth. Hair could not reach the shirt collar.

We had to wear a suit, as long as the suit was not made of corduroy. And whatever the suit was made of, the thread used for the stitching must match the predominant color of the material. Employees could take their suit jackets off when they were working at their desks, but they had to put their suit jackets on if they were going to ride on an elevator.

Neckties were required; bow ties, however, were not allowed. The top of your shoes could not go above your ankle bone.

And only one shirt color was allowed: white.

Safeco's home office was in the U District, just two blocks from the University of Washington campus, which had 30,000 students. None of these students wore suits and ties with white shirts. While going to and from work, Safeco employees stuck out like a sore thumb.

Chuck Solves His Problem

One morning, a coworker of mine named Chuck woke up and could not find a clean white shirt.

Chuck had some blue shirts, but Safeco would not allow him to wear a suit and tie with a blue shirt. Chuck had some white shirts with stripes, but Safeco would not allow him to wear a suit and tie with a striped shirt.

There was only one way Chuck could go to work without a white shirt.

He put on a rumpled sweatshirt and some jeans. He did not shower; he did not shave. He got to the office early. Chuck spent the day pretending that his

151

Career

beeper had gone off in the middle of the night and that he had to come in to fix a production problem.

When the Muzak Stops

Safeco also had some work rules.

Everyone had to start work at 8:00 AM. When you arrived at your desk, you would hear Muzak playing. At precisely 8:00 AM, the Muzak stopped, and the entire building would start working. You were not allowed to come in late.

The entire company took the same coffee break (the Muzak would play during coffee break); lunch hours were staggered according to which floor you worked on.

At precisely 4:30 PM, the Muzak would come back on. Everyone would stop working, and the entire building would go home. You were not allowed to work late.

Many of my friends wondered how I could work for a company with such a restrictive dress code and with such strict work rules. But I really enjoyed working there. Safeco cared about its employees: it provided me with training, my manager was supportive, I was learning a lot, and, of course, I never had to work past 4:30 PM.

I didn't mind dressing like a 1927 insurance salesman.

Career

MY CHILDHOOD BANK HAS DISAPPEARED

Brooklyn in the Good Old Days

"My childhood bank has disappeared." Mabel Mifflin said this to me in 1983, and I detected some wistfulness in her voice.

Mabel was my mother's best friend; they were both born in 1907 and grew up together in Brooklyn. They remained friends throughout their entire lives.

I imagine Mom and Mabel as little girls in the good old days walking down a street in Brooklyn. They would stroll past an imposing stone building with the letters B-A-N-K carved in granite over the doorway. This bank would have impressed the girls as being very solid and very permanent.

However, that bank did not survive the savings and loan crisis of the 1980s, when over 1,000 banks failed and were absorbed into other banks.

In 1983, Mabel was wistful because a pillar of her childhood had disappeared. Her comment did not make me wistful --- it made me nervous because I was working for a bank.

What Name Should I Use

In 1983, the bank I was working for was healthy and not in danger of collapsing. In fact, it was absorbing a lot of the banks that had failed. But a healthy bank faces a different type of danger --- being acquired.

During my computer programming career, I have worked for three banks, and none of the three banks has the same name now as it did when I worked there. This is a problem for me: I don't know what to say when I tell people where I used to work.

I worked at my first bank until 1984. After I left that bank, it was acquired by another bank, which changed its name to the name of a different bank that it had also acquired. I worked at my second bank until 1991. After I left that bank, it was acquired by a local bank, which was then acquired by a regional bank, which was then acquired by a nationwide bank. I worked at my third bank until 1997. After I left that bank, it acquired another bank and took the name of the bank it had acquired.

I solve my problem by giving people the current names of the banks rather than their historical names: I say that I worked for U.S. Bank, Bank of America, and Wells Fargo Bank, even though I never really worked for any of these banks.

Career

Looking for Persistence

There is a pattern: after I leave an employer, it either gets acquired or changes its name, even if it is not a bank.

I worked for May Department Stores until 2000. After I left May Company, it was acquired by Federated Department Stores, which changed its own name to Macy's Incorporated. I worked for A. G. Edwards until 2005. After I left, they were taken over by Wachovia Financial. Then Wachovia Financial was taken over by Wells Fargo Advisors.

Mabel Mifflin learned that what seemed so permanent in her youth did not remain permanent. And I learned in my career that companies that seem permanent do not remain permanent.

So I am not expecting permanence out of the company I am currently working for. I do expect persistence, however, and want the company to persist until I leave.

Of course, as soon as I leave, the company will be in imminent danger of being acquired or having its name changed.

Career

HE SHOOK MY HAND A COUPLE OF TIMES

First Day at the Brokerage Firm

Abraham Lincoln got married in Ben Edwards' great-grandfather's parlor. It was this great-grandfather who founded a brokerage firm in 1887 and named the firm after himself --- A.G. Edwards, Inc. Leadership of the firm was passed down through four generations of the Edwards family.

I started working for A.G. Edwards in May 2000. On my first day at the company, all the new employees were taken in a group to the CEO's office. This got my attention. Of all the companies I had worked for, I had never once set foot in a CEO's office. Here it was my first day, and I was getting to set foot in Ben Edwards' office.

I thought the new employees were going to the office to introduce themselves to the CEO. I was wrong; the purpose was for the CEO to introduce himself to the new employees. Ben seemed genuinely pleased that we had chosen to work for his firm. I felt honored.

He then went around and shook everyone's hand. I felt honored again but also a bit uncomfortable. Ben Edwards was an avid collector of Chinese Imari porcelain; his office was filled with plates, bowls, and vases. I was afraid a vigorous handshake might send a $25,000 vase crashing to the floor.

Later on, Ben would shake my hand in the cafeteria at the annual Thanksgiving lunch and at the annual Christmas lunch, when there was no porcelain around to make me nervous. But the effect of the man and his handshakes was clear: Instead of working for A.G. Edwards, Inc., I felt like I was working for Ben.

I think most of the 15,500 employees felt the same way: We all felt like we were working for Ben.

Back to the Middle Ages

Ben believed in the Golden Rule. He publicly stated that the customer came first, the employee came second, and the shareholders came third.

As an employee, I was proud of the company's growth into the largest brokerage firm outside New York City. I was proud of the amenities available in the corporate headquarters. I was proud that the company encouraged us to volunteer to mentor in a grade school during lunchtime. The company even provided a shuttle bus to take us to the school.

155

Career

Then Ben retired. I had expected the position of CEO to go to Ben's son. The board of directors chose someone else --- someone who was not a descendent of A.G. Edwards. I was reminded of the Middle Ages and wondered if Ben's son was a hemophiliac, and they were trying to avoid passing the crown to him.

The new CEO started changing things. He divided us into groups and had us herded into the auditorium to be branded.

We did not have our flesh seared with hot irons in the auditorium. Instead, we were shown a movie about the new company logo, which was a wing and a flame. The wing and a flame reminded me of a medieval coat-of-arms.

The movie said that the wing reflects the freedom of a financial consultant to do what is right for the customer; the flame reflects an enduring dedication to professional integrity. The flame was colored Sedona red --- the color of the rocks near Sedona, Arizona, a place of special regard by native Americans.

Do what is right and practice integrity - a nice message, bathed in the color of the rocks in Sedona.

But soon after the branding session, the new CEO took away the lunchtime shuttle bus that carried mentors to the grade school. And the new CEO started laying off employees --- something that had never happened when the company was in the hands of a descendent of A.G. Edwards, not even during the Great Depression.

Reading the Obituary

I left A.G. Edwards before it became clear why the board of directors had not made Ben Edwards' son CEO. It had nothing to do with hemophilia.

They wanted a CEO who would steer the company toward being acquired. Their goal was not to do what was right for the customer; they wanted to do what was good for their own wallets. They were not interested in personal integrity; instead, they were interested in personal income growth. So much for the wing and the flame.

The brokerage firm was sold to a large bank six years after Ben Edwards retired. His legacy was destroyed.

Ben Edwards died in April 2009.

Reading an obituary about the man who shook my hand a couple of times, I was reminded that there once was a brokerage firm that lived by the Golden Rule. I know because I worked there; I worked for Ben.

MOTHER

Mother

Mother

WHEN EDITH MET HENRY

At the Matchmaker's Apartment

Here is how Edith, my mother, met Henry, my father.

When Mom left high school in the 1920s, she found a job in an office running a Monroe calculator. This was one of the first mass-produced adding machines. Mom liked the Monroe calculator because it made a racket, and they made her work out in the hallway where she could enjoy some solitude.

Ruth, who was one of Mom's coworkers, got married.

Ruth believed that everyone should get married. She decided to match up some of the girls in her office with some of the guys in her husband's office. They were all invited to Ruth's apartment in Manhattan for a party --- something like a mass blind date, with Ruth being the matchmaker.

Ruth had chosen George as a good match for my mother.

Fresh from the Speakeasy

The girls arrived early for the party and were waiting in the apartment. The guys, however, had stopped at a speakeasy on the way over to Ruth's.

When the guys finally arrived, Ruth introduced them around. Mom did not hear the name "George" mentioned. Mom asked where her blind date was.

One of the guys took Mom to the window and pointed down at the sidewalk below.

There, Mom saw a very drunk man holding himself upright by hugging a lamppost for support. He looked just like one of those drunks she had seen in cartoons. George had had too much to drink at the speakeasy, and when the guys got to Ruth's building, they left him on the sidewalk. They were too embarrassed to bring him up to Ruth's apartment.

So Mom forgot about George and started socializing. She talked to a fellow named Henry. She liked him.

A Marriage That Started in a Mirror

Ruth's matchmaking instincts quickly told her that a possible romance was about to begin. She pulled Henry aside into an alcove so they would be out of

Mother

Mom's line of sight. Ruth asked Dad if he liked Edith. Dad vigorously nodded his head yes.

What Ruth and Dad did not realize was that Mom was watching them. By positioning herself near a mirror in the living room, Mom could watch the clandestine conversation in the alcove. Mom saw Dad's vigorous nod. Mom knew that he was the man for her.

Edith and Henry got married on June 21, 1930.

Their marriage produced three children, four grandchildren, and seven great-grandchildren. Together, Edith and Henry lived through the Depression, through a world war, through postwar suburbia, through the social changes of the sixties, and into the calm of retirement.

Their marriage, which had started in a mirror, ended when Dad died, ninety-six days short of their fiftieth wedding anniversary.

Mother

A LITTLE WHITE DUCK DOING WHAT HE OUGHTA

An Early Form of Karaoke

Back when I was a kid, I serenaded my aunt when she came over to our house for a visit. I was about three years old. The tune was "The Farmer in the Dell", but I wanted to sing something original for my aunt, so I changed the words to: "The Farmer Jumped over the Fence." This song is one of my earliest childhood memories.

Back when I was a kid, everybody sang.

At home, I would sing duets with my mother. Our favorite song was "Little White Duck", which we learned from a Burl Ives record: "There's a little white duck, sitting in the water; a little white duck, doing what he oughta." Mom and I sang our duet with gusto.

At my father's company picnics, they would hand out books with song lyrics and everybody sang. Singing was as much a part of the picnic as food and softball. One of Dad's coworkers grew up in Indianapolis. Every year when we sang "When the moon shines bright upon the Wabash, how I long for my Indiana home," I would watch my Dad's coworker closely to see if her eyes were glistening with tears of nostalgia.

In grade school music class, everybody sang. Our grade school even had music assemblies, which were an early 1950s form of karaoke. The music teacher had a projector that showed typewritten lyrics on a large screen on the stage of the auditorium, and 200 kids would sing, following the lyrics on the screen.

People Who Could not Sing

As an adult, I have met blind people who could not see. I have met deaf people who could not hear. I have met people in wheelchairs who could not walk.

Sometime around 1980, I started to meet people who could not sing. At least, they said they could not sing. They claimed they could not carry a tune; they warned people that nobody in the world would want to hear them sing.

Of course, these people could sing. Everybody can sing.

What changed is the meaning of the phrase "I can sing."

Mother

Nowadays, if you say you can sing, it means that you have a great voice, you sing with sweetness, and you deserve a recording contract. So, given that definition, people say they cannot sing.

We have become a nation of people too shy to sing.

If I Could Only Hear My Mother Sing Again

A couple of months ago, I heard Janis Ian sing a song which was written by Woody Guthrie: "If I could only hear my mother sing again, if I could only close my eyes and hear your voice as then."

What a wonderful image. My mother has been dead for a long time now. It would be wonderful to hear her sing again.

Hey, Mom, how about singing "Little White Duck"?

My mother would not say "But I can't sing." My mother would not say that she could not carry a tune. My mother would not say that nobody in the world would want to hear her sing.

She would say "Yes."

And I would be transported back to my childhood --- back to a time when people were not too shy to sing, back to a time when everybody sang. My mother, of course, would sing, with gusto, about the little white duck, doing what he oughta.

Mother

BOB HOPE MADE MY MOTHER WEEP

Keep Your Eyes Closed

February 06, 1968, was the date for my induction into the United States Army. At that time, I did not want my parents to drive me to the army induction center; I had a neighbor drive me there. My parents had to say their farewells to me at 21 Beacon Drive.

Basic training was at Fort Jackson, South Carolina.

One night in the barracks, our platoon had a discussion about what happened when we left home. Spaventa talked about how his mother had advised him, "Keep your eyes open, son." Sowinski talked about how his mother had given him the same advice, "Keep your eyes open, son."

But my mother, when I was leaving 21 Beacon Drive for the army induction center, had advised me, "Keep your eyes closed, son."

I never knew if that advice was deliberate or was a slip of the tongue. But I took my mother's advice to heart. I kept my eyes closed for two years. I shut out the Army so that the Army could not get me down.

I was treating the Army like sitting in a dentist's chair. Close my eyes, and let the dentist drill away. And then, after two years, on February 05, 1970, I opened my eyes.

Thanks, Mom, for the advice.

Squish and Puff-Puff

When I was in the 101st Aviation Division of the Sixth Army at Fort Lewis, Washington, one of my buddies was nicknamed Squish because of his general body shape. Another buddy was nicknamed Puff-Puff because of his hamster-like cheeks.

After I got out of the Army, I was visiting Cleveland and went to see Squish. We called up Puff-Puff in Buffalo and persuaded him to come to Cleveland so that the three of us could have a mini 101st Aviation Division reunion.

Having spent most of my two years in the Army at Fort Lewis, I never served in Vietnam, but both Squish and Puff-Puff had. I was looking forward to finding out what two recent returnees from Nam would talk about.

Mother

Mortar attacks? (No.) Body bags? (No.) Gooks? (No.) The nearness of death? (No.)

These guys, fresh from the war, quickly became immersed in a discussion of the USO shows that had toured their bases in Nam. Puff-Puff declared that he had seen more shows than Squish. Squish declared that he had seen better shows than Puff-Puff.

But neither one had seen the ultimate USO show: Bob Hope.

Imagining Her Son in the Audience

Bob Hope's USO Christmas tours in Vietnam got televised back to the United States, and my mother would always watch them. After I had left the Army, my mother confessed to me that during my years in the service, she would watch Bob Hope with tears in her eyes.

Mom looked at the television screen and imagined that I was in Bob Hope's USO audience. It generated tears.

Until her comment about Bob Hope's USO show, I had never realized how much my being in the Army had affected my mother. I had thought that life at 21 Beacon Drive was going on as normal while I spent my two years wearing a green Army uniform and black Army boots.

Thanks, Bob Hope, for showing me how concerned my mother was.

Mother

SALTWATER DREAMS

Edith Schneider and Saltwater

Saltwater was important to my mother, Edith Schneider. Her grandfather was a boatswain on an oceangoing freighter. Her father worked in the shipyards and built oceangoing ships. She grew up in Brooklyn, five blocks from the harbor.

Mom loved to swim. When I was growing up, summertime meant going to the beach with Mom and her friends during the week and going to the beach with Mom and Dad on the weekends.

We lived in Port Washington, Long Island. It was on a peninsula on an island, surrounded by saltwater on three sides. We had plenty of choices for swimming: the bay, the sound, the ocean, or the harbor.

Mom never grew tired of going to the beach; she never grew tired of saltwater.

Coming Home from School in Wintertime

Mom's dream was to live in a home that had a view of saltwater. But the houses she lived in did not have a view. They were usually a couple of miles from the water.

However, when I was a teenager, we lived in a three-bedroom house on a hill just a quarter of a mile from the harbor. My bedroom was the one in the back of the house, and my window overlooked some woods.

Mom was a stay-at-home mother, and I would come home from school to find that she had made my bed, cleaned my room, and picked up my clothes. Sometimes, when it was wintertime, I would come home from school and find that Mom had shifted all the stuff on my desk over to one side.

It took me a couple of years to figure out what was going on.

My desk was underneath a window. I tried climbing on top of my desk and looking out the window. There it was: a patch of blue water. You could see the harbor if you stood on my desk and all the leaves were off the trees. You could see saltwater.

Mother

How to Make Saltwater Dreams Come True

My mother knew that we would never have enough money to buy a house with a water view.

But she also knew there was one way she would have a water view. She told her children that she wanted to be cremated and scattered at sea. Her saltwater dreams would be realized.

I promised Mom that we would scatter her at sea, and since Dad had never mentioned a preference, he would be scattered with her.

The sea would be a fitting resting place for the woman who sometimes climbed up on her youngest son's desk when all the leaves were off the trees and gazed at the blue water of the harbor a quarter of a mile away.

A fitting resting place for the granddaughter of a boatswain and the daughter of a shipbuilder. A saltwater resting place.

Mother

EDITH LEARNS TO DRIVE AT AGE 75

Dreading the Hanky

My mother, Edith Schneider, did not have a driver's license when I was a kid. She did not need to drive. We had a good bus system in the Long Island suburb where we lived, and Mom took me on the bus to the dentist, the doctor, and my aunt's house.

The main drawback about these journeys was waiting at the bus stop. There was time to kill waiting for the bus, and my mother would look me over. Invariably, she would declare that my ears were dirty. We should not go to see the dentist, the doctor, or my aunt with dirty ears.

Mom would take a hanky out of her purse --- the dreaded hanky. She would wet a corner of it with her saliva and proceed to clean my ears right at the bus stop --- in plain view of everyone.

Driving to the Bank

When we moved to a house that was not on a bus route, my mother still did not need to drive. She had lots of friends who picked her up and dropped her off.

When my parents retired to eastern Long Island, my mother still did not need to drive. My father took her wherever she needed to go.

But after my father died, Mom decided that she needed to drive. She started taking driving lessons, and the state of New York issued her a driver's license at age seventy-five. Then Mom bought her first car, a little Chevrolet.

Mom did not need to drive to the supermarket. The village where she lived had a senior citizens' bus that went to the supermarket on Wednesdays; the kindly driver would carry people's shopping bags into their homes for them.

But Mom did need to drive to the bank. And she went often. I think she found every sort of excuse to go. It was a social event for her. Sometimes she would put the dog in the car because the drive-up teller gave out dog biscuits.

Mother

Selling the Little Chevrolet

Most of my friends were elated that my mother had the gumption to go out and get her license at age seventy-five.

But I was not so elated. My mother had spent seventy-four years being a passenger; she did not have the instincts to be a good driver.

One day my brother took me on a tour of Mom's village.

He showed me the sign near the drive-up teller window that our mother had run into with her little Chevrolet. He showed me the metal post she had bent with her car; the post held up a canopy over the drive-up teller window. He showed me a mailbox she had uprooted despite the mailbox's having been anchored in a chunk of cement. The mailbox was located across the street from the drive-up teller window.

If Mom continued to drive, I worried that something really bad was going to happen.

One day, three years after Mom got her license, the police found her sitting dazed in her car with the car up on a sidewalk near the bank. The state of New York revoked her license, and I did not have to worry about something really bad happening.

No longer having a license meant that Mom had to sell her car. I was visiting Mom on the weekend that she sold her little Chevrolet. When the man showed up to buy the car, I went over to the neighbor's to let Mom handle the transaction herself.

I looked out the neighbor's window to watch the little Chevrolet drive away from Mom's house for the last time. I saw the new owner in the driver's seat, and my mother was in the passenger seat. What in the world was going on?

The neighbor quickly figured it out. Mom had sold the car and had asked the new owner to take her to the bank.

IN GREAT BRITAIN

In Great Britain

In Great Britain

DRINKING WITH WALTER

There Is a Drink for Everyone

American bars are dark and foreboding, and only certain segments of American society go to bars.

British pubs are light, lively, and filled with chatting grandmothers, guys playing darts, young couples with baby carriages, lushes, teetotalers. All segments of British society go to pubs.

How do the British do it?

In Britain there is a drink for everyone. Chatting grandmothers drink sherry; guys playing darts drink bitter; young couples drink lager-and-lime (a combination of beer and sweetened lime juice); lushes drink hard cider because cider gets you drunk quickest and cheapest; teetotalers have soft drinks.

There Is a Pub for Everyone

In Britain, not only is there a drink for everyone, there is also a pub for everyone. There are posh pubs, there are neighborhood pubs, and there are trendy pubs. There are pubs where you walk in and find everyone dressed in tweed; other pubs you enter and find everyone wearing blue jeans.

Some pubs are even two pubs in one. One door says "lounge" and has a carpeted floor and cushioned chairs; the other door says "public" and has a wooden floor and wooden chairs. The bar is located in the middle between the lounge and the public. You can actually order the same drink from the same pubkeeper --- but if you are standing on the carpeted side you pay more for the drink than when you are standing on the wooden-floor public side.

There is a pub for everyone, but I did not realize the full impact of this until I went drinking with Walter.

Free from the Burden

When I lived in London, my friend Elizabeth lived in the small village of Whitchurch in Hampshire. I decided to go visit Elizabeth near Christmas time. Her friend Walter was also visiting. Elizabeth went off for the day and left us two guys with some time to kill.

"Walter, what shall we do?" "Let's go down to the pub." "OK, but not the Red

In Great Britain

House Inn; it's Elizabeth's favorite and she always takes me there. Let's try out some new pubs."

The village of Whitchurch was small, but it had twenty-three pubs. Walter and I walked past the Red House Inn and entered the Prince Regent. I went up to the pubkeeper and got drinks for Walter and me. After finishing these drinks, we crossed the trout stream that ran through the center of Whitchurch and went to the Fox and Goose.

The Fox and Goose was a real treat. It had parsnip wine; I tried it for the first time and it was great. At no other time during my two years in Britain did I find another pub with parsnip wine. While we were in the Fox and Goose, a cockle man came in. He had baskets with cockles and mussels (but, disappointingly, he did not sing "alive alive-o".) I ordered a little paper cup full of cockles and sampled them along with my parsnip wine. It was a golden moment for me.

When Walter and I got back to Elizabeth's house, I found that our pub visit was also a golden moment for Walter. He actually thanked me for taking him to these pubs. He then said that he was treated nicely because he was with me.

I was stunned. I had no idea that the pubkeepers would have treated Walter differently if he had not come in with me. Walter was Irish, and the Irish are looked down upon in England. Walter also worked as a sculptor and did not have a high income.

Walter entering a pub alone would have been treated according to his class. The pubkeepers at the Prince Regent or at the Fox and Goose would have made him feel unwelcome. Because I am American born, I am not aware of class and I act classlessly. Therefore the pubkeepers react classlessly to me and --- by extension --- they react classlessly to Walter when we were drinking together.

Drinking with Walter, I discovered that the idea of "class" bound Walter and determined his behavior and which pubs he would go to. Class was a burden to Walter, but I, being oblivious to "class," was free from the burden.

In Great Britain

BREAKFAST ON PLUTO

Friends with a Sword over their Heads

In 2005, seven people joined me for lunch at an Italian restaurant in St. Louis.

We talked about how things were going at work. Three of the people at the lunch, who worked for the same employer, painted a disturbing picture.

Their company is losing its largest client. Their company is probably closing its St. Louis office. Their company may be bought out.

I asked the three what they were planning to do because of their company's situation. Certainly, such uncertainty required a plan. But the three looked surprised that they were supposed to have a plan. They were in a wait-and-see mode.

They had a sword hanging over their heads, and they were acting oblivious to it.

The whole conversation at the Italian restaurant made me remember times in my life when I had a sword hanging over my head.

Litter in My Coat Pockets

I had a sword hanging over my head when I lived in London for two years during the bombings. These were not the German bombings of World War II, but the Irish bombings of the mid-1970s.

While I was living in London, the Underground was bombed four times, Parliament was bombed, the Tower of London was bombed, clubs were bombed, hotels were bombed, and a number of streets and squares were targets of IRA car bombs.

Every time I left my flat --- and especially when I took the Underground --- I was in some danger. But I went about my business anyway.

Because the IRA had been planting bombs in trash containers, all the trash containers had been removed from the Underground. And all the trash containers in the city of London had been removed from the streets.

This meant that every time I wanted to dispose of some litter, there was no place to put it except in my coat pockets.

In Great Britain

My coat pockets often filled up with litter. The litter was a reminder of danger, but I continued to act oblivious to the sword hanging over my head.

Breakfast on Pluto

In 2006, I was plunged back into the turmoil of London in the mid-1970s when I saw a movie called *Breakfast on Pluto*.

The movie thrilled me. It captured the look and feel of London at the time I lived there. The main character is an Irish transvestite who moved to London. The role is played by Cillian Murphy; his remarkable performance got him a Golden Globe nomination.

The movie absorbed me. On the screen was someone who lived with a sword hanging over his head during the bombings. But he was Irish, which meant he was constantly a suspect in the bombings – a second sword hanging over his head. And he was living his life as a transvestite, which meant yet another sword hanging over his head.

The movie enlightened me: I now look back on the days when I lived in London during the bombings, and I appreciate that I had just one sword hanging over my head.

In Great Britain

WE ARE GLAD YOU ARE AN ANTI-ROYALIST

Let Me See the Corpse

When I first moved to London, I shared a flat in Kilburn with three women. When we discovered that there was a mouse in the flat, the three women turned to me and said that it was my job to kill the thing because I was a man.

I baited a mouse trap, set it in the kitchen, and went to bed. When I woke up the next morning, I saw that the trap had worked. The mouse was squashed lifeless with bloodstains on its torso.

Yvonne, who was still in bed, shouted from her bedroom, "Did you catch a mouse?" "Yes." "Let me see the corpse." I opened Yvonne's door and showed her the lifeless bloodstained mouse.

Then I heard Elizabeth shout that she wanted to see the corpse, and I showed it to her. I finally went to Diane's bedroom and showed the corpse to her.

I found it curious that the three women, who were so averse to setting a trap, were so eager to see the bloodied results.

Getting My Teeth Drilled During the Royal Wedding

Shortly after the mouse incident, I moved from Kilburn to Holland Park, where I rented a room from a woman named Caroline. Holland Park was so posh that Princess Anne had her bridesmaids' party in a restaurant down the street from Caroline's flat.

The royal wedding of Princess Anne and Mark Phillips was held on a Tuesday. I could not watch it on TV because I had unwittingly scheduled a dental appointment that conflicted with the ceremony. My dentist was so far from the wedding parade route that I could not watch the parade in person.

That night, I met some friends at a pub; they asked if I had watched the royal wedding. I told them that I had scheduled a dental appointment for the same time as the wedding.

My friends grew jubilant, "Good for you, Doug. We are so glad to hear that you are an anti-royalist!" My friends thought my dental appointment was a deliberate political statement against the British monarchy.

175

In Great Britain

But I wasn't an anti-royalist. I was just a poor planner.

The Cute Mouse in the Pitcher

A few days after the royal wedding, I came home to the flat in Holland Park and found a note from Caroline:

"A mouse fell into one of the pitchers. I could not bear to kill it. The mouse looked so cute that I gave it a cracker instead. Please get rid of the mouse."

It was my job to get rid of the mouse because I was a man. I went to the cupboard and found the pitcher. There, in the bottom of the pitcher, was a cute mouse, surrounded by crumbs from Caroline's cracker, staring up at me. I could not bear to kill the thing, either.

I decided to dump the mouse somewhere. And I decided that since my friends thought I was an anti-royalist, I was going to act like an anti-royalist.

After night fell, I walked up the street with the pitcher in my hand. When I got to the posh restaurant where Princess Anne had her bridesmaids' party, I took a few steps up the alley and dumped the mouse out of the pitcher, setting the mouse free --- and becoming a true anti-royalist in the process.

In Great Britain

THE SECRET OF HAPPINESS IN ENGLAND

Which Foxhunt Shall We Watch?

In 1974, I was visiting some friends in Yorkshire, England.

They gathered round the kitchen table and spread out the local newspaper. They looked like an American family deciding which high school football game to go watch or which movie to go watch.

But this English family was deciding which foxhunt to go watch. I was astonished; I had never imagined that foxhunting was a spectator sport.

Vermin vs. Poor Little Critters

Later that year, I did get to watch a foxhunt myself. It was on a typically gray English day with persistent drizzle.

I went with a friend who was riding in the hunt, and I had been asked to play an important role in the foxhunt: I was the gatecloser. After the hounds and horses thundered by and passed on through to the next field, I was supposed to go latch the farm gates behind them.

A foxhunt is held at the request of a farmer who wants to rid his farm of a fox. Farmers do not look at foxes as poor little critters; farmers consider them vermin. Although the foxhunters are performing a service for the farmer, they still are his guests, and it is important that no gate be left unlatched.

During that day's hunt, the fox did run by me once --- scared and heavily outnumbered, it was looking back anxiously over its shoulder at the wall of hounds and horses advancing on it. I did feel sorry for the fox, and definitely thought of it as a poor little critter.

But years later, my cousin in upstate New York showed me his henhouse, empty and void of life. A fox had systematically killed all my cousin's chickens. This killing was not for food; it was for the joy of killing.

That made me reconsider my feelings about the poor little foxes. Maybe they really are some kind of vermin after all.

In Great Britain

While the First Pair Dries Out

Being a gatecloser proved to be arduous, as I had trouble figuring out how English farm gate latches worked. I was befriended by an English couple who took pity on a befuddled American.

I could tell this couple was English because they looked like they had just walked out of the costume department at BBC television. Tweed caps firmly on their heads, tweed jackets keeping them warm from the drizzle, and Wellington boots keeping their feet dry. They drove a Rover touring sedan --- how English can you get?

The BBC couple latched a few more English farm gates with me. They asked if I were a tourist, and I said no, I was living in London. Upon hearing this, the wife turned to me and asked if I wanted to know the secret of happiness in England.

I, of course, was all ears; I wanted to know the secret.

"The secret of happiness in England is owning two pairs of Wellington boots. You can wear the second pair while the first pair dries out."

I, unfortunately, did not own even one pair of Wellington boots. I wondered if I was doomed to unhappiness in England.

178

In Great Britain

CHRISTMAS IN WALES

Marjorie Signs Up

Marjorie and I were in the same linguistics classes at the University of London in 1973.

Originally from Wales, Marjorie and her husband had lived in the United States for a number of years, until her husband was killed in an automobile accident. Marjorie decided to move back to Britain and enroll in the University of London.

In London, Marjorie lived in a student dormitory. One day she saw a notice on the dorm bulletin board: SIGN UP TO HOST A FOREIGN STUDENT FOR CHRISTMAS. Marjorie had visions of students in exotic saris eating a traditional Christmas dinner at her parents' house in Wales.

Marjorie was assigned two foreign students: one foreign student was a woman from Portland, Maine, and the other foreign student was a woman from Elmira, New York. Neither of them owned a sari.

Marjorie told me about the luck of the draw and had an invitation for me --- I might as well come along to her parents' house and make it three American guests for Christmas.

An Adult's Christmas in Wales

Marjorie's family lived in Llandaff, Wales, and consisted of: a colorless brother, a very ill mother confined to an oxygen tent, and a sad father who seemed overwhelmed by his wife's illness.

On December 24th, the three Americans announced that they wanted eggnog. We plunked ourselves in Marjorie's car and made Marjorie drive us around Wales for a couple of hours.

We never did find any eggnog in Wales, but we got to see the Welsh countryside where grim stone houses string themselves out along the roads in narrow Welsh valleys. Marjorie spoke of her childhood in Wales and pointed out that no matter how grim your house was, you could always lift your head and be inspired by the beauty of the surrounding Welsh hills.

Llandaff Cathedral, which holds the bones of St. Telios and the bones of St. Dyfrig (who is said to have crowned King Arthur) is within walking distance of Marjorie's parents' house.

In Great Britain

On Christmas Eve, I coaxed Marjorie's father to join us (her colorless brother was reluctant to leave his easy chair), and we walked over to Llandaff Cathedral for late-night services. The cathedral was built in the 1100's, and had suffered a direct hit from a Luftwaffe bomb in World War II. It has been magnificently restored.

To add to the Christmas spirit, a light snow fell as we walked back to Marjorie's parents' house.

On the morning of December 25th, the three Americans plus Marjorie squeezed into the kitchen. The three women cooked while I read Dylan Thomas' *A Child's Christmas in Wales* out loud. One by one we took breaks and went to talk to Marjorie's mother through her oxygen tent.

Then came Christmas dinner. Then came digestion. Then came December 26th, and it was time for the three Americans to leave Wales and return to London.

Marjorie's Mother

When Marjorie returned to London it was after New Year's. She told me that her mother had died on December 28th.

I immediately felt like I had been an intruder on a dying woman's last Christmas. Imposing on Marjorie's parents, bounding around their house, spouting Dylan Thomas, making people go to late-night church --- all of this while Marjorie's mother's life was fading away.

Then Marjorie told me what her dying mother had said about having all those people in the house: "What a wonderful Christmas it was, having the house filled with talking and laughter and the words of Dylan Thomas."

I no longer felt like an intruder.

In Great Britain

BEING CAROLINE'S LODGER

Next Door to the Maserati Dealer

I attended graduate school in London from 1973 to 1975. At the time, it seemed like everybody I knew in London either had a lodger or was a lodger.

In my case, I was a lodger. I was Caroline's lodger. This meant that I rented the extra room in her flat, and we shared the kitchen, the telephone, and the bathroom. Caroline's flat was in Holland Park, in the garret of a four-story Barclay's Bank building.

Living in the garret was not a big deal except at night. To save electricity, the stairwell was lit by a single light bulb on a timed light switch. Once you hit the switch, the stairwell light came on for only one minute, and I had to sprint up or down four flights of stairs to avoid being plunged into darkness.

The bank building was next door to a Maserati dealer, which was a clue that the majority of people in Holland Park had a higher income level than Caroline had and a much higher income level than I had.

The Jig Is Up

The neighborhood was interesting, and Caroline herself was interesting.

She was an artist and had a booth at Portobello Road Market (the largest antiques market in the world) where she sold her paintings, tin soldiers that she repaired and painted herself, and crockery.

When you walked into our kitchen, every surface was covered with stacks of plates, and every cupboard was filled with stacks of bowls. There were two kinds of bowls and plates: those that were so beat up that Caroline couldn't sell them at Portobello Road and those that were so nice that she could not bear to sell them.

I liked lodging with Caroline; the rent was affordable and Caroline was amiable. But Caroline did ask me to be inconspicuous. Her lease with the bank specified that she was not allowed to have lodgers. She was afraid the bank would kick her out if they found out she was renting a room to me.

Then one day I received a hand-written note in the mail.

It was from Barclay's Bank and said that the manager wanted to speak with me in person. Uh-oh --- I thought the jig was up. I had not been

181

In Great Britain

inconspicuous enough, and Barclay's had figured out that I was living at Caroline's illegally.

I talked to the manager and found out that my panic was unwarranted. A letter addressed to me on the fourth floor had been delivered to Barclay's Bank on the first floor by mistake. The manager simply wanted to pass the letter on to me. He did not intend to evict me or punish Caroline.

Mom Has a Suggestion

I made sure I was a good lodger. I kept the kitchen neat and tidy. I took messages when Caroline's friends phoned and she wasn't home. And I made sure I was not in the flat on Friday evenings.

Every Friday evening Caroline took a long luxurious bath. I knew that my presence in the flat, no matter how quiet I was, would disrupt the mood. So I would leave the flat on Friday evenings; often I just went to the neighborhood pub for a pint. I could see our bathroom window from the door of the pub. If the window was lit up, Caroline was still luxuriating in her bath. If the window was dark, I knew I could finish my pint and head home.

Then came the summer of 1974; I would be out of England for three months before returning for my final year of graduate school. I was worried that Caroline would rent out her extra room to another person while I was away.

I mentioned my worry to my parents, who were visiting London at the time. I also mentioned that the bathroom sorely needed painting, and I promised Caroline that I would paint it before I left for the summer. I knew that a nicely painted bathroom would make her Friday night baths even more luxurious.

My mother's suggestion: Paint three of the four walls in the bathroom and tell Caroline I would paint the fourth wall when I got back in the fall.

Mom's suggestion worked. I painted three bathroom walls and left England. When I came back in the fall, Caroline had not rented out her extra room to another person.

I got to spend another year being Caroline's lodger.

In Great Britain

RENDERING PEOPLE SPEECHLESS

Rendering Carol Speechless

When I was in high school, most seniors could drink legally because New York State's drinking age was eighteen at the time. And most seniors chose to drink New York State's most popular beer: Rheingold.

The father of my high school friend, Carol, worked for Rheingold. This meant whenever you visited Carol's house, she would offer you a beer from the family's well-stocked refrigerator. Being a good hostess, Carol always offered Rheingold in a bottle.

This was because every high school senior in New York State knew that drinking beer from a can was uncool --- cans in those days were made of steel and imparted a metallic taste to their contents. Glass, on the other hand, is tasteless, and drinking Rheingold from a bottle was cool.

I, however, enjoyed asking Carol for Rheingold in a can. I told her that I preferred cans to bottles because I could taste the glass in a bottled beer. This statement was such an inversion of logic and science and high-school drinking lore that Carol would start to sputter and became unable to speak.

This is how I rendered Carol speechless.

Rendering My Flatmates Speechless

I shared a flat in London with three flatmates.

One day they invited me to go someplace I did not want to go. My reply was, "I can't go with you because I never do anything I have not done before."

This statement was so illogical that all three flatmates became unable to speak.

Actually, not quite speechless. They spent a couple of weeks walking around the flat muttering. All three had taken my comment seriously and were trying to make sense of it. I could hear them muttering, "If Doug never does anything he has not done before, then how does he _____."

I knew that if you say something that is utterly untrue, you have a bigger impact than if you say something that is true.

183

In Great Britain

Rendering British People Speechless

Eventually, while living in London, I found an easy method for rendering British people speechless.

I would start by saying, "It's amazing how many cities in Britain are named after cities in the United States."

Then I would give examples, "For example, Glasgow is named after Glasgow, Kentucky, and Bristol is named after Bristol, Tennessee."

When I saw that I was about to be corrected, I would go to the next level, "And London is named after New London, Connecticut, and York is named after New York City."

By now, the British people would be unable to speak. It would be time to cap it all off, "Yes, it's all really amazing considering how Britain is so much older than the United States."

This is how I rendered British people speechless.

In Great Britain

THE CHANGING OF A GUARD

The Sky above Hyde Park

My two years as a graduate student at the University of London were drawing to a close, and my time in London was running out. I made a bucket list of London's highlights that I needed to see before I left the city for good.

My list started with Speakers' Corner in Hyde Park where people come, stand on a box, and start speaking. I took the tube four stops from my flat, and headed into the park, ready to see free speech at work.

I saw a dozen people speaking, but only six of them had an audience. The other six were speaking to thin air. I was curious what the six speakers without audiences were talking about. But I was afraid to go and stand in front of them. This would turn me into their total audience. I would be stuck there; guilt would keep me from walking away.

So I listened to some of the speakers that already had an audience. Until I noticed something special about Hyde Park --- the sky.

London was a sprawling city, and my horizon was always hemmed in by buildings. But Hyde Park had a giant field. I left Speakers' Corner, walked into the center of the field, and lay on my back.

Big sky! No buildings in sight!! I lay there enjoying looking up at the sky with nothing blocking my view --- except an occasional dog. Then I realized that this field was used by people for walking their dogs. My mind started to think of what could be in the grass I was lying in.

So much for Hyde Park. I quickly stood up, walked to the tube stop, went back to my flat, and changed clothes.

At the Palace at 11:30 AM

The changing of the guard was on my list. I took the tube seven stops from my flat and showed up at Buckingham Palace. I stationed myself at the fence surrounding the palace forecourt. I was looking forward to pomp and pageantry and band music.

There were only two other people standing at the fence. I wondered where the tourist buses were. I wondered where the people selling souvenir programs were.

While I was wondering, a small cadre, five guards in all, marched into the

185

In Great Britain

forecourt. They marched full of pomp. They stopped in front of a sentry box; the sentry marched out of the box and a new sentry marched in, full of pageantry. The same thing happened at the other sentry box.

I asked the other two people at the fence, "Where's the brass band?" "Oh, they only have a big show and a band every other day in the winter. Come back tomorrow and you'll get music, tourist buses, and souvenir programs."

I never went back for the big show. I felt like the five guards had put on a show just for me.

Mind the Hammersmith Bridge

Also on my list was the annual Henley Boat Race, when a quarter of a million Londoners line the banks of the River Thames to watch Oxford (in a dark blue eight-oar boat) row against Cambridge (in a light blue eight-oar boat).

I took the tube to Hammersmith, where London's oldest suspension bridge crosses the Thames. I decided that the best place to watch the race would be on the south bank of the river. But I wanted a pre-race drink, and all of Hammersmith's pubs were on the north bank of the river.

Coming out of the pub, police stopped me from walking across bridge to the south bank. No pedestrians allowed; apparently, they were afraid of people dropping things on the racing crews when they went under the bridge.

But the bridge was still open to motorized traffic. I solved my problem by hailing a taxi and asking him to take me across the bridge. The driver realized what I was doing, drove me to the other side of the bridge, where I paid for a 700-foot ride.

The two boats came into view and the crowd began to cheer. Some people were shouting "Go Blue!" --- A phrase that made no sense to me since both boats were blue.

One lone voice, however, was shouting something sensible. This fellow saw that the eight rowers in each boat were sitting backwards, and only the coxswain could see where the boat was heading. The fellow shouted, "Mind the Hammersmith Bridge! Mind the Hammersmith Bridge!"

The boats zipped by me; neither boat hit the Hammersmith Bridge. The crowds dispersed. I took the tube back home.

Another highlight crossed off my London list.

186

VOLUNTEERING

Volunteering

Volunteering

WHEAT BEER OR NOT WHEAT BEER

Where Is My Lemon?

Although I stopped drinking beer in 1987, I volunteered to be a beer tapper at a local music festival in 2002. The festival was called The Lot because it was held in the parking lot of a microbrewery.

They gave me three types of beer to tap at the festival, and all went well until a woman ordered a hefeweizen. I filled a cup and placed the cup and her change in front of her.

The woman looked down at her hefeweizen and her change. Then she looked up at me.

Something was missing. I had no idea what was missing: I had given her the correct change; I had filled the cup to the top; I had given her the type of beer she had asked for.

The woman looked down at her hefeweizen again and looked up at me again. "Where is my lemon?"

This woman wanted to put a lemon in her beer! Was this a joke? Was she a weirdo? Her ID said that she was from Illinois --- did that explain it?

I did some quick thinking, "We just ran out of lemons, and I will go get some more." I ran inside the microbrewery and got some lemon slices for the joking weirdo woman from Illinois.

Only later did I find out that lemon is considered a natural accompaniment to wheat beer --- and hefeweizen is a wheat beer.

Brewing Is 90% Sanitation

At a graduation party, I found myself sitting next to a brewmaster who works at the Augusta Brewing Company in Augusta, Missouri.

I started asking the brewmaster a bunch of questions about hops, yeast, and brewing. I envisioned the brewmaster spending his days sampling the contents of each vat, dreaming up catchy names for new types of beer, carefully nursing batches of mash, deciding what types of beer to brew next.

My vision was too romantic. The Augusta brewmaster set me straight, "Brewing is 90% sanitation." He spends his days in rubber boots, scrubbing --- not very romantic at all.

Volunteering

Two-Row vs. Six-Row

Then I asked the brewmaster a question that had been on my mind since I tapped hefeweizen at the music festival, "If wheat beer is brewed from wheat, what is regular beer brewed from?"

"Regular beer is brewed from grain."

"What kind of grain?"

"Brewer's grain."

Was he pulling my leg? "Grain" was way too vague. There was an empty Budweiser bottle on the table where we were sitting. The label on the bottle clearly said that Budweiser is brewed from barley. "Is brewer's grain the same as barley?"

"No. There are only two kinds of brewer's grain: two-row and six-row. That refers to the rows of whiskers on a head of brewer's grain." I was dumbfounded. This guy brewed beer and he didn't even know what kind of grain he was brewing it from.

I decided it was not a matter of ignorance --- it was a matter of the brewmaster being so focused on the trees that he could not see the forest. Maybe his supply catalogs only talked of brewer's grain and he never stopped to ask what that grain was.

I only needed a quick visit to the internet to find out that two-row and six-row are types of barley. And six-row is better than two-row for brewing regular beer.

190

Volunteering

AND THE WINNER IS...

He Was Nineteen Years Old

In 1964, I was a student at Brown University, and I organized an intercollegiate film festival. As far as I could tell, it was the first festival ever for films made by college students.

We had a nice response with a variety of entries: a film about the wages of sin, a film with a soundtrack of Indian tabla music, a film in which animal carcasses evoke sensual overtones, a film about race relations "brought to you by Melanin."

But the clear winner of first prize was a student at New York University. His film, *What's a Nice Girl Like You Doing in a Place Like This?*, was humorous, well-edited, and showed signs of talent.

As festival director, I did not treat the losers very well. Second- and third-place winners got a hand-calligraphed certificate, and their films were returned by cheap surface mail, uninsured. The remainder of the entrants simply got their films returned by cheap surface mail, uninsured.

The first-place winner got a hand-calligraphed certificate and the grand prize: twenty-five dollars. I mailed the film, the certificate, and a check for twenty-five dollars to our first-place winner.

His name was Martin Scorsese; he was nineteen years old.

What If Marty Came in Second?

The second place winner in 1964 was Tom Barker.

Tom Barker was a photography student at the Rochester Institute of Technology (RIT) who had bought a second-hand 8mm movie camera for eighteen bucks. Tom is now on the faculty at RIT as an Associate Professor of Applied Statistics, and holds six U.S. patents.

Coming in second to Martin Scorsese definitely had an impact on Tom Barker. Forty years later, Tom displayed his second-place hand-calligraphed certificate on his website, along with the letter I sent him informing him that he lost to Martin Scorsese.

On his website, Tom fantasized, "What if I had come in first and Marty Scorsese had come in second? Would I be directing Hollywood movies while

191

Volunteering

Marty teaches applied statistics?"

The Twenty-Five Dollars

I have often wondered what impact winning first place had on Martin Scorsese. Did our twenty-five dollars give him the resolve to become a professional filmmaker? Did the intercollegiate film festival that I organized in 1964 make a difference?

Mean Streets was Scorsese's first film to get distributed on the art theater circuit. When I saw it in London, I had a twinge of pride. Maybe our twenty-five dollars had helped created a director whose films where showing around the world. *Taxi Driver, Raging Bull, The Last Waltz, Goodfellas, Casino*, to name a few of his films.

Alice Doesn't Live Here Anymore was my favorite Scorsese film. When I saw it in Seattle, I had a twinge of pride. I was convinced that our twenty-five dollars had played a role in Scorsese's success.

But then I saw *Gangs of New York* in St. Louis. I felt no twinge of pride, only a sense of disappointment. While watching it, a question popped into my mind, "Can we get our twenty-five dollars back?"

192

Volunteering

SPIN, LULU, SPIN

Hot Lips Hits the Lamppost

One of my lifelong dreams came true on the Fourth of July in 2003: I held one of the ropes on a giant helium balloon in a grand parade.

Our team of twenty-four volunteers carried a balloon named LuLu. She was a fifty-foot woman wearing a kimono, and in her hands she carried a wrapped gift, the gift of peace and understanding.

Two balloons in front of us was the Hot Lips balloon, a giant yellow fish with brilliant red lips. The Hot Lips team released the balloon from the restraining sandbags, and it floated up and hit a lamppost. A crossbar on the lamppost put a large gash in Hot Lips, and the balloon collapsed. Hot Lips was out of the Fourth of July parade.

Suddenly, our team's goal was not simply to walk our giant helium balloon through downtown St. Louis; our goal was to walk the parade and keep our balloon from hitting anything. Our goal was to make sure that LuLu survived.

The Flying Wedge of John Deeres

Our place in the parade was right in back of the Collinsville, Illinois, high school band and right in front of a flying wedge of antique green John Deere tractors driven by menacing-looking men in coveralls and green caps.

Spectators clapped their hands as LuLu passed by. Some spectators would start making circular motions with their hands and shouting, "Spin, spin, spin!" They wanted us to stop and make LuLu rotate 360 degrees. I learned that the spinning of a giant helium balloon is a highlight of the parade for a spectator.

We could not fulfill all the requests to spin --- only when the parade had ground to a halt and we needed to kill time.

When we approached the reviewing stand with the mayor and Stan Musial, we heard a voice boom out over the loudspeaker, "Spin, LuLu, spin" --- and we did spin LuLu for the mayor and for Stan the Man.

Volunteering

The Ethereal Fifty-foot Woman

My rope attached to LuLu's right foot. They gave me gloves for gripping the rope --- actually, two right hand gloves, but I put them on anyway.

Guiding LuLu took a lot of concentration.

Sometimes LuLu wanted to rise, and I had to rein her in. Sometimes LuLu wanted to sink; to keep her from scraping the street, I had to walk with her foot resting on my head.   The people guiding LuLu's head were getting too far in front of the feet people, which made LuLu go horizontal, and I had to hustle to close the gap. The guy holding the rope for LuLu's left foot was a joker and wanted us to move the feet back and forth to make it look like LuLu was marching.

Traffic lights arched over intersections, and we needed to swerve to dodge them.

Look straight up at the right foot, hold the rope with even pressure, wear the mismatched gloves, ignore the summer heat, listen to the excited applause, spin the giant helium balloon for Stan Musial, humor the joker holding the left foot, hustle to keep ahead of the antique John Deere tractors, don't get dusted by the high school band – I was busy while I walked in the parade.

Then we went past a glass office building.

I saw LuLu's reflection in the windows of the office building. I realized what the spectators saw. The spectators did not see ropes or gloves or a team of twenty-four volunteers moving a giant helium balloon through the streets of downtown St. Louis.

They saw a woman floating through the air, an ethereal fifty-foot woman in a kimono floating gently through the air, while bearing the gift of peace and understanding.

LuLu inspired awe, and I was proud to help make that inspiration happen.

Volunteering

MASSAGING DEAN MURPHY

The Weakness of His Immune System

I was living in Minneapolis when I decided to put my massage skills to good use.

The newspaper had an article about the AIDS Massage Project, where people gave free massages to people with AIDS. Since massage strengthens the immune system, AIDS massage seemed like a good use of my skills.

I signed up, took the orientation course, and got assigned an AIDS client named Dean Murphy. Dean was to come to my apartment every Wednesday evening for a massage.

On the first Wednesday, I was nervous. I had never massaged a person with AIDS before. In fact, I had never even met someone with AIDS before.

Dean showed up that first night, and got his massage. He looked pretty normal. He looked so normal that after a few weeks I started to wonder if he was pretending to have AIDS so that he could get a free massage once a week.

The Hickman in His Chest

Then one Wednesday Dean showed up for his massage, took off his shirt, and showed me a Hickman newly implanted in his chest. A Hickman catheter is a device for delivering medication directly into a vein so that you no longer need to inject medication with a needle.

What I could see of the Hickman was two little tubes sticking out of Dean's chest. Dean no longer looked normal.

I had no idea how to massage someone with a Hickman. What if I squashed it or dislodged it? What if I contaminated it?

Finally, I came to the realization that I should view the Hickman as part of Dean, just like his ear or his foot. I did my regular massage routine, avoiding the Hickman, while pretending it is no big deal to have two little tubes sticking out of your chest.

Volunteering

__The Whites of His Eyes__

Dean came over every Wednesday evening for about a year. Then one Wednesday, he told me that he was going to rent a hospital bed and have it set up in his dining room. The doctor had given him ten days to live.

The news shook me up, but I calmly told Dean that I would come to his house the next Wednesday and do a massage in his dining room.

That next Wednesday, I massaged Dean in his dining room. He definitely did not look normal: He had lost control of his eyeballs, and his pupils would roll up into his skull leaving only the whites of his eyes showing.

After the massage was finished, Dean's neighbor showed up to keep him company for the rest of the evening. His neighbor told me that she was a professional massage therapist, and I told her that I was thinking of going to massage school to improve my skills.

Dean, who was listening in his hospital bed, spoke up, "Doug! You don't need to go to massage school. Your massage is wonderful just the way it is."

I was so honored. Dean was on his deathbed, only the whites of his eyes showing, and yet he had the graciousness to compliment me.

That was the last time I saw Dean Murphy alive. He died three days later, on schedule.

Volunteering

LIKE NO OTHER SOUND

The Hottest Ticket in Town

My buddy Randy and I both volunteered to help out at the 2001 NCAA Women's Final Four Basketball Tournament. At the volunteer bracket party a couple of weeks before the event, we put our names in a fishbowl for a raffle --- not to win tickets, but for the chance to buy tickets.

And we did win the chance to buy Final Four tickets --- at $100 per ticket. Sounds like a lot of money, but the tournament consisted of two semi-final games on Friday night, plus the final game on Sunday night so it really was $33.33 per game. We bought the tickets.

As the day of the semi-finals approached, the St. Louis media were abuzz with ticket scalping news. Newspapers said that people were desperate for Final Four tickets, and the scalping price was $1000 per ticket. The radio said $1100 per ticket. Our friends constantly reminded us how valuable those tickets were. The TV news said $1800 per ticket.

Scalping is attractive, but it was illegal at the time. Since the tickets were sold to us because we won the volunteer raffle, we felt scalping the tickets would be breaking a trust. Plus, we would have to watch the tournament at home on TV.

So, we decided not to scalp, which means we decided to forego the opportunity to clear a $3,400 profit. We went to the Final Four and had a great time.

Building an Earthen Dam in China

If the tournament games are on Friday and again on Sunday, the question is, how does St. Louis keep the attention of all the Final Four press people in town who are at loose ends on Saturday? Simple: We set a Guinness world record for the most people dribbling basketballs simultaneously.

As a volunteer, I was assigned to help out at "The March to the Arch."

We were to give out 2,000 free basketballs to the first 2,000 people who showed up. These people would then dribble their free basketballs simultaneously for seven city blocks with a percussion band leading the crowd and the Budweiser Clydesdales following behind. This would create a new world record for the largest number of people dribbling basketballs simultaneously.

197

Volunteering

But first we had to unload 2,000 basketballs (packed four to a carton) from the trucks.

We formed a human chain, each person taking a carton of basketballs from the person in front of them and passing the carton to the person behind them. Take --- pass --- take --- pass.

We set up a rhythm, and I quickly realized that this task required complete concentration. If my mind wandered, I lost the group rhythm. Had to keep focused, keep the cartons moving.

Then I had a vision: This was just like working at one of those vast dam-building projects in Communist China, where they had lots of human labor but hardly any earth-moving equipment. Those dams in China were built one basket of dirt at a time.

Take the basket of dirt from the person in front of you; pass the basket to the person behind you. Take --- pass --- take --- pass.

Dribbling En Masse

When all 2,000 basketballs were distributed, it was time to start dribbling en masse.

Yes, the sight of a huge group of people dribbling down Market Street was amazing.

But much more amazing was the sound of 2,000 basketballs being dribbled down Market Street. Because we were dribbling in the midst of tall buildings, the sound was multiplied. The sound bounced off the downtown buildings, the sound echoed in your ears, the sound reverberated in the very basketball you were dribbling.

At the end of seven blocks, having set a world record, there was a post-dribbling party. We got to keep our basketballs. We each got a free cup of frozen custard.

Hey, I was a happy Final Four volunteer.

Volunteering

SCRAPING THE EASTER PLATES

For Camaraderie

It sounded good to me; I volunteered to help serve a free Easter dinner to the homeless in a large church in downtown Minneapolis. I pictured the benefits of volunteering: camaraderie (chatting with other volunteers), altruism (helping feed the homeless), and gratitude (feeling appreciated).

When I showed up at the church, the coordinator told me I would be a scraper. I was to stand next to a garbage can and accept trays from the diners when they had finished eating. I would scrape any excess food off the plates and pass the plates through an opening in the wall to the dishwasher.

Didn't sound very challenging: How much food would the homeless leave on their plates? I stood by my garbage can.

The opening in the wall was too small for me to see the dishwasher and chat with him. So I started to chat with the other scraper, who was standing by a second garbage can. I quickly found out that he was passionate about the stock market and boasted about watching his portfolio grow and grow.

I made the mistake of asking if he had ever sold any of his stocks. He turned sour and stopped chatting. Apparently, stocks are for watching, not for making a profit.

For Altruism

There was little time for chatting as the first wave of people started bringing us their trays.

The first plate I scraped had a lot of food still on it. So did the second plate. Into my garbage can went corn, mashed potatoes, slices of ham, candy wrappers.

What was going on? I watched the serving line, staffed mainly by perky teenaged volunteers. They smiled as they were piling food on people's plates. Piling on? Maybe they thought the needy wouldn't get to have another meal for another week or so. Maybe they thought the needy would eat a lot of Easter dinner and store fat just like bears before they hibernate.

At the end of the serving line, I saw people putting pie on people's trays, and, if there was a kid, they would add pieces of wrapped candy to the tray.

199

Volunteering

I then noticed parents at tables pleading with their kids to eat some ham. The kids had filled up on the candy and pie; the kids were in no mood for mashed potatoes. No one had figured out to serve the kids dessert after they had eaten their ham, corn, and mashed potatoes.

More people came up with trays. I was scraping and scraping; a lot of food was going into my garbage can. I noticed that most diners actually didn't look needy. They looked like they were freeloading on the church and getting a free Easter dinner.

For Gratitude

I was beginning to get annoyed when a man came up to me and handed me a tray with a clean plate on it. He had eaten everything. He looked like he was down on his luck. Clearly, he was the target for this free Easter dinner.

He looked at me, and said, "Thank you." He was so appreciative of a free Easter dinner that he even thanked the scraper.

The pastor came and greeted all the volunteers and all the diners. It dawned on me that the church had to cast its net wide to put on a free Easter dinner.

It had to cast wide to get diners whether they were homeless or freeloaders. And the church had to cast its net wide to get volunteers, whether they were perky teenagers who wanted to fatten the homeless or me - - - who was looking for some camaraderie and some altruism and some gratitude.

Volunteering

THE GRAND GLAIZE GROUP

It's an ELetter

The Grand Glaize Library takes its name from nearby Grand Glaize Creek. One day at the library, I spotted a sign: Come to the Grand Glaize Writers' Group. It meets once a month, and it is free.

This sounded like a good way to improve my writing, so I showed up at the next meeting carrying a printout of an ELetter (which is what I called my weekly e-mail vignettes). When I sat down, I was handed a clipboard. I needed to fill in my name and the type of writing I had brought to read.

Looking on the clipboard, I saw that other people had brought poems, short stories, and chapters of novels to read. I wrote down my name and that I had brought an ELetter to read.

At the Grand Glaize Writers' Group, the leader calls on people to read a piece, and then the group comments on it. The leader does an amazing job of keeping egos from being bruised and keeping feathers from being ruffled. He also stops people from going off on tangents so that the comments stay focused on the writing.

That night, the leader asked people to read poems; I listened and I commented. The leader asked people to read short stories; I listened and I commented. People read chapters of novels; I listened and commented. But he never called on me to read my ELetter.

The next month, it was the same story: I listened and I commented, but I was never called on to read. I began to wonder what the value in going to the writers' group was if I did not get to read --- this was not a good way to improve my writing.

It's Excellent

Finally, after a couple of months, the leader of the Grand Glaize Writers' Group decided to take a risk and asked me to read an ELetter.

I prefaced my reading with an explanation. I had invented the ELetter and it has a strict form, like a sonnet. (I thought that the reference to a sonnet would give me some credibility.) An ELetter comes in three sections, each with its own title, and should be about a page-and-a-half in twelve-point font.

Volunteering

People listened to me read my ELetter, and I waited for comments. Lots of people in the group said, "It's excellent." That was a nice thing to say, but I didn't learn anything from this comment; I may as well have stayed at home.

I began to wonder what the value in going to the writers' group was if everyone there told me my writing was excellent --- this was not a good way to improve my writing.

It's Annoying

The next month at the Grand Glaize Writers' Group, I was asked to read another ELetter.

People listened to me read my ELetter, and I waited for comments. Someone spoke up: "You overused a particular phrase, and it annoyed me. You should stop using it so much."

I perked up; I smiled; I said, "Thank you." Finally I had received a useful suggestion.

It looks like the best way to improve my writing is to annoy people.

IN THE USA

In the USA

In the USA

MANURE FOR SALE, BY APPOINTMENT ONLY

In the Wealthy Part of Town

Whenever I visited my mother on Long Island and she wanted a chuckle, she would ask me to drive her over to the wealthy part of town. Here, some of the yards were large enough so that people could keep horses.

We went in search of a particular house with horses. It was surrounded by a white wooden fence, and on the fence was a sign: MANURE FOR SALE, BY APPOINTMENT ONLY.

When she saw the sign, my mother would always chuckle at the incongruity of manure being so desirable that you needed to make an appointment to buy it.

But people in other countries would not chuckle at the idea of manure being desirable.

Livestock in the African Garden

Where I lived in northern Nigeria, manure was vital.

The landscape there was not lush; only a handful of trees broke a flat vista of soil tinted red from iron ore. It was not the dark rich soil that you see in the United States.

Yet the soil managed to feed a population of millions. The Nigerians accomplished this with manure. People would keep goats and sheep in their gardens and then sweep up the droppings and take them out to their fields.

In fact, one definition of poverty in northern Nigeria is being so poor you have to sell your livestock droppings rather than use them on your own fields.

Manure is the only readily available fertilizer, and it makes this part of the world flourish. Nigerians would never chuckle at a sign saying MANURE FOR SALE, BY APPOINTMENT ONLY.

At The Spanish Christmas Market

The Christmas Market in Barcelona consists of stalls set up in a large plaza in front of a church near the Old City.

In the USA

I spent a week in Barcelona and visited the Christmas Market a couple of times. The market comes to life at night, when you stroll through the aisles looking at all kinds of Christmas decorations for sale, all of high craftsmanship.

There was a huge variety of nativity scenes for sale. You could buy the three-centimeter size, the six-centimeter size, and the nine-centimeter size. You created your own nativity: buying a manger and then choosing the pieces to go in the manger --- Mary, Joseph, the Baby Jesus, camels, sheep, wise men, shepherds, and guys in a crouch with their pants pulled down, defecating.

Defecating in the manger with the Baby Jesus nearby? What was going on?

The landscape outside the city of Barcelona provided an explanation. The landscape is harsh --- rocks, hills, sandy soil. Obviously, the only way people can survive here is to manure the soil.

The guy in a crouch with his pants pulled down, defecating, is called a caganer. He is the symbol of soil fertility in this part of Spain. Because he is the source of prosperity, the caganer earns a place in the Christmas manger.

As I walked through the Barcelona Christmas Market, looking at the three-centimeter caganers, the six-centimeter caganers, and the nine-centimeter caganers; I kept thinking of how my mother would chuckle if she had been there.

In the USA

THE GREAT SHIP WENT DOWN

A Titanic Joke with an Underlying Lesson

In the world after 9/11, it is time to retell this joke; it has a lesson about not lumping people together.

Mr. Lee and Mr. Greenberg were sitting at a bar. Greenberg stands up and shouts, "This is for Pearl Harbor!" He proceeds to slug Mr. Lee, knocking him to the floor. Mr. Lee groggily protests, "Hey, what did you do that for? I am Chinese; I had nothing to do with Pearl Harbor." Greenberg responds, "Chinese - Japanese - they're all the same!"

A week later the same two are sitting at the same bar. Lee stands up and shouts: "This is for the Titanic!" He slugs Mr. Greenberg, knocking him to the floor. Mr. Greenberg groggily protests, "Hey, what did you do that for? I am Jewish; I had nothing to do with the Titanic." Lee responds, "Greenberg - Iceberg - they're all the same!"

The Titanic as Object of Humor

I used to think of the sinking of the Titanic as an object of humor. This attitude came from the many times I sang the Titanic song with great gusto, sitting around the campfire at summer camp:

1. Oh, it was sad, it was sad
2. It was sad when that great ship went down
3. (To the bottom of the...)
4. Husbands and wives
5. Little children lost their lives
6. It was sad when that great ship went down

Of course, I hammed up line 3 with a big bass voice and sang line 5 with a childish voice. The most daring campfire singers changed lines 4 and 5: "Uncles and aunts, little children lost their pants." Yes, the loss of life on the Titanic was something humorous.

The Titanic as an Object of Sadness

That campfire classic lost its appeal after I went to the Titanic Artifacts Exhibit at the St. Louis Science Center in 2002.

The artifacts, all recovered from the debris field (not from the ship itself), are amazing. You look at things that sat on the ocean floor for decades after that

In the USA

night in 1912. All had been carefully cleaned and preserved by a center in France. A delicate china bowl, unbroken. A leather valise, looking ready for the next journey. A letter, still legible, "I am counting the days until we are together..."

That letter sent a shiver up my spine.

To help bring back that night in 1912, the exhibit had a slab of frozen salt water, an iceberg, for you to touch. The slab was exceedingly cold; another shiver.

But nothing brought back the night of the sinking like the boarding pass you were issued upon entering the exhibit. You carried it through the exhibit, and by the exit were lists of those who survived and those who did not.

The name on my boarding pass was Jovan Dimic, a third-class passenger with an Eastern European name. My buddy Randy told me, "You will not survive." Randy's sister told me, "You will not survive." I had some hope, but when I reached the exit and read the lists, it was clear that Dimic had gone down with the ship.

Suddenly, the loss of life on the Titanic was not humorous; it became personal.

In the USA

MY HEART WILL SPLURT OUT AND LAND ON THE FLOORMAT

The Missing Sofa Pillows

Three weeks had gone by since my heart surgeon had ripped my chest open, repaired a heart valve, and super-glued my chest back together. I went to the surgeon for a checkup; he told me I was now allowed to drive and I was now allowed to return to work.

I had one final day at home before going back to work. This was the day for the new sofa to be delivered. The furniture delivery guys showed up, carried in the new sofa, and announced that the delivery was complete.

But where were the two decorative pillows that were supposed to come with the sofa? At the furniture store, we had gone through a book of cloth swatches to pick out the pattern for the pillows. The delivery guys checked the invoice: no pillows.

I called up the salesman who claimed that pillows do not come with the sofa. I decided I needed to go to the store and straighten this out face-to-face.

The delivery guys left. I started to get ready to drive for the first time in three weeks.

Then the phone rang.

Linda Is Reminded of Her Father

It was Linda on the phone. She wanted to find out how I was doing after my open heart surgery. I proudly told her that I was going to drive for the first time in three weeks.

This comment reminded Linda of her father.

She told me that her father had open heart surgery and driving made him nervous because of the surgery. He was afraid that a sudden stop would cause him to lurch forward into the steering wheel, popping his chest open, causing his heart to splurt out of his chest and land on the floormat.

I hung up the phone and got in the car to drive for the first time in three weeks.

Then the electricity went off.

209

In the USA

With a Hunter Lantern in Hand

A neighbor came over and told me the electricity was out all over the county.

This meant a darkened furniture store. I grabbed a hunter lantern, hobbled out to the car, and started driving toward the store.

No electricity meant that none of the traffic signals was working. Each intersection became a scary opportunity for sudden stops. Thanks to Linda's phone call, I kept on thinking about my heart splurting out of my chest and landing on the floormat.

I made it to the furniture store. I found the salesman's desk, shined the hunter's lantern in his face, and told him to follow me back to the sofa display area. The floor model for our new sofa had decorative pillows on it, and there was no indication that you needed to pay extra for the pillows.

I had made my point. The salesman said that the store would mail us the pillows.

I hobbled back to the car and crept home slowly through all the nonworking traffic lights.

When I got home, I was happy that I had avoided any sudden stops. I was happy that my newly repaired heart was still safely inside my chest and not on the floormat.

In the USA

I MISS MY MARINES

Semper Fi

I heard a feature on the radio about medical care for U.S. soldiers. They interviewed a Marine who had been wounded in Iraq. His shinbone had been shattered, and his leg was being held together by a latticework of metal hoops and bolts.

The interviewer talked to the marine about the wound, about the metal hoops, about physical therapy. Then the interviewer asked the marine a big question: What is the main thing that goes through your mind as you lie here in this hospital bed?

I expected the marine to answer that he missed being able to walk or being able to go places. Instead, he told the reporter: "I miss my marines."

He did not think of his leg first. He was a marine, and he thought of his comrades first. Semper Fi; the marines have always had a special kind of camaraderie.

Earning Money for Combat Boots

When I was growing up, I had a friend in the neighborhood named Donny. He dreamed of becoming a marine.

Donny would spend his allowance on GI Joe comic books. He got a paper route and earned enough money for his dream purchase: a pair of combat boots.

Donny did go into the marines after college and was selected for OCS --- Officer Candidate School. Anyone who can pass OCS qualifies to become commissioned as an officer in the United States Marine Corps. I thought Donny would be in seventh heaven.

I was in the army when Donny sent me a letter from Camp Pendleton.

Donny wrote that soon after he joined the marines, he had discovered that he hated being in the marines. In OCS, he was studying very hard so he could be number one in his graduating class. He was looking forward to graduation day, when the marines would proudly spotlight him as first in his class, and then he would then publicly refuse the commission offered to him.

Donny was a marine who hated the marines, and this moment at graduation would be his sweet revenge.

211

In the USA

They Are Not Troopies

When I got out of the army, I drove to Camp Pendleton to visit Donny for a couple of days. We went down to Tijuana and looked around. We drove through Oceanside, California, which has an incredible number of pawn shops ready to service the largest marine base in the country.

And we went through the base, which stretches for seventeen miles along the Pacific coastline. At one point, I spotted a platoon of marines practicing for a parade. I said to Donny, "Ah, the troopies are marching."

This would have been a perfectly normal thing to say on an army post, but I was now on a marine base. Donny grew serious and looked me straight in the eye, "They are not troopies; they are marines."

Even a marine who hated the marines could not allow his comrades to be called anything except "marines." Semper Fi; the marines have always had a special kind of camaraderie.

In the USA

CHRIST OF THE BLUE RIDGE

Swans Mate for Life

In 1985, when I was driving across Virginia, I stopped at Swannanoa.

Swannanoa is a fifty-two-room replica of Rome's Villa di Medici. It took 300 artisans to build it in 1912 on top of one of the foothills of the Blue Ridge Mountains. The person who owned it, a railroad magnate, adored his wife and named their mansion Swannanoa because swans mate for life.

After the railroad magnate and his wife died, the mansion became a country club, and then it became derelict --- until it was spotted by two newlyweds on their honeymoon. The newlywed wife had once had a vision of a large statue of Jesus standing on a hilltop, and Swannanoa's hilltop location matched her vision exactly.

The newlyweds bought the house. They were from New York. Walter Russell was forty-four years older than his wife, and they were both sculptors. Together, they renovated the mansion and created a large statue of Jesus that stood in the garden at Swannanoa: Christ of the Blue Ridge.

The University of Science and Religion

Walter Russell and his wife had strong religious beliefs.

He turned Swannanoa into a religious center, where he promoted his idea that there was no dichotomy between religion and science. He turned the mansion into the University of Religion and Philosophy, and people came from all over the world to take classes there.

When I got to Swannanoa, Walter Russell was no longer alive, but the university was still in existence. I went on a guided tour, led by a sincere young woman who spoke with great reverence of Walter Russell.

We got to tour the first floor. The guide proudly showed off the numerous books that Walter Russell had published. She showed us his paintings depicting the energy of the universe. She took us into the garden to get a closer look at the statue. And she listed some famous people who had visited Swannanoa: such as Norman Vincent Peale and Gloria Swanson.

She brought us back into the house to visit the gift shop. That is when something on the grand staircase caught my eye.

213

In the USA

In a Diaphanous Nightgown

It was Walter Russell's widow, then in her eighties. She had a lot of makeup on, her hair was dyed, and she was wearing a diaphanous nightgown in the middle of the day. She was clinging to the banister and creeping down the stairs.

Where had I seen this before? Of course: Gloria Swanson in *Sunset Boulevard*.

The widow got to the bottom of the grand staircase and glanced at the tour group in the gift shop. I was tempted to ask her if she was ready for her close-up, but she scampered into the kitchen, acting as if she was in need of some medicine.

I can only guess that the medicine she was looking for was not kept in a medicine cabinet. It was probably kept in a liquor cabinet.

You can still visit Swannanoa today. The university has moved into a nearby town. Walter Russell's widow is no longer alive.

The mansion must still be impressive, but you will no longer get the chance to see an aged woman in a diaphanous nightgown looking like the ghost of Gloria Swanson searching for a bottle of medicine.

In the USA

OMEN SPELLED BACKWARDS

Schooner across the Prairie

2007 was the year to go to the annual Motorcycle Rally in Sturgis, South Dakota.

Sturgis sits on the edge of the Black Hills; the town covers four square miles and boasts a population of 6,500 people for fifty-one weeks a year. During the first week in August, Harley motorcycle riders descend on the town. According to the South Dakota State Department of Transportation, there were 451,507 motorcycles in Sturgis that year.

My buddy Randy wanted to take his Harley to the event, and I wanted to see what happens when a town of 6,500 people is overrun by half a million motorcycles.

We drove our truck. There were four people in the cab of the truck, two dogs on an air mattress in the back of truck, and two Harleys (plus luggage and dog food) in a trailer behind the truck. We headed west; I felt like I was in a prairie schooner as we drove for hours through endless stretches of flat South Dakota countryside.

We finally reached our goal, the town of Nemo, where we were renting a cottage in the Benchmark Valley. The cottage sat on five acres of forest land. The owners of the cottage lived on the ground floor and rented out the upper floor. The owners not only allowed dogs, but they also played with our dogs and took the dogs out for potty breaks in the middle of the day when we were out motorcycle riding.

The setup was perfect.

Thick with Ponderosa

The Black Hills are black because they are thick with ponderosa. The roads are scenic. The air is clean.

The people are friendly because they know the economic boon that the motorcycles bring. In fact, the Nemo Fire Department gets its yearly budget by serving breakfast during Rally Week.

After breakfast, we would get on the Harleys and zoom through forests and canyons, past deer and buffalo, until we came to Sturgis. Traffic. Lots and lots of two-wheeled traffic, which meant we had to crawl into town.

215

In the USA

We would park and stroll down Main Street. For block after block, Main Street was thick with lines of parked Harleys: one line at the curb, two lines down the middle of the street, and one line at the other curb. Lots of chrome gleaming in the South Dakota sun. In fact, a local had set up a ladder and charged me five dollars to climb the ladder and take photos of all the motorcycles gleaming in the sun.

We visited lots of shops in Sturgis. Every shop sold T-shirts. I did see a bank, but I did not see a pharmacy, a dry cleaner, a barber shop, or hardware store. Just T-shirt shops, interspersed with tattoo parlors and bars.

I wondered what this town looks like when the bikers are not there. I imagined going back to Sturgis in January and finding that the town consists of one bank and 100 empty stores with signs in their windows: "Closed --- be back in August."

Lewd Acts in Public

The crowds in Sturgis were orderly during the day. At night the crowds were pretty orderly as well, although a few of the scantily clad barmaids did put on little shows, but nothing remarkable.

After a week in South Dakota, we drove back home. My friends asked me what Sturgis was like. They asked me that question with a gleam in their eyes.

I realized that my friends had certain expectations of the Motorcycle Rally. They expected to hear stories of tattooed drunks brawling in the streets and motorcycle women performing lewd acts in public. They expected to hear about gangs of Hells Angels pillaging defenseless South Dakota villages.

I am afraid I disappointed my friends. I told them that the weather was perfect for motorcycles, the Black Hills were scenic, the locals were friendly, and the bikers were orderly. No brawls, no lewdness, no pillaging.

I told them that it was special to spend all those days in a landscape dominated by motorcycles. So dominated that when a car appeared, you would look at the car in astonishment: What is that thing? It has four wheels, and it is enclosed --- how strange.

And it was extra special because Sturgis is like Brigadoon, a city of chrome and black leather, half a million strong, that appears out of the mists once a year and then disappears.

216

In the USA

THE WALTZ MADE ME HOMESICK

Dancing in England

When I was a student at the University of London in 1973, I always took the tube to Tottenham Court Station to get to my classes. One morning, when I was walking up the stairs at Tottenham Court, I noticed that the person next to me looked familiar. I tapped him on the shoulder. He was a friend of mine from America who was in London for a couple of months doing graduate research.

Fate gave me a nice surprise that morning in London.

My friend told me that his big passion was international folkdancing. The folkdancers in London were pretty snooty, so he always rented a car and got a bunch of people together to go to Oxford to dance there. The dancers in Oxford were not snooty.

I did not know anything about international folkdancing, but I asked to go along because I wanted to see Oxford. There were six people in the rental car: five Americans and one Australian. The Australian was a woman named Rae.

My friend took country roads to drive from London to Oxford. There were numerous blackberry bushes growing on the roadside, and we made a stop to snack on berries. After dinner at an Indian restaurant in Oxford, we arrived rather early at the church hall where the international folkdancers met. We were the only ones there.

One of the Americans, named Barbara, had brought along her fiddle. She started to play a waltz that sounded very American, like something you might hear at a barn dance. Rae and one of the Americans started to waltz in that empty hall.

While watching them waltz to that music, I suddenly felt homesick for America.

Dancing In British Columbia

By 1978, when I was living in Seattle, I had learned how to Scottish country dance. It was time to go to my first grand Scottish ball with live music. The ball was in Canada in the city of Victoria, British Columbia.

I was nervous because it was my first time dancing at a formal event. I made it through the first four dances on the program, enjoying the live music. Then

In the USA

the fiddle player went up to the microphone and announced that the band was taking a break. Her voice sounded familiar.

My mind recalled an empty church hall in England five years before. It was Barbara.

I went up to her in hopes that she would remember me and remember the waltz that made me homesick. Barbara didn't really remember me or the waltz, but she did remember snacking on blackberries by the side of the road to Oxford.

Fate gave me a nice surprise that day in Victoria.

Dancing in Massachusetts

The next time I saw Barbara was when I moved to Boston in 1984. I knew that Barbara was living in Boston and that I would probably run across her at a Scottish country dance class.

When I did meet Barbara at a class in Boston, I mentioned the blackberries by the side of the road to Oxford. Yes, Barbara still remembered that trip to Oxford.

Then she had a question for me: did I remember the woman from Australia named Rae? I answered yes. Barbara pointed to a corner of the room; Rae was standing there.

Turns out that Rae was on a round-the-world trip and was spending a couple of days in Boston.

She was leaving the next morning to go back to Australia.

I went up to Rae to see if she could recall stopping to snack on blackberries by the side of the road. She did not remember the blackberries, but she did remember the Indian restaurant where we had dinner in Oxford. I then told Rae about how watching her waltz in an empty church hall in England eleven years before had made me homesick.

Fate gave me a nice surprise that evening in Boston.

218

LUCK

Luck

YOU HAVE A NICE CATAHOULA LEOPARD

At the Hospital

In 2006, I took Petey, our therapy dog, to Forest Park Hospital on one of his monthly visits to see the mental patients there. We parked and then stopped at some bushes so that Petey could empty himself outside the hospital rather than inside the hospital.

After stopping at the last bush, Petey and I met a man coming out of the hospital; he looked at me and said: "You have a nice catahoula leopard." I had no idea what he meant, but I nodded. I wondered if he was one of the mental patients.

After entering the hospital, Petey and I met a nurse. She looked at me and said, "You have a nice catahoula leopard." I nodded. Now I started wondering if the hospital staff was playing a practical joke on me.

When Petey and I passed the employees' lounge, one of the hospital employees told me, "I like your dog." I decided to turn the tables and replied, "Isn't he a nice catahoula leopard?"

The hospital employee agreed, "Yes, you have a nice catahoula leopard there."

At the Xerox Machine

At work the next day, I went to the Xerox machine and found that someone was using it. Out of the blue, I asked him if he knew what a catahoula leopard was. This question startled him, and in a loud voice, he said, "A cata-WHAT?"

By the time I had finished explaining to him where I had heard the term, another coworker showed up at the Xerox machine holding a copy of *Dog Breeds of America*. She had overheard the conversation and had the book opened to a page with a photo of a dog that resembled Petey. It was a photo of a catahoula leopard dog.

We had adopted Petey from a rescue group. All we knew is that he had been found roaming the streets of Jefferson County and that he is a mixed breed. We could tell he is half chow because of his purple tongue; we did not know what the other half was.

Suddenly, I had evidence that the other half is catahoula leopard. Petey now has a heritage. He is the state dog of Louisiana, a breed developed

Luck

by Louisiana's original French settlers in the 1700s. Catahoula leopards are used for herding cattle and for hunting squirrels. I don't think Petey has ever seen a cow, but he has done a great job of hunting down the unwitting squirrels that venture into our back yard to raid our bird feeder.

My coworker with the dog book mentioned that rednecks like catahoulas. Jefferson County has a high percentage of rednecks, so it all fell into place.

Make Your Own Luck

There is a theory that you can make your own luck.

You make your own luck by putting yourself in situations where you think and behave in ways that create good fortune. You open yourself up to possibilities. You speak up. For example, you approach the Xerox machine and startle the guy there by asking him if he knows what a catahoula leopard is.

If I had asked the guy something ordinary, like, "How are you doing?" Petey would still be a half-chow-half-something-else dog. Now Petey has a heritage, and the guy at the Xerox machine knows a new dog breed.

I made some luck.

CROSSING THE BOUNDARY WITH JOIE DE VIVRE

k. d. lang on the Carousel

When I was a kid, my birthday meant two things: Mom would bake some gingerbread, and I would get some presents.

The gingerbread was memorable because I don't like frosting and everyone else in my family does. My birthday was the only time during the year when there was a cake without frosting.

The gifts were not so memorable except for my eighth birthday, when I asked for a wood carving kit with a nice sharp razor knife. Of course, I wound up cutting my hand with the knife, causing copious amounts of blood to flow and putting a halt to my wood-carving career.

Cutting my hand might have planted a seed in my head. As an adult, I decided that instead of getting presents for my birthday, I would give other people presents.

For one birthday, I rented a trolley car and hired a banjo player, who sang "Clang, Clang, Clang" as my friends and I rode the trolley. Once I rented an indoor carousel, and my friends rode the carousel while the carousel played music by k. d. lang. And I rented a planetarium, where the person narrating the planetarium show mentioned that there are a few things in the universe older than Doug Schneider.

The Big XL

The very first birthday where I gave other people presents was my fortieth birthday: the big XL (in Roman numerals).

I had noticed that some friends turned forty quietly. They did not want it made public. Perhaps they thought that if no one knew you were forty years old, you would not be forty years old.

But I saw turning forty as an accomplishment, and I wanted to make it public. It was my big XL birthday, and people were going to dance.

I rented a dance hall and hired a four-piece dance band. I arranged for friends to teach folk dances, ranging from simple to intriguing. There were English dances, Scottish dances, and American dances. Plus a long conga line mimicking Rosalind Russell in the movie *Wonderful Town*.

Luck

Years later, one of the party guests would remember my big XL birthday as "such fun, and one of the first parties I ever really enjoyed dancing at."

I had given my friends a present.

A Box of Triangles

I want to cross the boundary with joie de vivre. I want my milestone birthday parties to show people the spirit in which I plan to live the next five years.

For the sixty-fifth birthday, I gathered people at the Atomic Cowboy, a funky bar/restaurant celebrating the apocalyptic Wild West, with free salsa lessons. For the sixtieth: rented a flea market building and hired a disk jockey. For the fiftieth-fifth: rented an apartment complex party room and hired a Scottish band. For the fiftieth: rented the Czechoslovakian Cultural Center, hired a band, got up on stage, and sang to my guests. For the forty-fifth, rented a church hall and asked friends to sing or play music for my guests.

These parties were a present to everyone --- with one exception.

A friend who sang at my forty-fifth was an elementary school music teacher. She brought along a box full of maracas, triangles, and rhythm sticks. She handed them out for people to play while she sang.

After the party, a guest said to me, "You know, Doug, all those years I was in elementary school and the music teachers handed out maracas and triangles and rhythm sticks, I never got an instrument to play. So, here I am an adult and I come to your forty-fifth birthday party and your teacher friend hands out instruments --- and I still didn't get an instrument to play."

His joie de vivre was dampened that night. But mine was intact.

See you the next time I cross the boundary.

Luck

THERE IS NO RUM IN THE LIFE SAVERS

It's Made of Cold Black Granite

Whenever I visit the Vietnam Memorial in Washington DC, I look up Tom Temple's name.

Etched in the black granite of the wall are the names of all the Americans who died in service during the Vietnam War. I use the book at the entrance to the memorial to locate the exact granite slab where Tom Temple's name is etched.

I go to the slab, I find Tom Temple's name, and I run my fingers over the name. There are dozens of people around me, but everyone is hushed. We all feel that this is a sacred place.

Then I take out a pen and paper and write him a note.

There is a space in between the slabs in the wall big enough for me to wedge my note into it. I feel like I have made a connection with Tom, even though I know that the National Park Service will take my note down at night.

The Least Distracting Room

When I was at university, there were two types of people --- those who studied in their dormitories and those who studied in the library.

I studied in the library, out of necessity. I needed to get away from all the distractions in my dorm room. Because the library offered its own types of distractions, I found the least distracting room to study in.

It was the English Literature Reserved Book Room, just big enough to hold a table that seated four people. Every night, the same four people showed up this room to study: myself, Annette, Ellen, and Tom Temple.

I usually brought a roll of Life Savers with me and would offer some to Annette, Ellen, and Tom. They were my favorite flavor: butter rum. I always reassured them that there was no actual rum in the Life Savers.

Over time we bonded as a group, becoming friends.

Shortly before graduation, Tom went to a presentation by a Marine recruiter. He signed up for Officer Candidate School. Tom was the only classmate I knew who went into the military directly after graduation. .

Luck

It was 1965. The Vietnam War was just beginning to heat up.

Checking the Armoire

After graduation, I went off to Nigeria to serve in the Peace Corps. I served for two years and came back to the U.S. for a visit in 1967 before returning to Nigeria. I had signed up to serve an additional year.

During my visit in the U.S., I caught up with a friend from university. His first words to me were, "Did you hear that Tom Temple was killed? It was in the *Alumni Monthly*."

My heart sank. I did not know about Tom's death.

The university had been mailing the *Alumni Monthly* to me in Nigeria. I would read them and stack them up. But I had thrown the entire stack in the trash as part of a cleanup effort before going on my trip back to the U.S. Somehow, I had missed reading about my friend's death.

I returned to Nigeria, saddened. While unpacking my suitcase, I noticed something in the bottom of my armoire. It was a single issue of the *Alumni Monthly*.

I took the *Alumni Monthly* out of the armoire and opened it to the obituary section.   I read that Lieutenant Thomas Temple was killed while leading a Marine patrol in Quang Nam province in October of 1966.

I wondered if this issue of the magazine, knowing that it had such important news about my classmate, had deliberately avoided my cleanup efforts. It patiently sat there, in the bottom of my armoire, waiting for me.

Luck

THE ULTIMATE ST. LOUIS MOMENT

Got Some Music to Recommend

When I went from St. Louis to visit Minneapolis in 2002, I was looking for some fresh ideas about music. I asked my friend Jackie, "What music should I be listening to?"

Jackie immediately recommended Kelley Hunt.

I had never heard of Kelley Hunt, even though she lives in Missouri, on the western side of the state. So I bought Kelley Hunt's latest CD at the nearest Minneapolis record store. I listened to the CD in my rental car and liked Kelley Hunt's high energy. I quickly became enamored of her blues and boogie woogie style.

The next day I visited my friend Jon in Minneapolis. I told him that I wanted to recommend some music.

Jon needed no further clue; he immediately said, "You're going to recommend Kelley Hunt, aren't you?"

The Queen of the 88's

I got to hear Kelley Hunt perform live in St. Louis. The venue was the Route 66 Microbrewery, located in Union Station.

Kelley sang her autobiographical "The Queen of the 88's." The song tells about choosing a piano teacher. At age ten, Kelley Hunt could play by ear, but her parents wanted her to take formal piano lessons so she could read music.

They took her to piano teacher number one, who asked Kelley what she wanted to learn. Kelly told her she wanted to learn boogie woogie, and piano teacher number one responded, "No lessons for you!" And so on down the line to piano teacher number five, who responded "No lessons for you!"

The song goes on to tell how Kelley Hunt's mother decided to take her daughter to the other side of the tracks, to a piano teacher named The Queen of the 88's. This piano teacher lived in a tiny house, wore a bright red wig, had a cigarette dangling from her mouth, and wore a ring on every finger.

Kelley told her she wanted to learn boogie woogie. The Queen of the 88's responded, "Come on in. As soon as I change my wig, we will start your

Luck

lessons."

Fingers Like Cigars

Kelley Hunt continued with her autobiographical song, singing about the time decades ago when her sister put her first Chuck Berry record on a 45 RPM record player. The sister told Kelley, "Listen to Chuck Berry play that guitar," but Kelley was entranced by Chuck Berry's piano player. Kelley told her sister, "Listen to Johnnie Johnson play that piano."

When Kelley Hunt finished her song, she pointed out her mother sitting in the audience there at the Route 66 Microbrewery. Applause. Then she pointed out Johnnie Johnson sitting in the audience there at the Route 66 Microbrewery. Applause, cheers, stomping of feet.

Then Johnnie Johnson rose from the audience and sat down at Kelley Hunt's piano. I noticed how huge his fingers were, like large fat cigars. He started to play "The St. Louis Blues." His playing was effortless. Kelley Hunt started to sing.

And I suddenly realized that this is what I had expected to find in St. Louis when I moved here in 1997. Sitting in a bar named after the legendary Route 66, located in what was once the world's largest train station, listening to a high-energy Missouri woman sing "The St. Louis Blues," while she was accompanied by a legendary piano player.

It was the ultimate St. Louis music moment.

228

Luck

YOU PULL THE DUCK AND RUN

In Minneapolis in 1995

It was thirty years after I had left Providence, Rhode Island, and I was chatting with a fellow at a party in Minneapolis, Minnesota.

When I found out that he and his wife used to live in Providence, I asked him how often they went back to Providence for a visit.

He answered, "My wife and I don't go back any longer ever since one of our favorite people moved from Providence to Vermont."

Hmm... One of my favorite people had moved from Providence to Vermont. Could we be thinking of the same person?

So I asked the guy, "Was that Dian Parker?" I hit the nail on the head. Although we had never met before, this guy and I had a favorite person in common.

In The Old Corner Bookstore

I was a college sophomore in 1962 when I went to the Old Corner Bookstore in downtown Providence to order a book on Appalachian dulcimers.

The bookstore was at basement level, reached by a steep narrow stairwell. The descent was heightened by Alice in Wonderland characters painted on the walls.

This was when I first met Dian Parker, who was a clerk at the bookstore. She took my order for the book on Appalachian dulcimers and then told me that she was in the process of repairing a European dulcimer. She asked me to stop by her apartment and take a look at the European dulcimer.

Dian gave me her address and her apartment number and told me that I had to "pull the duck and run."

This required explanation. The apartment buzzers at the front door did not work, so Dian had rigged up a bell outside her third-floor kitchen window. Attached to the clapper was a long string tied around the neck of a cement duck hung down near ground level.

You pulled the duck, the bell outside the third-floor kitchen window rang, and then you ran around to the front door and waited for Dian to buzz you in.

Luck

In Dian's Apartment

I went to the address, found the cement duck, pulled, and ran.

Once Dian buzzed me in, I discovered that the only similarity between an Appalachian dulcimer and a European dulcimer was the name. I could not help in her repair effort.

I found Dian's apartment exotic. It was unlike any place I was used to. I had grown up in a suburban house where every wall was wallpapered. I lived in a college dormitory where every wall was painted institutional green.

But Dian's place had off-white walls. I had never even heard the word "off-white" before.

Because she was earning a bookstore clerk's salary, Dian could not afford artwork for her walls. So her friends would take a pencil and draw pictures on her off-white walls for her; she hung empty garage-sale frames around the drawings.

Even more exotic, Dian was not a college student. Every friend I had in Providence was going to the same college I was. But not Dian. This was a door to another world.

I cherished my friendship with Dian, and, yes, she became one of my favorite people. And three decades later and 1,400 miles away in Minneapolis, I discovered that other people considered her a favorite, too.

I am glad that I pulled the duck and ran.

Luck

BLOWING IN THE NARRAGANSETT WIND

<u>Worshipping Peter, Paul, and Mary</u>

I had the chance to go to the 1963 Newport Folk Festival, which was held on a July weekend at Fort Adams in Newport, Rhode Island --- three nights of solid folk music, from Friday through Sunday.

Newport's Fort Adams had a panoramic view over Newport Harbor and Narragansett Bay. The fort was large enough to accommodate 13,000 festival-goers sitting in chairs on the parade ground.

My favorite folk singer, Theodore Bikel, who sang international music, was scheduled to perform.

But the vast majority of the festival-goers were there because of the headline act --- Peter, Paul, and Mary. Peter, Paul, and Mary, with their smooth harmonies and slick arrangements, were a big commercial success. Whenever the festival emcee mentioned their names, the audience would sit up and take notice.

I decided that most people had come to the Newport Folk Festival to do more than listen to Peter, Paul, and Mary --- they came to worship them.

<u>A Shudder in the Crowd</u>

The crowd listened politely to Theodore Bikel, listened respectfully to Mississippi John Hurt, and was patient when a taxi driver from Montreal played a fiddle. The crowd grew restless waiting for Peter, Paul, and Mary.

Peter, Paul, and Mary finally took the stage. And then they proceeded to devastate the audience.

They said they were going to sing something by the most important person in American folk music. The massed worshippers could not believe their ears. A shudder ran through the audience. Weren't Peter, Paul, and Mary the most important people in American folk music?

There was going to be an abdication, a passing of the crown.

Peter, Paul, and Mary announced that the most important person in American folk music was Bob Dylan. The audience gasped.

Luck

Most gasped because they had never heard of Bob Dylan. The rest gasped because they had heard Dylan's one album, which had been released just two months before the Newport Folk Festival. No smooth harmonies. No slick arrangements. Only raw and untutored music.

Newport, 1963: The crown was passed.

The Narragansett Fog Rolls In

On the final night of the festival, Bob Dylan was the closing act.

The light of the summer evening started to fade. A chill could be felt in the air. As the show was coming to a close, fog started to roll in from Narragansett Bay. Bob Dylan got up to perform.

When Dylan finished his set, it was time for the finale and the fog-shrouded stage filled with the weekend's performers, and they all joined in on Dylan's song "Blowing in the Wind." As if on cue, the wind started blowing in from Narragansett Bay.

A year later, I realized that I had been a witness to history. At Newport, Bob Dylan had gone from being an obscure Minnesota singer on Friday to being the most important person in American folk music on Sunday.

Two years later, the United States had gone from being a peaceful, well-behaved country to a country at war, with its generations split apart by radical social change.

In 1963, Bob Dylan was right: Something was blowing in the wind.

Luck

THIS WEATHER IS ELEVEN HOURS OLD

Driving Off the Ferry

When I lived in Boston, I would take a ferry to go visit my mother, who lived on Long Island. The ferry left from Connecticut, went across Long Island Sound, and landed on the North Fork of Long Island. I would take the ferry to the island on Friday night, and I would take the ferry back to Connecticut on Sunday night.

You are not allowed to stay in your car on the ferry. You have to exit from your car and sit on the passenger deck. At the end of the journey across the sound, I would wait for the comforting bump that signals that the ferry has made contact with the dock. The PA system then announced that we were free to go down to our cars.

On Sunday evenings, when the ferry docked in Connecticut, I would start the car, drive onto the dock, and immediately turn on the radio to listen to the "Sunday Night Folk Festival." I really enjoyed this show. It was hosted by Susan Forbes Hansen, broadcasting from a small public radio station in central Connecticut.

One Sunday night, when I drove off the ferry onto the dock and turned on the radio, the station was doing a fund-raiser. For a pledge of $75, you would get to be a guest co-host for an hour on Susan Forbes Hansen's show.

I made a beeline for a phone booth and made a $75 pledge.

Formidable Audio Equipment

On that day I was to be a co-host with Susan Hansen, I drove to Connecticut with a box full of my folk music tapes. Most were commercial tapes that I had bought, but some tapes had been recorded in my living room. I had hosted some house concerts, designed to raise money for Boston dance musicians.

Susan Forbes Hansen welcomed me into the studio, we chatted briefly, and then came the beginning of my hour. "We have a guest host tonight from Massachusetts."

I was impressed by the ease with which Susan queued up my tapes on the formidable audio equipment, and I was impressed by how comfortable she made me feel as we introduced each song I had chosen.

Then she handed me a weather report to read. However, I pointed out that the report was eleven hours old. Susan jumped up and headed down the hall

233

Luck

to the Teletype to get a fresh weather report.

She left me sitting alone in a strange radio studio full of formidable audio equipment. I started to panic. What if the tape that was playing at the moment came to an end before Susan returned from the Teletype? I had no idea which buttons to push. She seemed to be taking forever...

But she was back in the nick of time, and I got to tell central Connecticut what their weather was going to be for the next two days.

Near the end of my hour, Susan asked me why I put on house concerts. I told her that I appreciated having live dance music in Boston and I wanted to help out the musicians. I also told Susan that I take advantage of the office Xerox machine to copy fliers for my house concerts.

Close the Door Behind You

At work the next day back in Boston, my boss asked me to come to his office. When I entered his office, he asked me to close the door and sit down.

Oh no, the jig was up. I had been so stupid!

I had publicly stated on the radio that I made copies on the office Xerox for personal use. Somehow, my boss found out. Maybe Sunday night's atmospheric conditions were so good that the signal from the little station in central Connecticut had reached all the way to his house in Boston.

I sat there rigid in front of my boss, prepared to be demoted. Or reprimanded. Or fired.

"Doug," my boss began, "you have been promoted to assistant vice president. You will get a salary increase. Business cards are being printed up for you."

My boss must have seen delight in my eyes at that point. He probably thought my delight was due to the new title or the new salary or the new business cards.

Little did he know that my delight was due to my expectation that assistant vice presidents are permitted to make copies on the office Xerox for personal use.

FAMILY

Family

Family

THE DUKE OF WINDSOR ORDERS A PIZZA

Dad's High School Classmate

Dad graduated from the High School of Commerce in Manhattan in 1921. He kept in touch with a lot of people who were in his graduating class.

One of Dad's high school classmates was Joe Lauder. After high school, Joe tried a number of commercial ventures. At one point, he bought a lipstick machine and turned out inexpensive lipstick for small variety stores in The Bronx and Manhattan. At another point, Joe Lauder married a woman named Estee, who knew the formula for a skin cream invented by her uncle.

Lipstick plus skin cream eventually became the Estee Lauder Company, a world leader in the cosmetics industry.

Dad admired Joe Lauder because Joe never forgot his original customers and continued to make inexpensive lipstick for the dwindling number of small variety stores in The Bronx and Manhattan.

A Fragrance-free Mother

Estee Lauder loved being in the spotlight, mingling with the jet set, and showing off her posh corporate headquarters in Manhattan. Joe Lauder did not mind mingling with the jet set, but he preferred to spend his time at the Estee Lauder factory, which was in an ordinary building in an ordinary industrial park in ordinary Mehlville, Long Island.

Dad would take Mom and me to go visit Joe in Mehlville. Mom disliked our visits to the Estee Lauder factory because Mom was anti-fragrance. There wasn't a single perfume bottle on Mom's dresser; fragrances annoyed her.

It was hard for Mom to avoid fragrances while visiting the Estee Lauder factory. And the hardest part for Mom was the end of each visit, when Joe Lauder would load her down with gift baskets brimming with Estee Lauder products. Mom had to pretend to be grateful for these annoyingly fragrant gifts.

Wasn't That a Great Pepperoni and Mushroom Pizza?

During one Mehlville visit, I was staring at Joe Lauder's bookcase and spotted a photo of the Duke of Windsor. The photo was black-and-white and showed the duke wearing some dapper clothes in elegant surroundings.

Family

"Is that the Duke of Windsor?"

"Yes, the duke is a very good friend of ours. But I want you to know that although he wears dapper clothing and lives in elegant surroundings, the Duke of Windsor is really just a regular guy. He's the kind of guy who enjoys ordering take-out pizza."

This news was devastating.

The Duke of Windsor, once known as Edward VIII, the man who abdicated the throne of England so he could be with the woman he loved, the center of one of the most famous love stories of the twentieth century --- this man is just a regular guy? The Duke of Windsor is such a regular guy that he enjoys take-out pizza?

I was so devastated that I decided not to walk over to Joe Lauder's bookcase. Yes, I was curious about what the Duke of Windsor had inscribed on the photo, but I was afraid.

I was afraid that the former King Edward VIII had inscribed, "Dear Joe and Estee, wasn't that a great pepperoni and mushroom pizza?" Signed, Ed.

Family

THE SAINT AND THE WOBBLY

Do Not Interrupt the Dodgers

My brothers and I are not certain if our grandfather was a Wobbly, but we are certain that he was a mystery.

This was our mother's father. He worked at the Brooklyn Navy Yard, where he installed asbestos. But he never had a respiratory problem in his life. Instead, he had a cloudy eyeball. But he never explained how a piece of steel got in his eye. He had twin daughters, and he was a twin himself. He never made an effort to keep in touch with his twin brother.

I only knew him after he retired from the Navy Yard.

At that age he was very quiet with a gruff exterior, and his main passion in life was the Brooklyn Dodgers. I vividly remember Grandpa sitting in an armchair, focused on the television set, watching a baseball game. And I remember the unwritten rule of his household: You must never interrupt the Dodgers.

I was not sure what this gruff man would do if I interrupted the baseball game, but I would tread very lightly when I was at my grandparents' house.

As a child, I had no idea that this quiet man in an armchair used to be a labor union activist.

Her Sewing Rescued the Family

Mabel asked me to sit down because she wanted me to know that my grandmother was a saint.

Mabel's parents lived next door to my mother's parents in a Swedish neighborhood in Brooklyn. Mabel was four years old when she became friends with my mother, also four years old. That friendship lasted over eighty years.

I sat down, and I learned from Mabel that my grandfather had been active in the labor movement, and he was always on strike. To get income, my grandmother took in sewing. Her sewing rescued the family and put food on the table. My grandmother was a saint.

My mother did not talk much about her childhood in Brooklyn.

Family

However, she did talk about the excitement of getting ready to move to Seattle when she was a little girl. Grandpa had gotten a job out in Washington State, and the family was to follow him. The bags were packed, and Mom was eagerly looking forward to a cross-country train trip.

Then the word came from the West: Grandpa had "gotten in a fight" and was returning to Brooklyn. They unpacked the bags and got the train tickets refunded.

I Dreamed I Saw Joe Hill Last Night

Mom never moved to Seattle, but I did. When I was living there in the 1970s, I read up on Seattle history and found out that the International Workers of the World (IWW) was a strong organization in Seattle in the early twentieth century.

The IWW was a radical organization. Members were called Wobblies, and their goal was to end wage labor. I read further and looked at the chronology.

My mother had a clear memory of getting ready to move to Seattle; she could have been nine years old then, which was 1916.

If Grandpa had been in Seattle in 1916, he could have joined the IWW. He could have been a Wobbly.

On Sunday, November 5, 1916, a group of Wobblies boarded a steamer to go to Everett, Washington. Their steamer was met at the Everett dock by the sheriff and 200 vigilantes. After ten minutes of intense gunfire, five Wobblies were killed and twenty-seven were injured. The steamer left the dock and went back to Seattle.

The most famous Wobbly was Joe Hill. Whenever I hear the song "I Dreamed I Saw Joe Hill Last Night," I get goose bumps.

Are these goose bumps a result of the haunting lyrics of the song, or do I get goose bumps because my grandfather may have been a Wobbly?

I have no evidence that Grandpa was on that steamer in 1916. I have no evidence that the Everett massacre was the reason he went back to the safety of Brooklyn. But I do know that I feel an extraordinary connection with a song.

Family

ALL MY SUFFERINGS ARE NOTHING

<u>Married to a River Pilot</u>

I visited Romania in the spring of 1975 to do some work on the family tree.

While I was there, I talked to my father's third cousins, Adelbert and Ladislaus Schneider. They had a request for me. They had not heard from their sister Josephine who had immigrated to the United States. Could I please ask Josephine to write them a letter?

The request sounded simple enough, but later I found out that it wasn't simple.

Josephine Schneider had married a Hungarian in the late 1930s and moved from Romania to Hungary. Her husband was a river pilot on the Danube River. At the start of World War II, he was exempt from military service because his occupation was vital to Hungary's national security.

But the war turned bad for Hungary, and Russian troops started invading from the east. Josephine's husband was drafted, went to the front, and was captured by the Russians. They sent him to a slave labor camp in Siberia.

In the meantime, Josephine took their two young sons and fled eastward into Germany to avoid the advancing Russian troops.

<u>Miami Sweatshop</u>

As a refugee in postwar Germany, Josephine lived by her wits. She and the boys were taken in by a kindly farmer. She helped the farmer sell meat on the black market, walking along mountain paths with a backpack full of beef.

In postwar Germany, Josephine heard nothing from her husband.

Josephine managed to immigrate with the boys to Miami. She got a job as a seamstress in a small alterations shop. The job involved hard work, low pay, long hours, and a very demanding boss.

In Miami, Josephine heard nothing from her husband.

President Eisenhower went before the United Nations in 1953 and gave a speech in which he quoted statistics. He mentioned the number of enemy combatants captured by the Russians and the number of enemy combatants released by the Russians. There was a gap. The gap proved that the Russians were still holding combatants, eight years after the war had ended.

241

Family

This speech embarrassed the Russians into releasing all the enemy combatants they had been holding in slave labor camps since the end of World War II.

In Miami, Josephine finally heard from her husband. The Russians had released him from the slave labor camp. But he was now back in Hungary. This did Josephine no good because Hungary was shut solidly behind the Iron Curtain at the time. There was no way for her husband to join her in Miami.

But then the Hungarian Revolution of 1956 broke out. And while Hungarian citizens used Molotov cocktails to battle Russian tanks in the streets of Budapest, the Iron Curtain opened for a brief moment. Josephine's husband managed to escape into Austria.

He was flown to Miami and reunited with his family. He got a job as a school custodian.

But the years in the slave labor camp had made him a sullen man. And the years away from the family had made him a stranger to his sons. He died after a few years.

Married to a Cincinnati Red

It was early October 1975 when I went to visit Josephine and her second husband at their home. Josephine had remarried; her husband was a former professional baseball player for the Cincinnati Reds. She was living quite comfortably.

I sat in their living room as Josephine told me the story of the war, postwar Germany, the sweatshop in Miami, and being reunited with a husband who had turned sullen. I had never met anyone who had so much suffering in their life.

I mentioned to her that her brothers back in Romania, Adelbert and Ladislaus, would like her to write them a letter. About that time, Josephine's husband announced that he was taking us for a drive and went down to get the car ready.

Now that her husband was out of earshot, Josephine looked me in the eye, and said: "Doug, all my sufferings during the war and after the war are nothing compared to the way my brothers treated me when I was a little girl."

I asked for no details. We went down to the car and went for a pleasant afternoon drive. I knew that Adelbert and Ladislaus would never be getting a letter from their sister.

242

Family

THE HYMN IN THE DULCIMER

Just Across the Harbor

I was a teenager, swept up in the folk music craze, when I heard my first dulcimer. I decided that the instrument is cool and that I must save up some money to buy one.

The Appalachian mountain dulcimer is cool because of its sound --- three strings, but you only play the melody on one string while the other two are drones. It is cool because of its elongated hourglass shape. And it is cool because of its intimacy; it rests on your lap as you play it, and it is not very loud.

Back in the 1960s, the foremost dulcimer player in the United States was Jean Ritchie. She was born in Viper, Kentucky, and was the youngest of fourteen children. Song was an integral part of life in this family. After graduating from college, Jean was awarded a Fulbright scholarship and went to Great Britain to research the origins of the songs she sang as a child.

She also wrote a book about dulcimers and praised the dulcimers made by Ake Tugel of Sea Cliff, Long Island.

Sea Cliff --- it was right across the harbor from my hometown. When I saved up enough money, I went to Sea Cliff to buy one of Ake Tugel's dulcimers.

My Seafaring Ancestor

Ake Tugel was a Swede who had immigrated to Sea Cliff and earned his living as a cabinet maker.

Ake told me that he started crafting Appalachian mountain dulcimers because he was fascinated by their shape. I bought one made of dark wood, with an elegant scrolled head and wooden tuning pegs. Its beauty took my breath away.

At home, I opened up Jean Ritchie's book and set about teaching myself how to play my instrument. I managed to find a turkey feather for strumming the dulcimer. But tuning the dulcimer was a pain; finding music for it was a pain; and discovering that I was supposed to re-tune it to match various keys was discouraging.

I wound up mastering only a handful of tunes on the dulcimer; the tune which sounded the best was "In the Sweet Bye and Bye." One day, my

Family

grandmother walked by while I was playing the tune, and she stopped still. "That was your great-grandfather's favorite hymn."

My great-grandfather was a Swede who spent most of his life at sea, working as a ship's boatswain. It was a nice connection playing the favorite hymn of my seafaring ancestor from Sweden on a dulcimer made by a cabinet maker from Sweden.

She Has Fat Hips

I didn't play my dulcimer for many people in my hometown, but I did tell lots of people about it.

A friend's mother heard me talk about my dulcimer and how Jean Ritchie had praised the man who crafted it. Her reaction, "Jean Ritchie has fat hips and shouldn't wear Bermuda shorts when she goes to the supermarket."

I was surprised. I had no idea that Jean Ritchie, who grew up dirt-poor in rural Kentucky, was living in my hometown, where she goes grocery shopping in Bermuda shorts.

I ran home and checked the cover photo on Jean Ritchie's dulcimer book. Jean was wearing a print dress and leaning up against a tree. The photo was supposed to make you think she was leaning against a tree in rural Kentucky, but now I saw that the tree was in a park in my hometown in suburban Long Island. I was deflated.

I did get over the shock of discovering that my dulcimer heroine was a suburban housewife. But I never did master the dulcimer. Eventually, my instrument's beauty was its undoing. The wooden pegs put too much stress on the body, and eventually it split and became unplayable.

Now the dulcimer hangs stringless and silent on our living room wall.

If you look inside, you will see a little tag: Sea Cliff-FEB 1961-Ake Tugel. Besides the tag, I know there is also a hymn inside the dulcimer. It is a hymn I once managed to coax out of the instrument --- a hymn my seafaring great-grandfather knew well.

Family

MY EMBARRASSING AUNT MARGARET

Rabbit Cookies

Aunt Margaret (my father's sister) and Uncle John did not have any children. My brother and I decided that lack of children is what made our aunt and uncle so embarrassing.

Aunt Margaret cooked embarrassing ethnic German food. Aunt Margaret and Uncle John lived in an embarrassing old house. Aunt Margaret had the same embarrassing out-of-style hairdo for years. Aunt Margaret wore embarrassing cheap cotton dresses.

When she visited our house, Aunt Margaret would usually bring a tray of cookies.

One Easter I mentioned that she had not baked any rabbit cookies --- plain sugar cookies made with a rabbit-shaped cookie cutter with a fluffy meringue tail. Aunt Margaret latched on to my comment; from that day forward, every time she visited our house, she made sure she had baked some rabbit cookies for me.

Easter, Christmas, my father's birthday --- you name it, I got some rabbit cookies.

She probably thought she was pleasing me; but I felt she was overdoing it, and I found it embarrassing.

All my childhood, I kept my fingers crossed and hoped that none of my friends would find out that I had such an embarrassing aunt.

Pretty Paper

Every Christmas, when the family gathered around the tree to open presents, I would cringe because I knew exactly what Aunt Margaret would do.

When she was handed a present to open, she would exclaim that it was wrapped in pretty paper. She would very carefully unwrap the paper from the present, flattening the paper with her hands so that she could save it. She would try her best to save the ribbon as well.

Family

This made me cringe. Why save wrapping paper? Why re-use the paper? Just rip the paper off the present and wad it up. It's so easy to buy new wrapping paper.

I grew up and moved overseas. Aunt Margaret died while I was living in London. My father mailed me a photo of her.

Beautiful Cheekbones

A friend of mine in London saw Aunt Margaret's photo. "What beautiful cheekbones!" he exclaimed. I was impressed; this guy was a professional model, and he called my aunt beautiful.

When I moved back to the United States, my cousin showed me the love letters that Uncle John had written when he was courting Aunt Margaret. The two of them were profoundly in love. They were so much in love throughout their lives that Uncle John could not live without Aunt Margaret. He died less than a year after she did.

Now that I have learned to recognize that my Aunt Margaret was beautiful and my Aunt Margaret was beloved, I no longer feel embarrassed by her.

Now I no longer mock her careful saving of wrapping paper; instead, I am proud of her for being a recycling pioneer. Now I am deeply touched by the food she used to bring to our house; it was her gesture of family love.

And I miss Aunt Margaret's rabbit cookies.

Family

WE HAVE NO BISHOPS HERE

Catholics vs. Protestants

In the 1960s and 1970s in northern Nigeria, only large cities had hotels. If you were traveling and had to spend the night in a small town, your best bet was to ask to stay with a missionary. Sometimes a small town would have two missionaries, and you needed to decide if you were going to ask a Catholic or a Protestant for a place to spend the night.

The Catholic missionaries were members of the Society of Apostolic Life, founded in 1868. Because of their white robes they were known as White Fathers. Besides proselytizing, the White Fathers sponsored projects to help alleviate poverty.

The Protestant missionaries were from the Sudan Interior Mission (SIM), founded in 1893. Besides proselytizing, the SIM missionaries sponsored projects to improve health in Nigeria.

For me, it was easy to choose between the Catholics and the Protestants. The Protestant missionaries were teetotalers. The White Fathers, who were from Wisconsin, kept a supply of cold beer. I always asked to stay at the Catholic mission.

The city I lived in had a large Protestant mission station. I heard that two new Americans had arrived in town and were staying at the mission. The new folks were called Mr. and Mrs. Bishop. They were not missionaries; the husband was a linguist and was helping translate the Bible into an obscure Nigerian language.

I drove my motorcycle to the Protestant mission station to meet the new Americans. Walking in the door, I said, "I would like to meet the Bishops." I got an indignant response, "We have no bishops here." I realized that the missionaries assumed I was seeking out a bishop --- as in bishop, archbishop, cardinal. The Sudan Interior Mission had no such hierarchy

I quickly rephrased my request, "I would like to meet Mr. and Mrs. Bishop."

Plagiarism and Graffiti

While Mr. Bishop worked on his Bible translation, Mrs. Bishop took a job teaching English at the same school where I taught. Her desk in the staff room was next to mine.

Family

One day, she told me that she was worried because the students had invited her to judge a poetry contest. She was worried because the poetry was not in English. The poetry was in Hausa, a language she did not know.

I told her not to worry. As a judge she didn't need to understand the poetry, she just needed to watch the audience. The audience reaction would tell her which one was the best poem.

Mrs. Bishop did a fine job of judging the poetry contest but later became upset when she found out the winner had plagiarized a famous poem. I calmed her down; in the world of Hausa poetry, plagiarism is the highest form of flattery.

Our school was all male. One day I mentioned to Mrs. Bishop that there was suggestive graffiti mentioning her name written on the walls in the student latrine. I expected Mrs. Bishop to become irate.

Instead, she blushed. She was not irate; in fact, I think Mrs. Bishop was flattered.

Northern Nigeria was a place where both plagiarism and graffiti were considered flattery.

Grab My Spare Helmet

Then Mr. Bishop's mother, who was the same age as my parents, came to Nigeria for a visit.

When I met her, she took one look at my motorcycle and asked for a ride. I grabbed my spare helmet, put her on the back of the motorcycle, and we went off on a jaunt around the city. The city was walled in the eleventh century and had twelve gates. We saw the market, which has been running daily for centuries; we saw the central mosque; we saw camel caravans.

Mr. Bishop's mother went back to the United States, where she lived an hour's drive away from my parents. When I went home on vacation, I arranged for her to come one evening and meet my folks and tell them about her trip to Nigeria.

My parents were astonished. Here was someone the same age as they were, who flew off to Nigeria with all its heat and weird food and insects and disease and dirt and strange languages - and she did not die the minute she stepped off the airplane in Nigeria.

Mr. Bishop's mother capped off the evening by giving me a copy of her favorite photo from her visit to Nigeria. It showed her smiling, clutching my spare helmet, sitting on the back of my motorcycle.

TRAVEL

Travel

Travel

LIKE THE ARM OF A TATTOOED LADY

Crossing Borders with Stamps

In the 1970s, I lived in West Africa and I traveled a lot in West Africa, which meant that my passport got quite a workout.

Nigeria, where I lived, stamped my passport with a residence visa, then stamped my passport every time I entered or exited Nigeria. Neighboring countries stamped it with visitors' visas. Some countries even had stamps for currency exchange.

At borders, immigration officials wielded their rubber stamps with great flair. The stamps were as big as an entire page in my passport. But before they stamped, the officials did two things. 1. They perused all the stamps already in my passport, whether they pertained to their country or not. 2. They would decide which page to stamp, and they never chose the next available blank page.

My passport was filling up. The U.S. consulate came to my rescue and glued an extender into my passport. This was an accordion fold of blank pages.

My passport was slowing me down. It was almost a hindrance as border officials took a long time to go through all the regular pages of my passport, and then unfold the extender, perusing everything. Even with an extender, they never chose to stamp the next available blank page.

Eventually, my accordion fold-out filled up with stamps and looked like the arm of a tattooed lady.

Crossing Borders with Fun

Usually I was tense crossing a border. So many things could go wrong. I usually felt like I was in one of those black-and-white films where an immigration official asks, "Where Are Your Papers?" Sometimes, however, it was fun crossing borders.

I entered Japan with a large jar of Marshmallow Fluff.

I had Marshmallow Fluff because an American friend living in Osaka was craving the stuff, which was unavailable in Japan. At the Osaka airport, I saw a sign "Declare agricultural products here." I was not sure if Marshmallow Fluff was an agricultural product, but I placed it on the counter in front of two Japanese officials. I liked the puzzled look on their faces as they tried to figure out what it was and whether to confiscate it or not. The jar was OK'd, and my friend in Osaka was happy to be reunited with Marshmallow Fluff.

Travel

The border with Mexico is easy to cross.

When I was staying in El Paso, I discovered the art center just across the Rio Grande in Ciudad Juarez. The Mexican government had built the art center to promote the sale of Mexican arts and crafts. To make sure tourists lingered and looked over the merchandise, the art center sold seventy-five-cent margaritas. Well worth the drive across the river

On the way back to El Paso, the U.S. border guards made me pop my car trunk to check for illegal drugs. They never noticed the smell of margaritas on my breath. But they did notice a brown paper bag in my trunk. The border guards would always dive in and grab the bag with glee.

I had recently finished active duty with the U.S. Army. Being a good soldier, I always carried shoe polish with me. I enjoyed the look of disappointment on the border officials' faces when they found cans of black shoe polish instead of something illegal to smoke.

Crossing Borders with Ease

I first noticed it in 1976 while I was traveling from France to Belgium on a bus. At the border, I expected an immigration official to get on our bus, look at our passports, and stamp them. The bus driver did not even stop at the border; instead, he passed around a clipboard. We wrote our names and nationalities on the clipboard. Borders were becoming easier to cross.

In 2008, I was traveling with friends, going from Austria to Italy by train. This time, no clipboard. In fact, nothing happened to make you aware that the train had crossed the border into Italy.

Leaving Italy was very lax. There were five of us traveling together. The airline asked to see our passports; when they handed them back, they got two of them mixed up. I made it through all the immigration formalities without anyone realizing I had someone else's passport.

With borders so easy to cross now, I worry about the old black-and-white movies. How will people appreciate those tense moments in the film when the hero and heroine are stopped at the border and asked, in a sinister Nazi accent, "Where Are Your Papers?"

The days of myriad immigration stamps are gone. And my passport with its accordion fold-out pages is gone. It would have made a nice souvenir, but I had considered it such a hindrance that I threw my passport away when it expired. I did not keep my tattooed lady.

Travel

COME SEE MY ARCHEOLOGY

Perhaps a Glass of Wine and a Plate of Brie

I spent ten days in French Guiana on vacation in 1989. French Guiana is in South America, just north of Brazil. The country is mostly jungle.

I was staying with a friend, and a friend of my friend invited me to come visit his house on Sunday. The phrase he used, in French, was "Come see my archeology."

On that Sunday, I took a taxi out to his house. I did not know exactly what the fellow meant by "come see my archeology." I was picturing a pleasant day looking at artifacts; perhaps my host would hand me pot shards or old bottles and describe how he found them.

Since my host was French, I guessed that he would hand me a glass of wine and a plate of brie as we looked at his artifacts.

I got out of the taxi, was shown inside the house, and waited to see what my host would hand me.

He handed me a shiny, freshly sharpened machete.

Snacking on Jungle Eggs

My host grabbed his machete, and we headed out his back door, straight into the jungle.

After fifteen minutes of hacking our way down a path, my host asked me if I was hungry. I said yes, hoping that he had some nice French snacks in his backpack.

Instead of reaching in his backpack, my host proceeded to hack a branch off of a nearby shrub. The branch had yellow puffballs on it, and my host said that these were jungle eggs and tasted quite pleasant. He popped one in his mouth to prove they were edible.

I tried a few. Not quite as good as a plate of brie, but they were pleasant.

We continued hacking down the path through the jungle until we reached a clearing. When I stepped into the clearing, I was speechless.

253

Travel

Looming over the Clearing

There, looming over the clearing, was the oldest steam engine in the world.

A bunch of men were working on the steam engine; they dropped their tools and came over to greet me. I expected them to say "bonjour"; instead, they said, in French: "Goody, you brought a shiny, freshly sharpened machete!" They proceeded to assign me a section of the clearing where I was to whack at the fast-growing weeds.

As I wielded my machete that Sunday, I figured out what was going on.

This once was a large sugar plantation in the eighteenth and nineteenth century, a plantation that used slave labor. Sugar was so profitable that the plantation could afford to order a giant steam engine from England. The steam engine replaced a donkey-driven mill that crushed sugar cane.

In 1848 France abolished slavery. The newly freed slaves in French Guiana did not want to become wage earners working on the sugar plantation. They all moved into town. The plantation shut down, and the jungle took over.

In the rest of the world, old steam engines were scrapped when newer models were available. But this steam engine sat untouched in the jungle in French Guiana for well over 100 years --- until a group of men decided to uncover the steam engine and try to get it working again.

When my friend's friend said, "Come see my archaeology," he really meant, "Come work alongside a group of men who dream of getting the world's oldest steam engine working again."

At the end of the day, I told my host that I was glad he invited me to come see his archeology.

Travel

MY CAMERA AS PASSPORT

Belgium: Passport to the Front of the Crowd

When I was living in Belgium for a few months in 1976, a friend of mine got a gig as a model in a fashion show. I thought it would be nice to take some photos of him during the show.

The show was in a Brussels nightclub; there were no rows of chairs or a stage or a runway. The show was taking place in the middle of the room, which was filled with fashion-conscious people --- all of them stylishly dressed, sporting stylish hairdos.

Except for me --- I had an ordinary haircut, and I hadn't bought any new clothes in a year. I hung out at the back of the crowd, even though that meant I would not get any good pictures of the fashion show.

The show started. I hoisted my camera and flashed a photo from the back of the crowd. Suddenly, the stylish crowd parted in front of me. I stepped forward and flashed again. The crowd continued to part, and I wound up in the front.

I took a bunch of photos and then retreated to the back of the crowd. I realized that the crowd had not parted for me; they had parted for the camera. They probably thought I was some hot-shot fashion photographer.

In Brussels, I got my photos, and my camera was a passport to the front of the crowd.

Norway: Passport to Confiscation

When I was visiting Norway in 1995, someone suggested that I should go to a McDonald's just to see the menu posted above the counter.

I found a McDonald's in downtown Oslo, stepped inside, read the menu, and started chuckling. There, on the menu, was McSalmon. Not only did the Norwegian McDonald's serve salmon, but it was also cheaper than a hamburger.

I took out my camera and took a photo of the menu, certain that my friends back home in Minneapolis would also get a chuckle from seeing a menu with McSalmon on it.

As soon as my camera's flash subsided, the manager of the downtown Oslo McDonald's was standing next to me. "You cannot take photographs in here."

255

Travel

"Why not?" "You might be working for a competitor; we need to inspect your camera."

Uh-oh, McDonald's competitor is Burger King, which is owned by Pillsbury, which is headquartered in Minneapolis. If the manager found out I lived in Minneapolis, I would never see my camera again.

"I am just a tourist, and I wanted to show that you serve salmon in a McDonald's." This remark distracted the Norwegian manager. He must have been amazed to hear that you could not get McSalmon at a McDonald's in America. So he decided not to inspect my camera.

In Oslo, I got my photo, and I did not get my camera confiscated.

Nigeria: Passport to Prison

A building caught my eye when I was visiting Lagos, Nigeria, in 1970. Painted up in vivid colors, the building was a century older than the surrounding buildings. It was a colonial era building, and I wanted to photograph it.

However, in 1970, Nigeria had just gotten over a civil war. During the war, the government had banned taking photographs of anything with military significance. If you were caught taking a photo of something significant, the police would throw you in jail.

The ban was still in effect.

I did not know if the brightly painted building had any military significance, but I did not want to take any chances. There was a Nigerian policeman nearby, and I was afraid that he would arrest me and I would get thrown in prison.

The solution was simple. There was no ban on taking photographs of policemen.

I went over to the policeman, and I told the fellow that I wanted to take his photo. Could he please stand over there in front of that colorful building? The policeman was glad to comply and posed for me.

In Lagos, I got my photo, and I did not go to prison.

256

Travel

IT SURE SMELLS GENUINE

Grandstands at the Two-year Anniversary

I had been in Germany when it was a divided country, back in 1967. So I was eager to see what a united Germany was like when I went to visit Berlin in November 1991.

I stayed with an American friend, and we went to see the Brandenburg Gate. The gate is a powerful symbol for Germany, and in a divided Germany, the gate was shut. Now, with a united Germany, the Brandenburg Gate is kept open so people can pass freely through it.

We found workers setting up grandstands near the gate. We were there on November 8, 1991.

The next day, November 9, would be the two-year anniversary of the fall of the Berlin Wall. They must be preparing for some kind of anniversary ceremony. I asked a worker what was going to happen the next day. The answer: They were not setting up the grandstands for a ceremony; they were setting up grandstands for the finish line of a bicycle race.

So, I thought that Berliners had forgotten about the fall of the wall.

A Laughingstock Parked on the Street

But people did not need a ceremony to be reminded that the wall had fallen.

For a reminder, all they had to do was try to make a phone call in Berlin. I needed to contact an airline and had to dial nine times before I got a call through. The East Berlin phone system was very antiquated and trying to incorporate it with the West Berlin phone system caused all calls in the city to bog down.

For another reminder, look at the cars parked on the street. For four decades under Communist rule, the only car an East German could aspire to was a Trabant. Made in East Germany, the Trabant had a two-stroke engine, like a lawnmower. The East Germans had to wait for years to get a car. They meticulously maintained their Trabants and were very proud of them.

But once the wall fell, all kinds of cars could be seen on the streets of East Berlin. These were snazzy modern cars that made the Trabants look shabby and pathetic. The once-proud Trabant became a laughingstock on the streets.

257

Travel

I talked to some West Germans about East Germans. They said the East Germans were backwards and ungrateful. The West Germans wished the country had never been unified. They were better off separate; let's bring back the wall.

I talked to some East Germans about West Germans. They said the West Germans were arrogant and looked down upon the East Germans. The East Germans wished the country had never been unified. They were better off separate; let's bring back the wall.

All this animosity took me by surprise.

<u>Sharing the Berlin Wall</u>

Although some Germans did not appear to be totally happy that the Berlin Wall had fallen, I was glad it had fallen and that the Cold War was over.

The fallen wall was now material for souvenirs. The friend I was visiting had personally pried pieces off the wall back in 1989. He gave me a piece that was about eight inches by six inches and was covered in colorful graffiti. My plan was to break it into smaller pieces to share with my friends back home.

I put the piece of the wall in my suitcase along with another souvenir of Berlin --- a can of German beer. However, I didn't pack carefully enough. During the flight back from Germany, the Berlin Wall punctured the German beer can, and the contents of my suitcase got soaked.

Once home, I broke my piece of the Berlin Wall into smaller pieces and distributed them to friends.

"Here, I brought you a genuine piece of the Berlin Wall."

My friends would look at the piece, ponder it, and then sniff it. The aroma of beer was unmistakable.

"Yep, it sure smells genuine."

258

Travel

THE VOLCANO WILL BLOW TONIGHT

Moving the Furniture Around

My buddy Randy and I had just arrived at the cabin we were renting in Arenal, Costa Rica.

I was standing on the porch when I heard rumbling. I yelled into the cabin window to ask Randy why he was moving the furniture around inside the cabin.

Simultaneously, Randy was standing inside the cabin when he heard rumbling. He yelled out the cabin window to ask me why I was moving the furniture around on the porch.

But neither one of us was moving furniture. There was another source of the rumbling. We scanned the horizon; our cabin faced the Arenal volcano. That was where the rumbling was coming from.

We had come to Arenal to see an active volcano; we just didn't expect that we would be hearing an active volcano.

Rumble, Cough, Spit, Plink, Plink, Plink

We booked a twilight volcano walk. When our Costa Rican guide drove up to our cabin to pick us up, there was a look of relief in his eyes. "You guys are young!"

Our guide's English was excellent because he had attended the University of Wisconsin at Milwaukee. He went on to explain that most of his customers were senior citizens, and his tour consisted of taking them to a nice safe viewing platform.

Because we were fit and we were the only customers that night, we would be hiking to the base of the volcano. The guide had his camera with him; he had a hunch that the volcano was going to do something this night.

Our hike consisted of going through a farmer's field, through a path in the forest, down and up a ravine with the help of a vine, and across part of the lava field. The lava field consisted of large boulders, and we settled down on one that gave us a good view of the top of the volcano.

Costa Rican volcanoes have high-silicate lava. Costa Rican lava does not flow. Instead, the volcano will rumble, then cough, then spit up some lava.

Travel

The lava instantly cools into a boulder, which then bounces down the side of the volcano: plink, plink, plink.

While we were sitting there, the volcano gave us a lot of rumble, cough, spit, plink, plink, plink. I began to wonder what we would do if one of these freshly-spat-out boulders started plinking down directly toward us.

The volcano was rumbling, but no grand eruption. The sun set, the guide sighed, pocketed his camera, and we headed back across the lava field, down and up the ravine, through the forest, and into the farmer's field.

Designed by Hollywood

That was the moment the volcano was waiting for.

When we were in the farmer's field, the volcano blew; it blew with all its might.

The volcano bellowed as the entire top turned red from spitting out hundreds and hundreds of boulders. The plink, plink, plink became a roar. The redness was so bright that we could see our shadows. It was like the inferno of Hell was overflowing.

Then came darkness. Followed quickly by quiet. The volcano had put on a spectacular show for us, almost as if it were in a movie straight out of Hollywood.

We had come to Costa Rica to see an active volcano, and we would be going home satisfied.

Travel

I WANT A FRIGATE FOR MY BIRTHDAY

The Friendliest City in the World

I have been in fifty-one countries and have visited a lot of cities. In my experience, the friendliest city in the world is Kuching, in Sarawak.

In the early 1800s, most British boys would have said that they wanted a toy frigate for their birthday. But James Brooke had come into a large inheritance, and for his twenty-first birthday, he got a real frigate.

That's right, his very own 140-ton war vessel, complete with cannon, ammunition, and a crew of twenty.

So what is a guy with a frigate to do? James Brooke sailed off to Southeast Asia in 1838 to see if he could be of use to someone. In his case, the Sultan of Brunei was having trouble with rebels and asked Brooke to help.

Brooke successfully defeated the rebels, and the sultan rewarded him with his very own country, called Sarawak, on the island of Borneo.

We Call that a Kitty Cat

Sailing up the main river in his own country, James Brooke came to the main town. He stood on deck, pointed to the town, and asked his guide in Malay, "What do you call that?" The guide didn't realize that Brooke was pointing at the town; he thought that Brooke was pointing to an animal sitting on the riverbank. The guide replied in Malay "We call that a kitty cat."

That is how Kuching, which means kitty cat in Malay, got its name.

What impressed me about visiting Kuching was how no one treated me as a stranger. Everyone I met acted as if they knew me. In Kuching, people constantly greeted me on the street; people asked me to join them at tables in restaurants; people engaged me in conversation.

I was delighted. I wondered why this city was so friendly and decided it was due to how the Brooke family administered Sarawak.

Honoring Diversity Pays Off

James Brooke saw that his country contained three major ethnic groups: the Malay, the Chinese, and the indigenous Iban. He made wise decisions about how he would rule these diverse groups.

Travel

He called himself the Rajah of Sarawak and built a palace across the river from Kuching. The palace door was open every day from 4:00 PM to 5:00 PM, and any citizen, however humble, could come and talk to the rajah.

Rajah Brooke created a handful of laws that covered all the groups: Slavery was outlawed, and headhunting was outlawed. Otherwise, he honored the diversity he found in Sarawak: Each of the three ethnic groups would be under its own traditional legal systems. An Iban accused of thievery would be tried in Iban court; a Chinese accused of thievery would be tried in Chinese court; a Malay would be tried in Malay court.

This way, all the people in Sarawak learned to get along.

Over time, the country was handed down within the Brooke family from James Brooke to his nephew, then to that nephew's oldest son. In 1945, the family gave the country to Great Britain. And nowadays, Sarawak is part of Malaysia.

The people in Sarawak still get along, a legacy of James Brooke and how he honored diversity. When everyone gets along, you wind up with the friendliest city in the world.

Travel

SEVEN FLOORS OF JAPANESE HANDICRAFTS

Never in a Million Years

I took a train to Kyoto during my visit to Japan in 1988.

Kyoto is a historic city, full of traditional arts. My goal in visiting Kyoto was to buy a high-class souvenir. Specifically, I wanted an antique Japanese woodblock print. These prints were made by a tedious process: drawing on a block of wood, carving the wood, and then inking the wood to make the print.

The main train station in Kyoto was filled with billboards encouraging tourists to visit the Kyoto Handicrafts Center at 21 Etomi Street. An art mall! Seven floors of Japanese handicrafts!! Tour busses welcome!!!

Upon seeing these billboards, I vowed that I would never set foot in that place, never in a million years. It had to be a big tourist trap, selling overpriced stuff.

But my wanderings in Kyoto took me down Etomi Street, and I broke my vow. I did set foot in the Kyoto Handicrafts Center to see if they had any antique woodblock prints.

Passing through the Alarm Clocks

They did have nice antique woodblock prints on the fifth floor, the same floor as the alarm clocks.

Japanese alarm clocks are anything but ordinary. They are full of whimsy; large plastic animals that make all kinds of sounds to wake people up. Cows that mooed; donkeys that played music; pigs whose eyes moved.

Although I was in Kyoto to buy a high-class souvenir, I could not resist the alarm clocks.

I bought a plastic dog with a clock in his stomach and a bugle in his right paw. His name was Norakiru, and when you tap his head, he closes his eyes and goes into alarm mode. At wake-up time, Norakiru's eyes fly open; he plays reveille on the bugle and screams at you in Japanese, calling you a sleepyhead. You turn off the alarm by tapping the dog on his head again, and Norakiru tells you to have a nice day in Japanese.

263

Travel

This was definitely a lowbrow purchase, but I was going to balance it out by buying a highbrow art print.

I Began to Get Nervous

In the print room at the Kyoto Handicrafts Center, I chose a print by Ando Hiroshige from his series "Fifty-Three Stations of the Tokkaido Road." The print was from the eleventh edition in 1842; I could never have afforded a first-edition print.

As the salesman took my credit card, I noticed that I was starting to get nervous.

I realized that I was nervous because I was still under the influence of my experience in Africa two decades before. In Africa, governments actively discouraged the purchase of antiques. It was illegal for a foreigner to purchase antiques, and it was illegal for anyone to take antiques out of the country.

But here in Kyoto, the Japanese were allowing me to buy a piece of their history and take it home. I looked around to see if a Japanese government official was about to swoop down on me, but the purchase went smoothly.

I got on the elevator, and went down to street level. I exited from the Kyoto Handicrafts Center and stood on Etomi Street.

I had a bugle-playing plastic dog in one hand and an antique Hiroshige woodblock print in the other. I was culturally balanced.

Travel

LINING UP TO RUB JULIET'S RIGHT BREAST

Verona is in New Jersey

When I was a kid, I knew that Verona is in New Jersey. But then, to my surprise, I discovered that there is also a Verona in Italy.

Shakespeare knew about the one in Italy: it's in the title of *Two Gentlemen of Verona*, and it is the setting of *Romeo and Juliet*.

For our 2008 vacation, we decided to visit the Verona in Italy. It was a good decision.

From the city of Verona, you can see the Alps on the horizon. Verona was a major outpost of the Roman Empire and nowadays has lots of Roman ruins, including a large coliseum. The acoustics are so good in Verona's coliseum that they put on operas for 22,000 people without using microphones.

The Adige River meanders through the city; many lovely bridges cross over it. The center of the city is car-free and is filled with sidewalk cafes and gelato shops. There are piazzas with lots of ancient buildings and the city has an architecturally-significant church and castle.

Verona was a lovely place to stroll around, and there were photo opportunities everywhere.

Do They Ever Get Any Work Done?

When I got back to the United States, I showed my Verona vacation photos to a coworker. Sidewalk cafes! Roman ruins! Streets ideal for strolling! A meandering river!

His reaction was, "Wow." I thought he meant "Wow, what a beautiful place." Instead, he meant "Wow, how do the people in Verona ever get any work done?"

His question made me notice how relaxed the city looked in my photos. The photos showed people walking rather than driving, people enjoying gelato, people lounging in cafes, and people smiling.

I could only answer my coworker's question by saying that somehow work does get done in Verona. It is a thriving city, but life there does move at a slower pace than what I am used to in the United States.

Travel

A Bronze Goldmine

The number one tourist attraction in Verona is a good example of how relaxed the place is.

After centuries of having tourists ask to see Juliet's balcony, the Verona Chamber of Commerce got tired of telling people that Juliet was fictional and there is no balcony. Early in the twentieth century, they picked a balcony in a courtyard near the main piazza. They put up a sign, "This Way to Juliet's Balcony." They filled the courtyard with souvenir shops. They added a bronze statue of Juliet.

Then they started a rumor about the statue: Rubbing the right breast will bring you good luck.

Tourists now flock here by the thousands --- thousands of tourists who are fully aware that Juliet is fictional.

They know the balcony is not hers, and they know that rubbing a statue's breast is unlikely to bring good luck. But the tourists come. They stand under the balcony and pretend to be Romeo; they line up to be photographed rubbing Juliet's right breast; they buy any kind of souvenir as long as it has Juliet's name on it.

When I got to Juliet's balcony, I fell under its allure. I knew full well that Juliet was fictional; I knew full well that it was not really her balcony --- but it felt fulfilling to see the balcony anyway.

It did not take much work for the city of Verona to come up with this low-cost tourist attraction, which turned out to be a gold mine. All the city needed to do was pay for a sign and a statue, and people come from all over the world to gawk at a balcony and rub a breast.

No wonder Verona is relaxed --- at least the Verona in Italy is relaxed; I am not so sure about the Verona in New Jersey.

Travel

WIPING YOURSELF WITH YESTERDAY'S NEWS

Making My Eyes Ache

One nice thing about living in Africa is that you get to stop in Europe every time you go back and forth to visit the United States. I decided to stop in Ireland in the spring of 1972.

The plane landed in Shannon Airport, which was built back in the days before jet aircraft, and Shannon was the closest European airport to New York. It must have been busy in the pre-jet days, but when I arrived the airport appeared cavernous and very under-utilized.

My plane must have been one of only a handful of flights that day, because when I got to the rental car area it was like running a gauntlet. The rental car agents yelled at us disembarked passengers, just like carnival barkers, trying to get us to rent with their agency.

Since it was a renter's market, I got real fussy, asking each counter if they had a blue Volkswagen beetle to rent. I found a blue beetle, and the rental agent did not blink an eye when I presented a Nigerian drivers' license to him.

Once I drove out of the Shannon Airport, it did not take very long to realize that I had never been any place as green as Ireland. Ireland was so green it made my eyes ache.

An Entire Country in one Phonebook

And it did not take long to realize that Ireland once had many more people than it did in 1972.

The hills were crisscrossed with stone walls from farms abandoned during the Potato Famine. The famine took place in the 1840s --- 130 years previously. So many Irish had emigrated that the population still had not caught up to its pre-famine level.

In fact, the population of Ireland was still small enough that the entire country fits in one phonebook.

My visit to Ireland included tourist highlights such as castles and Celtic oratories and historic churches and the Blarney Stone. But just as intriguing as the tourist highlights were the Irish people.

267

Travel

I remember an Irishman on the pier in Tralee harbor. He told me that his dog could dance. His dog was a dingy white mutt and could have used a bath, especially since its name was Snowy. "Dance, Snowy!" The dog proceeded to bounce up and down in joy. Its owner was very pleased to show off his talented dog to a tourist.

Snowy the Dancing Dog is the only thing I remember about my visit to Tralee.

How Is My Cousin in California Doing?

The best place to meet Irish people was in pubs.

There is a problem, however, with meeting Irish people in pubs: They all have relatives living in the United States, and they all expect you to know their relatives. "I have a cousin in California. How is he doing?"

I invariably dashed people's hopes when it came to knowing their relatives. But I did not dash their hopes when it came time to use the pub's toilet.

The toilets were out back. To get to the toilet, you had to walk past the bar, where there was a stack of day-old newspapers. Once in the toilet, it dawned on you that there was no toilet paper. You sheepishly went back into the pub and asked for toilet paper. The bartender pointed to the stack of day-old newspapers. You even more sheepishly grabbed a couple of pages and went out back again.

I'm sure the locals couldn't wait for the tourists to need to use the toilet. It was great entertainment and generated lots of snickers.

Nowadays, I hear that Ireland is thriving as a member of the European Union. I hope that prosperity has not diminished the friendliness of the Irish people or enabled them to clean up the stone walls crisscrossing the hills.

But I also hope, for future tourists' sake, that prosperity has enabled Irish pubs to supply toilet paper so that the locals no longer snicker at you, and you no longer need to wipe yourself with yesterday's news.

ANIMALS

Animals

Animals

STEPPING ON HORSESHOE CRABS

<u>Horseshoe Crabs in Long Island Sound</u>

A horseshoe crab is an object of revulsion. It looks prehistoric, and it glides like a tank. It has numerous eyes all over its shell. Worst of all, it has a long pointed spike for a tail.

As a kid, I went swimming in Long Island Sound a couple of times a week in the summer. This was where I decided that a horseshoe crab can also be an object of fear. This creature can lurk on the sea bottom, and you could step on its spiked tail when it is sticking straight up.

I never stepped on a horseshoe crab. But my friends fed my fear by telling me scary stories about how they knew someone who knew someone who knew someone who had stepped on a horseshoe crab. Yes, the spiked tail had pierced all the way through that kid's foot. And the lifeguards had to take the kid to the hospital in an ambulance.

So I was always nervous when I had to stand on the sea bottom; not only did horseshoe crabs lurk on the bottom, there were also lots of other unpleasant things you could step on: slimy seaweed, sharp sea shells, jagged rocks, pointy barnacles.

I think that is why I learned to swim at the age of four --- if you keep swimming on top of the water, your feet never have to touch the sea bottom.

<u>Horseshoe Crabs in Cancun</u>

The first thing that strikes you about Cancun is the color of the water. The water is azure and clear, very unlike the dark metallic green murkiness of Long Island Sound. And the beach sand in Cancun is clean and white. No rocks, no pebbles, no dried seaweed, not even a shell.

Swimming in Cancun was delightful; the sea bottom was pure sand. No slimy seaweed, no sharp sea shells, no jagged rocks, no pointy barnacles.

And, best of all, no horseshoe crabs to fear. I could step wherever I wanted.

Animals

__Horseshoe Crabs in St. Louis__

St. Louis has a colony of horseshoe crabs. They live in a pool on the first floor of the City Museum. They must be on display for their revulsion factor.

The City Museum is not really a museum; it is a place of whimsy. Hanging on a cable above the horseshoe crab colony is a 2,400-pound block of granite. Every morning this block of granite starts a slow descent from the third floor straight down toward the horseshoe crabs on the first floor. The block never gets to squash the creatures; it reverses and is hoisted back up to the third floor.

The cable holding the block of granite that daily threatens the lives of the horseshoe crabs is attached to a generator. This generator was once attached to the world's largest windmill in Medicine Bow, Wyoming. The City Museum salvaged the generator when a storm knocked over the windmill in 1994.

Whenever I go to the City Museum and see the horseshoe crabs, I remember my childhood fear when swimming in Long Island Sound. And I secretly wish that someday the City Museum's electrical system will malfunction, and the 24,000-pound block of granite will drop all the way and wipe out the entire horseshoe crab colony on the first floor.

Animals

PUPPIES AS A CROP

Puppies as a Crop

Missouri leads the nation. But it is nothing to be proud of: Our state has more puppy mills than any other state.

A puppy mill is a place where dogs are bred for profit, usually under deplorable conditions. Dogs are kept caged all their adult lives, producing litter after litter, living in filthy conditions, often with substandard food and little veterinary care. Little attention is paid to genetics, and the resulting puppies often grow up to have health and temperament problems.

Missouri has 1,000 licensed mass breeders. This is twenty times the number of mass breeders in Illinois, and 1,000 times the number of mass breeders in Utah. The Missouri Department of Agriculture (Yes, puppies are a crop) is stepping up its supervision of the breeders, but we are still the Puppy Mill Capital of the United States.

An E-mail out of the Blue

I received an email from a woman in Buffalo, New York, named Karen. She found my name on a St. Louis Dogpark website that I designed, and she e-mailed me out of the blue because she was going to adopt a female Mallinois that was rescued from a puppy mill in Joplin, Missouri. (A Mallinois is a type of Belgian shepherd.) Karen did not explain how this all got set up (Buffalo, New York, is 1,000 miles from Joplin, Missouri), but she did have a request.

Karen was going to drive west from Buffalo, the rescuer was to drive the dog east from Joplin, and they were to meet in St. Louis. Could I recommend a park where they could meet?

I had a recommendation. Just off I-44 (the interstate from Joplin) is Tower Grove Park. The park was originally designed for nineteenth-century St. Louisans to see and be seen while riding in their horse-and-carriages.

In the park are a number of lovely pavilions, including one named "The Sons of Rest," which was built in 1883 and restored in 1997.

I emailed Karen, suggesting that they rendezvous at the Sons of Rest and even sent her a link to a photo of the pavilion.

Animals

After the Sons of Rest

The rendezvous was a success. The rescuer, the dog, and Karen all met, and the dog is now in Buffalo adapting to a life of cleanliness, care, freedom of movement, and affection. Karen summed it up: "I'm sure all impediments to her leading a happy life will be overcome."

Karen e-mailed her thanks to me and had two points to make:

1. She found the people in St. Louis incredibly friendly. She and the Joplin rescuer got lost heading to a restaurant for lunch. The first person they asked gave them directions; but the second person they asked got in his car and escorted them directly to the restaurant.

2. Every person that Karen spoke to in her brief stay in St. Louis knew someone who was involved in some aspect of rescuing dogs from puppy mills.

Missouri leads the nation, not just in puppy mills but also in rescuing dogs from puppy mills.

Animals

AN AFFINITY FOR WARTHOGS

Really Really Bad = Good

There is a tenet in our culture that if a movie is really, really bad, then it is a good movie. An example would be *The Attack of the Killer Tomatoes*. A movie so bad that people want to watch it simply because it is really, really bad.

And I would argue that if an animal is really, really ugly, then it is a beautiful animal.

And what could be uglier than a warthog? A slate-colored hide, shovel-shaped nose, bristly whiskers, discolored tusks protruding from a face bedecked with warts. Although it could dig its own burrows, the warthog prefers to live in burrows abandoned by aardvarks. And its diet consists of tasty roots, berries, and occasional carrion.

And the warthog itself is blissfully unaware of how repulsive it is.

The warthog must be the epitome of repulsiveness. But, living in West Africa, I found myself drawn to warthogs. They are so repulsive that they transcend their repulsiveness; to me, a warthog really is a beautiful animal.

The Warthogs at the St. Louis Zoo

I am not the only person drawn to warthogs.

The St. Louis Zoo has just opened a new exhibit area called "The River's Edge." The hippos that live in the exhibit get lots of attention, as do the rare black rhinos; the graceful hippos and the majestic rhinos appear in all the zoo publicity photos.

But "The River's Edge" also has some warthogs, and the keeper of the exhibit does admit to a "special affinity for the warthog, even with its curved tusks, bulbous bumps, and beady eyes."

Animals

The Warthogs at the Jos Zoo

The best zoo for viewing warthogs, however, is in Jos, Nigeria.

The Jos Zoo disproves Hollywood's stereotype that Africans live amongst a constant daily menagerie of wild beasts. Northern Nigeria is actually more densely populated than The Netherlands, and Northern Nigerians have to go to the zoo to see animals.

What really makes the Jos Zoo so great is that they let you feed the animals. Right at the entrance gate you will find people selling peanuts and bananas.

Buy a banana to take to the monkey cage. Peel the banana, and you can feed it to a grateful monkey.

Now, what should you do with the banana peel?

No problem, you will soon be aware that there is a snorting and drooling animal in the next cage just begging for your peel. That's right --- it's the warthog. Throw your banana peel to the warthog, and it will snarf down the banana peel and then stare at you with a look of joyous gratitude in its beady eyes.

One zoo animal's trash is another zoo animal's treasure.

Animals

STILL SKITTISH AFTER ALL THESE YEARS

We Cannot Let You Adopt This Dog

When our dog Sydney disappeared, we found the house disturbingly empty.

We had to get a dog, and as a tribute to Sydney, we would rescue an Australian shepherd. We went to a rescue event and headed for the table staffed by the Australian shepherd rescue group. They had three dogs for adoption.

Dog number one was terrified of men, and was immediately ruled out. Dog number two was a big friendly full-blooded Australian shepherd with a lovely coat.

"We want to adopt dog number two."

"I'm sorry; we cannot let you adopt this dog."

It was a shock to be rejected so quickly. We were sure we were excellent dog owners: we like dogs, we have a fenced yard, and we buy high-quality dog food. That should qualify us to adopt any dog we wanted.

But the rescue group was looking for the right home for dog number two. The dog was being fostered in a home that had no cats. Our home had cats. The rescue group could not guarantee that dog number two would get along with cats.

They were afraid we would adopt the dog, take him home, find out he does not get along with cats, and return the dog. The rescue group would be right back where it started from.

That left dog number three.

Cringe and Cringe Again

Dog number three had a tail, so it was not a full-blooded Australian shepherd. But that tail constantly wagged, and the dog craved affection. Pet me, pet me. More, more, more. He was a merle. His fur was silver blue and indigo black, and his tongue was pink and indigo black. His tail made a complete 360-degree circle. The rescue group knew that he got along with cats.

His name is Petey; we adopted him.

Animals

We have a loving home with a fenced yard and high-priced dog food and lots of petting. We shower the dog with affection and treats, and take him for walks along Fishpot Creek. We want Petey to be comfortable, assured, and confident.

But whenever Petey sees me holding a whiffle ball bat, he cringes.

With a rescue dog, you never know its history. Petey had been found walking along a road in Jefferson County. Was Petey abused in his previous life? Was Petey hit with a whiffle ball bat? A co-worker has a rescue dog that cringes whenever it sees a belt; another co-worker has a rescue dog that cringes whenever it sees a flyswatter.

Why does Petey cringe? Can't he tell that we have no harm in mind?

Approached While Standing in Water

My two brothers were much older than me. Every time Mom and Dad took us kids to the beach, my brothers considered me prime dunking material. I would be standing in water about chest high, and my brothers would sneak up on me and dunk me. I did not like being dunked.

Nowadays, whenever I go swimming and I am standing in water about chest high, I start to get nervous. If a friend should approach me with no harm in mind, I tense up. I am an adult, my brothers are nowhere in sight, and I am still skittish after all these years.

When I think about my skittishness, I start to empathize with Petey.

Both the dog and I are skittish --- we are reacting to a situation that happened in the past. Both the dog and I cringe --- we are not reacting to the presence of harm, we are reacting to the persistence of memory.

Animals

THAT IS NOT A GIFT FROM GOD

Cute Little Kitten

When I first moved to Nigeria in 1965, I had no idea that Africans did not name their pets. In fact, they viewed cats and dogs in a utilitarian way. Cats, for example, were not really pets; they were rodent disposals.

In 1965 I had an American housemate, and the two of us hired a cook to take care of our house and our meals. One day, my housemate brought home a cute little kitten. We decided to ask the cook's son, who was eight years old, to name the kitten.

When we told the cook we wanted his son to name the kitten, he had a look of disbelief on his face. The look said: "You want to name a kitten?" The look on his face suggested that he probably thought we would start naming furniture or naming the vultures that liked to sit on the roof of our house.

The cook humored us and called his son to meet the kitten and give it a name. The son suggested "Gift from God." His father, horrified, said, "A cat is not a gift from God. You should call it 'David' instead."

So David grew up to be our rodent disposal. He did a decent job disposing of rodents until the time a mongoose walked into our house. When David saw that the mongoose was as large as he was, David ran in the opposite direction.

Our cook handled the situation: he bought a trap, caught the mongoose, and gave it to the neighbors, who ate it for dinner.

Cute Little Puppy

Africans view dogs as garbage disposals. One day, my housemate brought home a cute little puppy. We did not ask the cook's son to name the puppy because my housemate had already picked out a name: "Hankali."

Hankali means "common sense." Apparently, my housemate was tired of being told that he did not have common sense. Now, with this puppy, we both had common sense --- and we could prove it by pointing to the dog.

We fed Hankali. The dog did not have to scrounge for food like most dogs in Nigeria. Hankali grew up to be an affectionate dog and a pretty good watchdog. She was perceptive: She could tell by the sound of a car or motorcycle engine if the person approaching the house was a friend or a

279

Animals

stranger.

Cute Little Puppies

I never did like vultures sitting on our roof, especially when they would stare hungrily down at me as I sunbathed in the backyard. I eventually taught Hankali to get all growly and bark at the vultures to scare them off the roof. Once the vultures flew away, it would be a couple of hours before they dared to come back.

This was a talent that the neighbors liked, and whenever I would take Hankali for a walk, they would ask me to make Hankali scare the vultures sitting on their roofs. On command, the dog would become menacing toward the birds and get very agitated as she barked. The vultures would flap their wings and abandon the roofs. The neighbors would be highly amused.

Then Hankali got pregnant and gave birth to four cute little puppies. It was easy to give away the puppies to the neighbors, who expected the puppies to be as perceptive as their mother.

By this time the neighbors were used to the foreign idea of giving a name to a dog. So,when they got a puppy they followed the example of the Americans.

They all named their puppies Hankali. We now had five Hankalis in the neighborhood.

280

Animals

A FLUFFER AT THE NATIONALS

Maiming the Opposition

Once you get a dog, people assume that you will feed, train, and take good care of your dog. If the dog you get is an Australian shepherd, people assume that you will go beyond the basics. Australian shepherds are herding dogs, and you need to provide an outlet for their intelligence. You need to sign them up for an activity.

I signed up our first Australian shepherd, Sydney, for a beginner class in dog agility. Agility is a series of obstacles: jumps, chutes, teeter-totters, and ramps that the dog has to run through. The dogs are timed.

For the first couple of classes, we ran our dogs through the agility course while on a leash. Once the dogs were familiar with the equipment, they ran the course off-leash.

Sydney was intelligent enough to realize that agility was a competition. And she realized that she was not the fastest dog in the class.

One evening, after she ran the course off-leash, she dashed right past me. I heard screams coming from behind me and turned around. The owner of the fastest dog in the class was screaming because Sydney was attacking her dog. Sydney wanted to increase her chances of winning by maiming the star of the class.

I never took Sydney to another agility class.

Scaring the Head Nurse

When we got our second Australian shepherd, Skye, I took her out to Purina Farms to try out sheep herding.

I was amazed. Skye had never seen a sheep in her life, but she knew exactly what to do when I took her into the sheep pen. There were three sheep, and she immediately starting herding them --- herding them directly toward me. I jumped aside. She herded them directly at me again and again.

The herding instructor told me that a herding dog is supposed to herd the flock towards the human. Our dog was a candidate for sheepherding lessons.

But I was not a candidate for jumping around in a sheep pen with lots of sheep manure on the ground.

Animals

Cancel the sheepherding. I needed to find an activity that did not involve manure. Pet therapy seemed like a good option.

Skye took Canine Good Citizen classes and passed. I took her to Forest Park Hospital where our other dog did pet therapy. At the hospital Skye turned unfriendly and only let half of the patients pet her. She barked at the volunteer coordinator and proceeded to scare the head nurse by growling at her.

Skye failed her hospital audition. I never took her back to the hospital.

Best Bitch

I had failed to provide an outlet for Sidney or for Skye. But I could still help others who want to provide outlets for their Australian shepherds. I began volunteering as a steward at local dog shows.

A steward makes sure the competitors are lined up in the correct order. A steward makes sure that the judge is happy. A steward fetches the ribbons for the award part of show, and never snickers when he is asked to go fetch the ribbon for Best Bitch.

My big volunteer opportunity was the National Australian Shepherd Agility Trials in 2007. I was told that I would not be a steward, I would be a fluffer. I felt so important --- a fluffer for the Nationals! Little did I know it was the crummiest job at the agility trials.

For the agility trial, the dogs have to run through a chute --- a cylinder leading to a long collapsed nylon tube. The dog has to have the confidence to plunge into the cylinder and run in the darkness through the tube. After each run, the fluffer has to vault over the fence surrounding the agility area and quickly straighten out and flatten out the chute before the next dog starts its run.

A slight breeze that easily moved nylon did not help. But I was proud that I only fell once while vaulting over the fence. As a thank you, the organizers gave me a National Australian Shepherd Agility Trials commemorative bath towel.

We now have a third Australian shepherd named Sierra. She has found her own outlet for her intelligence: barking at the neighbors, shredding toilet paper, chasing the cat. I hope to find a different outlet for Sierra, and I hope that we can stick with it.

HOLIDAYS

Holidays

Holidays

YOU ARE AT THE PIRATE'S HOUSE

The Murphys' House

The Murphys had six kids, and the family squeezed happily into a modest house in the neighborhood where I grew up. I liked going over to the Murphys' house; there were always a couple of Murphy kids at home, and the door was always unlocked.

But the best time to visit the Murphy house was at Halloween.

When you rang the Murphy doorbell at Halloween, Mrs. Murphy let you inside and showed you a table where the treats were displayed. The treat you got was dependent on your age. Elementary school trick-or-treaters got a packet of chewing gum; junior high kids got a candy apple --- homemade by Mrs. Murphy herself; senior high kids got a deck of playing cards.

Oh, how I ached to be in senior high. Chewing gum was fine, candy apples were yummy, but getting a deck of playing cards was an incredible treat.

We moved away to another town in 1953 when I was ten years old. I never qualified for a candy apple or for some playing cards, and I never forgot the magic that Mrs. Murphy put into Halloween.

The Pagan's House

In 1976, I was housesitting for a friend in Tennessee.

It was late October, and the local radio stations were talking about Halloween.

The radio cautioned people that Halloween was a pagan holiday and warned them that good Christians do not celebrate it. Not only was Halloween pagan, but it was dangerous: Razor blades lurked in apples, scalding water could be dumped from second-story windows, candy could be laced with poison, and poorly-lit streets gave motorists plenty of opportunities to run over costumed kids carrying trick-or-treat bags.

In spite of the radio's warnings, I bought some candy. I turned on my friend's porch light on Halloween night, hoping that his neighbors would not consider him a pagan. Only two trick-or-treaters showed up.

That night in Tennessee made me feel sad --- the magic had gone out of Halloween.

Holidays

The Pirate's House

I lived in apartments from 1976 to 1998; apartment dwellers don't get trick-or-treaters. Then my buddy Randy and I bought a house, and I faced my first Halloween as a homeowner. I resolved that I would put some magic into the holiday.

Starting in 1998, I fly a skull-and-crossbones from our flagpole. I put on black clothing, a three-corner hat, and an eyepatch. When the doorbell rings, I open the door, step outside carrying a small treasure chest, and announce, "You are at the pirate's house!"

I tell each kid to expect three things: pirate treasure, pirate food, and pirate drink. The pirate treasure is Mardi Gras beads --- the green ones are emeralds, the purple ones are rubies, and the gold ones are real gold. The Pirate food is candy in silver or gold wrappers. The pirate drink is Kool-Aid. Kool-Aid always goes on sale in October --- even the special kind that turns colorless shortly after you mix it up --- and the kids get one packet each.

Many parents accompany their kids around the neighborhood. The parents hang back at the curbside and watch their kids go up to our front door. I really like it when I open the door, and the kids get excited and say "It's the pirate!" But I like it even more when the parents applaud me.

And I like to think that if Mrs. Murphy, bless her heart, were at the curbside, she would be applauding me also.

Holidays

THANKSGIVINGS WITHOUT TURKEY

<u>Taffy Helps Herself</u>

I hardly noticed that there was no turkey on the table for Thanksgiving.

When I was young, Thanksgiving was a big deal for me because I got to put sweet things on my dinner plate right alongside the mashed potatoes and Mom's tasty stuffing. Cranberry sauce was searingly sweet, and candied yams were loaded with sugar. In my mind, it was like eating dessert in the middle of the meal.

Every year, when the timer told Mom that the turkey had finished roasting, she would place the turkey in the pantry to cool. One year, when it came time to slice the turkey, Mom went back into the pantry; she found a turkey carcass instead of a turkey. Mom realized that our dog, Taffy, had wandered into the pantry and chomped into the turkey while it was cooling.

Mom considered Taffy the best-behaved dog in the world. Taffy liked to lie on our front stoop looking like one of the stone lions in front of the New York Public Library. She was a dog that never gave us any problems --- until she came face to face with a fragrant roast turkey and helped herself.

Mom sliced up the parts of the turkey that were unravaged by the dog and served them. I don't remember if people declined to eat any turkey or if they decided to share the bird with Taffy. I was too busy devouring cranberry sauce and candied yams to notice what other people were eating.

Plus, I was thinking about the pies we were having for dessert.

<u>When in Rome</u>

I was twenty-two years old when I was a tourist spending a couple of days in Rome by myself. One of those days was Thanksgiving. Rome was going about its daily business on Thanksgiving Day, with no indication that it was a big holiday over in the United States.

I knew there was little chance of finding a restaurant serving roast turkey in the capital of Italy. So I did the next best thing: I went to a restaurant and ordered chicken. It was not the same as eating turkey. In fact, I felt a little bereft.

I looked around the restaurant and noticed a number of other diners who appeared to be American. They had all ordered chicken. I wondered if they felt bereft as well.

Holidays

West Coast vs. East Coast

I grew up on the East Coast and had never been on the West Coast until 1968, when the army stationed me at a fort in the state of Washington.

As Thanksgiving approached, I decided that I did not want to eat my Thanksgiving dinner in a mess hall surrounded by soldiers. So I asked the Mathias family in Seattle if I could join them for the holiday. Mrs. Mathias told me I was very welcome, and she hoped that the salmon would be as good as it was the year before.

Salmon? For Thanksgiving? I was certain that Mrs. Mathias was pulling my leg. I figured it was some kind of holiday joke that West Coast people play on East Coast people.

On Thanksgiving Day, I put on my civilian clothes and drove from the army fort up to Seattle.

For dinner, the Mathias family was joined by Mrs. Mathias' sister, her sister's best friend, and me.

Ironically, her sister's best friend was born on the East Coast, and it turned out that we grew up in the same town. I'll bet she was just as surprised as me to watch Mrs. Mathias place a large salmon in the middle of the table.

Mrs. Mathias hadn't been kidding.

But all these Thanksgivings without turkey simply became practice for becoming vegetarian in 1992.

Nowadays, people know that I don't eat meat, and they ask me how I handle Thanksgiving. My answer is simple: As long as there is cranberry sauce and candied yams on the table, I will be fine.

Holidays

FAMOUS AS A HOLSTEIN COW

A Two-year-old License Plate

My first chance for fifteen minutes of fame came when I was ten years old. During the summer after I finished fifth grade, our elementary school had an activity camp five mornings a week. The camp had crafts and games; one day it had a scavenger hunt.

We were divided into scavenger teams and given lists. I thought our list was pretty demanding: It included a peach tree leaf, a 1943 steel penny, and a two-year-old license plate.

But I rose to the occasion and organized our team. Two kids were to go to the supermarket and get a steel penny in change. Two other kids were to ring doorbells asking people if they had a peach tree in their yard.

Another kid and I walked up and down streets looking for open garage doors. Back in those days, our state issued new automobile plates every year, and people liked to hang the old plates in their garages as decoration.

Finally we spotted a garage door with its door open and old license plates on the wall. We asked the lady of the house if we could borrow her husband's two-year-old license plate. We must have looked like trustworthy fifth graders because we got the license plate and won the scavenger hunt.

The activity camp people said that the winning team would have their names printed in the town's weekly newspaper.

On the day of publication, I opened up the paper to the article entitled "5th Graders Win Scavenger Hunt." I discovered that instead of printing "Doug Schneider," they had printed "Pete Schneider."

Pete Schneider was a sixth grader. I had been denied my fifteen minutes of fame.

The Conspiracy Continues

I volunteered when our company asked for employees to help out at the big Fourth of July celebration at the Gateway Arch in downtown St. Louis. Not only would we be doing our civic duty, we would have our names printed in the company monthly newsletter.

289

Holidays

As a volunteer, I spent a morning at the entrance to the arch grounds asking people to open up their picnic coolers and show me the contents. My job was to make sure that no one was bringing glass containers into the arch grounds.

Some of the people I turned away looked really mean and perfectly capable of snapping my spine in two. But everyone cooperated and took their contraband glass beer bottles and glass pickle jars back to their cars.

When the company newsletter was published, I opened it to discover that they had printed "David Schneider" instead of "Doug Schneider."

David Schneider worked in a different department from me and hadn't even volunteered for the Fourth of July celebration. I was denied my fifteen minutes of fame again.

New Year's Eve in New Hampshire

Portsmouth, New Hampshire, is a lovely city. In 1986, they held a First Night --- a nonalcoholic New Year's Eve event. There were all kinds of entertainment downtown: music, ice sculpting, dancing, fireworks, and a farmer who brought some sheep, goats, and a cow as a little petting zoo for the kids.

Our Scottish country dance group was among the performers. A reporter from the *Portsmouth Herald* interviewed me over the phone a week before the event. She came to our performance and had a photographer take some pictures of me dancing in my kilt.

I lived in Massachusetts at the time, so someone who lived in Portsmouth mailed me a copy of the newspaper with my interview in it.

I opened the *Portsmouth Herald* and found two features about First Night, both on the first page of the second section. One was the interview with me; the other was an interview with the farmer.

The reporter had spelled my name correctly. However, the typesetter had swapped the photos. Right above the article about the farmer was a photo of me in my kilt. Right above the article about me was a photo of a group of kids petting a Holstein cow.

The caption on the picture of the cow said: "DOUG SCHNEIDER PLEASES THE CROWD."

So, I did get my fifteen minutes of fame --- except I spent those fifteen minutes as a Holstein cow.

Holidays

FIRST CHRISTMAS IN AFRICA

Christmas Tree Shortage in Hawaii

A coworker e-mailed me a news item about a Christmas tree shortage in Hawaii.

The previous year, retailers in Hawaii ordered too many trees from Oregon and wound up giving trees away. So the next year the retailers cut way back on the ordering, resulting in a shortage. Some Hawaiians wound up paying $175 for a single Christmas tree.

I can understand why people in Hawaii would think that Christmas trees are necessary for celebrating a real Christmas. I used to think that certain things were necessary for Christmas until I spent my first Christmas in Africa.

No Snow, No Evergreens

When I first arrived in Kano, Nigeria, it was September. Kano had a landscape unlike any other I had ever seen. It was decidedly arid, with some palm trees but not much other vegetation. The city's flat dusty streets had lots of people passing by on foot and riding on donkeys. Sheep freely roamed about.

As December approached, I began to wonder if it was possible to have a real Christmas.

It has never snowed in Kano. There is not an evergreen in sight. One of the stores in town did hire a guy to dress up as Santa and stand at their front door, but the effect was diminished when you saw how much the tropical heat made him perspire under his Santa costume.

It was a downer. How could Christmas be real without snowmen and sleighbells and decorated evergreen trees?

Dirt Roads, Palm Trees

I expressed my Christmas despair to an American friend. He turned out to be a wise American friend.

My friend pointed to a palm tree and said that it was the same kind of tree they had in Bethlehem 2,000 years ago.

Holidays

He pointed to someone riding a donkey and said that this is how Joseph and Mary traveled to Bethlehem 2,000 years ago. And they traveled on dusty roads, just like the roads in Kano. He pointed to some sheep roaming the street and reminded me that there were sheep in the stable at Bethlehem.

I then realized that Christmas in Kano would be real.

It would be reminiscent of the time when Joseph walked down dusty roads beside Mary while she rode on a donkey; reminiscent of the time when the sheep and the other animals in a stable would witness the first Christmas ever.

Holidays

REMOVING WALLPAPER WITHOUT HARSH CHEMICALS

Romanticizing the House

When we bought our house in Valley Park, Missouri, from Paul and Vonda, it was clear that Vonda had romanticized the house. A closer reading of the house deed actually showed that Vonda had kicked Paul out at some point and then allowed him to move back in.

We were not certain at what point Vonda had romanticized the house, but she got very busy and put up flowered wallpaper. Some walls were fully covered in Vonda flowers; all rooms had borders with Vonda flowers; one room even had Vonda flowers on the ceiling. The dining room was the worst.

We really needed to strip Vonda's flowered wallpaper from the dining room, but we were reluctant to use harsh chemicals in the process.

Throw another Log on the Fire

Our first Christmas in the house: We invited nine guests to bring a dish and have Christmas dinner with us in our new home. When the guests arrived, they put their potluck dishes in the dining room, where Christmas candles glowed brightly.

My buddy Randy threw another log on the fire. And the smoke detector went off.

I assumed that the smoke from the new log on the fire had set off the alarm. I grabbed a large towel and stood under the smoke detector, fanning the smoke detector to get it to stop.

But an alert guest discovered the real reason the smoke detector went off: The dining room was on fire. There were flames working their way up the dining room wall. The flames were about four feet high; big black pieces of soot were swirling through the air.

Apparently, as we placed each guest's potluck dish on the dining room buffet, we wound up pushing the lit candles closer and closer to the wall.

Holidays

Concerned Hosts, Concerned Guests

Randy and I swung into action to put out the flames working their way up the dining room wall. We were concerned that the fire would spread and destroy our house. We took the large towel and started batting at the flames.

The nine guests also swung into action. They were concerned that the fire would spread and destroy Christmas dinner.

The guests ran into the dining room and rescued various dishes of food from the buffet.

The towel eventually put the fire out. We all stood in the living room. Randy and I were shaking because our house had been in danger of burning down. The guests were holding dishes of food and sampling them to make sure they hadn't been spoiled by the fire.

I looked in the dining room as the smoke cleared. Those big black pieces of soot were pieces of wallpaper. The fire had stripped the Vonda flowers from the wall.

We had removed the flowered wallpaper without using harsh chemicals.

Holidays

NO BETTER THAN A BILLY GOAT

Tweezers Made from Seashells

The town I grew up in was surrounded on three sides by salt water. There were plenty of beaches and lots of seashells.

In seventh grade, we learned about the Matinecock Indians who once inhabited our town. I was especially impressed by the fact that young Matinecock men would make tweezers out of seashell fragments and pull out all their facial hair.

That meant that Matinecock men never had to shave. As a twelve-year-old, tweezing out all my facial hair with seashell fragments sounded good to me.

Never having to shave meant that I would save time, and I would never have to worry about cutting myself with a razor. I would save lots of money never having to buy shaving cream or badger-hair shaving brushes. I would not have to go through the hassle of buying razor blades. It was 1955, and the best razor blades were imported from England; for some reason, these blades were only sold in stores that sold lawnmowers.

However, I never went down to the beach to find seashell fragments to tweeze out all my facial hair.

I shaved every day until I turned twenty-one when I was in college. Then I grew a beard, which came out red, showing my Viking heritage.

There were only two other men at college that had beards. My college beard was short-lived. When the yearbook announced they were taking senior photos, I shaved it off.

If You Can't Read or Write

In 1965, I moved to Nigeria, where my main means of transportation was a motorcycle. Nigerians would shout "hello" as I drove by. I decided to grow a beard again. And then Nigerians would shout "No better than a billy goat" as I drove by.

I was puzzled by this new greeting and tracked it down to a saying: "You with the beard, you are no better than a billy goat unless you can read or write." It was a taunt, but it was a good-natured taunt.

Holidays

Facial hair became an on-again-off-again thing throughout my life. Growing a beard or moustache was an easy way to change my look. Shaving off my facial hair was an easy way to change my look again.

When I lived in Minnesota, many men would grow beards to keep their face warm in winter and then shave their beards off in the summer. I became a Minnesota contrarian: I would shave my beard off in the winter and grow it back in the summer.

Just Like Salvatore Dali

A friend told me that his father had a moustache and his mother would often say, "Kissing a man without a moustache is like eating an egg without salt."

In 1970 I lived in Texas and had a moustache. When I discovered some moustache wax in a Dallas drugstore, I let the ends of my moustache grow long —-- very long. I waxed the moustache ends into a nice curl, and looked just like Salvatore Dali.

I worked for the Dallas Public Library and mistakenly thought I had the longest moustache in Texas.

One day at the library a coworker came back from lunch break and told me she had seen a man with a moustache longer than mine. "How did you know it was longer?" "I was walking behind him on the sidewalk and I could see the ends of his moustache sticking out on either side of his head."

I was invited to a friend's home in Dallas for Thanksgiving dinner. My moustache might not have been the longest in Texas, but it did attract the attention of the woman sitting next to me at the dinner table.

She told me that she had never kissed a man with a moustache. I took this as a request, and I turned to give her a kiss. However, as I turned, the waxed end of my moustache went up her nostril. She shrieked, and I quickly turned my head away; we both blushed and turned our attention to the food on our plates.

In the long run, I am glad that I never went down to the beach to find seashell fragments to make tweezers. I am glad I can be clean-shaven for photographs. I am glad I can have a beard that gets me taunted in Africa.

I am glad I can have a moustache that garners attention in Dallas, although that woman at Thanksgiving dinner never did find out if kissing a man with a moustache is like eating an egg with salt.

LIFE LESSONS

Life Lessons

Life Lessons

BLACK MUDDY RIVER

My Beatles Birthday

Paul McCartney wrote "When I'm Sixty-four" when he was sixteen years old and I was fifteen years old. The song was not recorded until the Sgt. Pepper album was released. I heard the song when I was twenty-three years old, and turning sixty-four seemed so incredibly far into the future.

I also wondered why he wrote a song about turning sixty-four instead of turning sixty-five.

But after years of losing my hair, the future became the present, and I turned sixty-four. I was very pleased to be sixty-four.

I had reached a milestone --- my Beatles birthday.

Roll Muddy River, Black Muddy River

Norma Waterson comes from a long line of Scottish troubadours.

When I heard Norma Waterson sing "Black Muddy River," I assumed it was a traditional Scottish song about growing old. The song begins "When the last rose of summer pricks my finger" and the song ends "And there's nothing left to do but count the years."

However, I found out that "Black Muddy River" wasn't traditional or Scottish. It was written by one of the Grateful Dead, who was dreading growing old. In his case, he was dreading his fortieth birthday.

I chuckled in amusement. I certainly had not dreaded my fortieth birthday.

In fact, I had not dreaded any birthday --- until I started approaching my sixty-fifth birthday.

The World Knows My Age

I did not dread turning one year older and becoming sixty-five; I dreaded going to the mailbox.

An astonishing number of strangers knew I was about to turn sixty-five. All these strangers wanted to sell me insurance. These strangers knew where I lived and what my phone number was. I don't know how they found out all this information, but there was no place to hide from them.

Life Lessons

Insurance agents called me to remind me that an important birthday was coming. Insurance companies sent me booklets about purchasing the Medicare supplementary insurance they offer. Health care providers sent me letters announcing that they were sending handbooks about purchasing the Medicare supplementary insurance they offer.

Some even told me that they weren't offering Medicare supplementary insurance; they were offering something much much better. And all of them told me that if I made a poor Medicare decision, it would haunt me for the rest of my life.

I did make a Medicare decision. I decided not to buy Medicare supplementary insurance because I am still working. I don't know if it was a poor decision or a good decision. I just wanted to stop the flood of phone calls and mail.

I celebrated my birthday when I turned sixty-five. But the mail kept on coming. This time, the letters said, "It's not too late to purchase our Medicare supplementary insurance."

No wonder Paul McCartney wrote a song about turning sixty-four instead of turning sixty-five.

Life Lessons

WAITING FOR INTESTINES

The Englishman Apologizes

Most people who choose to work overseas sign a contract to work for a fixed number of years; after their contract is up, they go back home. If they have a dog, they have to find a new home for their dog before they leave.

When I was working in Nigeria, I agreed to take someone's dog because he was going back to England. The guy brought the dog over to my house and told me about how smart and friendly the dog was.

But the Englishman wanted to make an apology. The dog had one major flaw: It had an Irish name. The dog was named Casey.

Dog on the Motorcycle

Casey and I got along very nicely, in spite of his Irish name.

He would sit on my motorcycle with me, and we would go on motorcycle rides together, visiting nearby villages.

Actually, Casey preferred to run along behind the motorcycle, but Nigerians are very conscious of animal abuse, and people would scold me for making the dog run so fast. So I put the dog on the motorcycle with me, and nobody got upset.

Nine Cents Every Evening

I fed Casey rice. He had rice for breakfast, but for dinner he had rice and intestines.

In Nigeria, intestines are a festive food. This is because meat in Nigeria comes from freshly killed animals.

The intestines, once cleaned, are the quickest part of an animal to cook. So Nigerians associate intestines with a big party like a wedding, when a goat or a sheep is slaughtered and the intestines are the first thing cooked up to feed the guests.

A number of my neighbors set up little stalls and sold food in front of their houses. One of the neighbors specialized in intestines. At dinnertime, Casey and I would go visit the intestine woman. She had a large wok and would fry up intestines in peanut oil.

301

Life Lessons

I would take a bowl, and we would line up at the food stall. I bought the dog nine cents worth of intestines every evening.

One day I noticed that the man standing in front of me was buying three cents of intestines for his family.

I became humbled. I realized how lucky I was to be able to afford all the food I wanted.

I still spent nine cents each evening on my dog, but I had gained a long-term reverence for food. Up until that point, I was callous about food.

Now I show reverence for food. I save every leftover at home. I shudder anytime I see someone waste food at a restaurant.

And it all started while standing in line, while waiting for intestines with my dog that had an Irish name.

Life Lessons

COINCIDENCE AFTER COINCIDENCE

Coincidence: St. Louis

In 2001, I took some out-of-town houseguests for some sightseeing in St. Louis and wound up having lunch at a restaurant near the Arch.

At lunch, one of our houseguests described her congressman as a slimeball. He was a slimeball because he kept on mentioning how he personally knew what it was like "to put a kid through college." The slimeball's son attends West Point, which is tuition-free, and can't be too big a strain on a congressman's pocketbook.

At lunch I also pointed out that each United States congressman gets to fill five slots in the freshman class at West Point. I wondered if the congressman nominated his own son, and was the son one of the five most qualified applicants in his district.

After lunch, we scattered to wander around the Arch grounds, and I went to visit the Old Cathedral. When I got there, I found a bagpiper in full kilt standing outside.

I spoke first, "Hello! Which St. Louis pipeband are you with?"

The bagpiper answered, "I am not from St. Louis; the bride and groom flew me out here to pipe at their wedding. Actually, I am the pipemaster for West Point."

Coincidence: Iowa

One of my favorite magazines is *Mental Floss*, "the magazine for information junkies."

There was an article about L. Frank Baum in the May 2010 issue. L. Frank Baum failed to make a living in the theater in upstate New York. He failed to make a living selling dry goods in Aberdeen, South Dakota. He found some success in Chicago, where he managed to get a couple of children's books published.

As Christmas 1899 was approaching, L. Frank Baum realized he had no money to buy presents for his children. He then bundled up some manuscripts he had lying around the house and took them to his publisher, William Riley.

303

Life Lessons

Riley read the manuscripts and gave L. Frank Baum an advance for one of them. When Baum got home, he looked at the check. He expected a small sum, enough to get him through Christmas. Instead he found that William Riley had advanced him $30,000, a princely sum, for *The Wizard of Oz*.

Shortly after reading this story in *Mental Floss*, I went up to Iowa for a Scottish dance event. During a break, I sat next to a woman named Marilyn. For some reason I told her the story of L. Frank Baum and his princely check for "The Wizard of Oz."

Marilyn said, "I like that story. William Riley was my great-uncle."

Coincidence: High School Cafeteria

In high school, I had a student-rate subscription to the *New York Times*, which was delivered to the high school lobby every morning.

Sitting in the high school cafeteria at lunchtime one day, I was listening to Weegie van Wagner. (Yes, back in the early 1960s lots of people had nicknames like that.) Weegie was describing how much she liked banana bread.

I had a sudden inspiration, "Weegie, do you think there is such a thing as applesauce bread?"

The very next morning, when I went to the high school lobby and picked up my copy of the *New York Times*, I opened the paper and saw a recipe for applesauce bread.

I cut out the recipe, and I still have the clipping because the *Times* obviously published the recipe expressly for my benefit.

Life Lessons

CENTERING THE CLAY

Yearning for Plastic

In eighth-grade shop class, once you finished your clay projects, you went on to plastic projects, and then you got to work with wood. I was stuck for a long time on my clay project --- I had to create a pot on the potter's wheel.

I yearned to move on to plastic, but clay was a big problem for me. I could never get the clay centered on the potter's wheel. I tried and tried, but the clay wobbled, the clay clumped, the clay refused to allow me to center it.

This Pot Is Too Junky

I decided to try to create a pot without centering. All I managed to produce with my off-center clay was an ugly off-center pot. It was awful.

I took one look at the pot and said, "This pot is too junky." I smashed it with my fist.

Lo and behold, I looked at the smashed clay and realized I had created an off-center ashtray, and it was beautiful. I glazed the ashtray, told the shop teacher I was not spending any more time on clay projects, and gave the ashtray to Mom.

Mom proudly displayed the ashtray on the desk in the living room. It was on the desk for thirty-four years, until we had to put Mom in a nursing home. Nowadays that ashtray sits on the desk in our living room in Valley Park, Missouri.

In eighth-grade shop class, one smash with my fist had taken trash and turned it into treasure.

This Pot Is Too Funky

The United States Army wants to encourage soldiers to follow wholesome pursuits; so, they had a large arts and crafts center at Fort Lewis, where I was stationed. It had been twelve years since eighth grade; I wondered if I would now be able to center clay.

I chose a potter's wheel, grabbed some clay, and tried to center it. The clay wobbled; the clay clumped; it still refused to be centered.

Looking out the window, I saw a car with Wyoming license plates pull into the

Life Lessons

parking lot of the Fort Lewis arts and crafts center. It was the first time I had ever seen a car with Wyoming license plates.

A soldier and his girlfriend got out of the car. I think the Wyoming soldier wanted to impress his girlfriend with his pottery skills. He sat down at the potter's wheel next to mine. He plopped some clay down on the wheel and took about two seconds to center it effortlessly. I was impressed.

As his potter's wheel spun around, the Wyoming soldier began to create a pot. The pot took shape effortlessly, magically, and if he intended to impress his girlfriend, he was certainly doing it.

She was in awe. I was also in awe. His pot was magnificent.

Then the Wyoming soldier took one look at his pot, and said "This pot is too funky." He smashed it with his fist.

His girlfriend gasped. I also gasped. If the girlfriend had burst into tears, I would probably have burst into tears as well.

At the Fort Lewis arts and crafts center, one smash of the Wyoming soldier's fist had taken treasure and turned it into trash.

Life Lessons

CONTINUOUS VS. CONTINUAL

Lay Lady Lay

Whenever I hear a new song on Pandora, my ears perk up. Likewise, whenever I hear a new song on a movie soundtrack, my ears perk up.

I am doing more than listening, I am making a decision: Is this song worth buying? Is it worth spending forty-nine cents at emusic.com or ninety-nine cents at iTunes.com? Is it destined to be added to my iPod?

If the song gets purchased and gets added to my iPod, it isn't safe. While I listen to the songs on my iPod, I am still making decisions: Is this song worthy of staying on my iPod, or should I delete it?

So the songs I listen to are being auditioned. If the song is new, it is auditioning for a place on my iPod. If it is on my iPod, it must keep on auditioning to remain on the iPod.

But some songs don't need to audition any more. "Lay Lady Lay" by Bob Dylan will never get deleted. It is a keeper.

Delicious and Pecans

Summertime in St. Louis is concrete time.

A concrete is a big cup of frozen custard, so thick that you can turn the cup upside down and the custard will not fall out. Concretes can be individualized; custard stands offer all kinds of fruits, nuts, and crumbled candy bars to mix in the frozen custard.

Once I was in line at our local custard stand when I heard the guy in front of me order a delicious and pecans. I immediately asked what that was. He said it was a concrete with blackberries and pecans mixed in --- a combination of sweet and tart that makes it addictive. The workers at the custard stand say "delicious" in place of "blackberry" so they won't confuse it with "black cherry."

I decided to skip my old standby (chocolate morsels and mint) and risk ordering a new combination. This new combo would be auditioning. It would try to get a permanent place on my list of favorite concretes.

What else auditions? Going to the nursery in the springtime, I have noticed flowers auditioning. Flowers try to look attractive and catch a human's eye so

307

Life Lessons

they will get purchased and planted. The flowers are not finished. Once they are planted they have to audition to get insects to come pollinate them.

At the supermarket, I saw sour cream auditioning: A new brand was at half-price, hoping people would try it and make it a keeper. Restaurants audition, hoping that your first visit is a good one and you will come back.

A lot of auditioning goes on in life.

The Years Melted Away

A friend told me about catching up with her roommate from college. She was amazed that their friendship was still as strong as it had been so many years before. It felt like the years had melted away.

I went to the dictionary.

I told my friend that there are two kinds of friendships: continuous and continual. A continuous friendship stays undiminished; whenever you get together with a continuous friend, it feels as if no time has passed. A continual friendship starts and stops and starts again; whenever you get together, you have to warm up to each other.

Now that I own an iPod, I would explain it differently. A continuous friend is a keeper; a continual friend has to audition for your friendship each time you meet.

Makes me wonder how many of my friends consider me a keeper and how many friends expect me to audition to maintain our friendship.

Life Lessons

CONFESSION IN THE PHARMACY

From Great Neck to Little Neck

We lived in Great Neck, Long Island, in 1949. I am pretty sure that Great Neck had a pharmacy, but my father used the pharmacy in Little Neck.

Sometimes Dad would take me with him when he went from Great Neck to Little Neck. I remember being around six years old when I was hit by a big realization in the Little Neck Pharmacy.

I realized that I needed to pay attention.

I needed to watch what adults did because I was going to grow up and be an adult. I was going to follow in my father's footsteps. I must copy him; it was the way to success in the future.

Dad always used the big step-on scale in the pharmacy. I studied how my father weighed himself. I filed away in my memory: Step on the platform first, then insert a nickel in the slot, then wait for the big needle to come to a stop.

My father liked to tell the story of watching someone use the scale in wintertime. That person was wearing a heavy winter coat and realized the coat would skew his weight. So he took off the coat, draped it over his arm, and then stepped on the scale, weighing just as much holding the coat as if he were wearing the coat.

The story always gave my father a chuckle. I filed away in my memory: Before getting on the big step-on scale, take off coat and place it on a nearby chair.

I started paying attention to everything my father did; there was so much to learn about being an adult. And it was urgent, because I only had thirty-four years of good life left.

Jack vs. Joanne

As a kid, I was an avid fan of Jack Benny's radio show. Every year on the radio Jack celebrated his thirty-ninth birthday; he was perpetually thirty-nine years old.

Clearly, after thirty-nine, it was all downhill; that is why Jack Benny avoided becoming forty years old. He would be washed up. Age forty was the moment when people were over-the-hill.

309

Life Lessons

According to Jack, life was a bell curve that hit its peak at thirty-nine.

Then I found out that Joanne Woodward disagreed with Jack Benny. I saw the movie *Rachel, Rachel* in 1968; in the movie Joanne Woodward talked about being thirty-five years old. She said it was her last ascending summer.

According to Joanne, life was a bell curve that hit its peak at thirty-five.

Yikes! I was twenty-five years old when I saw her movie; I had only ten years of good life left before I became washed-up and over-the-hill.

Still Ascending

When I reached age thirty-six, I did not feel washed-up. My thirty-sixth summer was just as ascending as my thirty-fifth summer. Then I reached forty, and life was still ascending.

I feel foolish for believing Jack Benny and for believing Joanne Woodward. Life does not appear to be a bell curve; life continues to ascend.

If my father were still alive, I think it would be fun to take him back to Little Neck, back to the pharmacy, where I studied how to use a large step-on scale. There, I would confess to my father that I once believed that life was static and that I had to mimic my father's ways in 1949 to achieve success in my adult life.

My confession would give my father a chuckle. He was born in a country that no longer exists; he lived through two world wars, and he survived the Depression. He knew that life is not static.

If my father were still alive, he could easily prove that life is not static. He could simply point to the big sign across the front of the Little Neck Pharmacy. Nowadays, the sign says *Pharmacy* in Korean.

Life Lessons

IN THE FIGHT BETWEEN YOU AND THE WORLD

Hunt Down 369 Quotations

I was invited to join the high school yearbook staff. The editor-in-chief had a big innovation in mind, and she asked me to be literary editor. I said yes.

One big advantage of saying yes is that the editorial staff got to hang out in the yearbook room, located in the back of the typing classroom. It was 1960, and typing was a popular subject since it was needed for lots of jobs back in those days.

The big innovation was to sprinkle the senior photographs throughout the yearbook instead of having all the seniors in one big section. Sprinkling the photos could lead to interesting possibilities: a senior who had never spoken a word of French winding up on the French Club page, or a senior without athletic prowess winding up on the football page.

Also, we were putting a quotation under each of the 369 senior photos.

My job as literary editor was to find 369 quotes. Not only did they need to be real quotes, but they also needed to fit the person. For a perky girl, "Sweet and neat and can't be beat." For a heartthrob boy, "So many girls; so little time." For an avid sailor, "Just give me a tall ship and a star to steer her by."

Those quotes took care of three seniors; 366 quotes to go. I kept pen and paper handy whenever I read a book. I enlisted my friends to keep their eyes open for usable quotes.   I sat in the high school library and scoured *Bartlett's Familiar Quotations*.

Dealing with Female Passions

I was the only guy on the yearbook editorial staff. This meant sharing the yearbook room with three girls, who were passionate.

They were passionate about hunky actors. One girl went to a Broadway play and saw William Shatner make his Broadway debut. Shatner was slim and trim in those days, and he made the three girls' hearts go pitter-pat. I had to listen to endless discussions of how dreamy he was.

Then the three girls came across a male model in a magazine. He made them forget all about William Shatner.

Life Lessons

The girls did some research, found out what agency the model worked for, and wrote a letter asking for his photo. They insisted that my name was to be included in the request, but I pointed out that an all-female letter would get a better response. The agency got a letter from "Sandra, Isabel, Carol, and Dougletta" asking for an 8x10 glossy.

The model, who was named Buck Class, sent us back an 8x10 glossy, graciously inscribed "Best wishes to Sandra, Isabel, Carol, and Douglas." The photo went up on the bulletin board in the yearbook room.

However, female passion in the yearbook room could run in the other direction. There was one senior boy whom the three girls detested. I had to listen to endless discussions of how vile he was.

A True Keepsake

I weathered all the talk of dreamy actors and vile classmates, and the editorial staff managed to produce a yearbook that we felt was a true keepsake.

The senior class liked that we broke the mold; they got a kick out of seeing senior photos sprinkled throughout the book. The junior class, however, was not impressed: For their yearbook the following year, they went back to having all the senior photos in one big section.

Finding 369 quotations, each one suited to a particular senior, had been hard work, but people seemed to like the quotations we had found for them.

I certainly liked the quotation I had found for myself, showing that I was a teen-aged smart-aleck with intellectual pretensions.

The quotation I put under my own yearbook photo was from Franz Kafka, "In the fight between you and the world --- back the world."

Life Lessons

YOUR TUNA SANDWICH WILL BE HERE AT 10:45

Registering at the Heart Center

A month before I was scheduled for open-heart surgery, my cardiologist wanted to see what was going on inside my heart.

I needed to check into the heart center for a half-day procedure. The procedure sounded unpleasant: They would make an incision in the groin area, insert a fiber-optic tube up an artery, snake the tube up into my heart, and then film my heart at work.

On the morning of the procedure, my buddy Randy and I arrived at the heart center at 6:30 AM. I sat down at the receptionist's desk, expecting to fill out all the paperwork that goes along with any medical procedure these days. But I was thrown off guard. I expected the receptionist to ask for a list of everything I am allergic to, and to ask me to describe all the medical events in my life, and request my medical plan card so she could Xerox it.

Instead, she asked me to pick out a sandwich. She handed us menus from the Panera Bread Company. Since Randy was going to wait with me at the heart center, he got to pick out a sandwich, too.

Once I had decided on a tuna fish sandwich, the receptionist then asked me to list what I am allergic to, asked me to fill out a form describing all the medical events in my life, and requested my medical plan card so she could Xerox it.

When all the paperwork was complete, she told me, "Your tuna sandwich will be here at 10:45."

And she sent us off to wait in room number one. Room number one was for the first patient of the day.

As Nice as a Marriott

The room impressed us because it was as nice as a Marriott hotel room.

Randy sat down in the armchair; I put on a hospital gown and lay on the bed. Unlike a Marriott bed, my bed had wheels. This was how I was to be transported into the procedure room.

313

Life Lessons

Some guy came in, checked my blood pressure, and said, "Your tuna sandwich will be here at 10:45."

The room had a TV with an old-fashioned VCR attached. A notebook on the coffee table listed all the movies on videotape that were available to help us while away the time. I wondered why the heart center was using tapes and had not switched to DVDs.

A nurse came in and described what I should expect to happen after I was wheeled into the procedure room. Then she said, "Your tuna sandwich will be here at 10:45."

I wondered why everyone at the heart center was so concerned about my sandwich.

An orderly came to wheel me away. As he was maneuvering the bed into the hallway, he told Randy, "His tuna sandwich will be here at 10:45."

A Movie to Watch during Lunch

Thanks to anesthesia, the procedure was no big deal. I was wheeled back to room number one by 10:15, and our sandwiches from the Panera Bread Company arrived a half hour later.

Then I realized why everyone had been fussing over my sandwich.

In all those hours at the center, the sandwich was the one thing I could control. I had no choice in the medical procedure, but I did have a choice regarding the sandwich. The sandwich not only gave me a sense of power, it also became something to look forward to besides having a fiber-optic tube snaking up an artery.

As I unwrapped my sandwich, the receptionist entered the room, holding a videotape. "Would you like to watch a videotape of the inside of your heart while you eat? I can put it in the VCR for you."

I declined the opportunity, but I now knew why the heart center had an old-fashioned VCR attached to the TV.

DEATH

Death

Death

LAST STOP, PENN STATION

Riding for Forty-Nine Years

Friday, March 21, 2003, was the 100th anniversary of my father's birth.

Born in the Hapsburg Empire, Dad was brought to this country at the age of three. When he was old enough to get his first job, the Schneider family was living in Whitestone in the Borough of Queens in New York City.

Dad's job was in Manhattan, and he started commuting to and from Penn Station, riding the Long Island Rail Road (LIRR). When Dad married Mom, he continued to ride the LIRR, and when he moved the family eastward to Great Neck and then further eastward to Port Washington, he continued to ride the LIRR.

One of the jobs of the conductors on the LIRR is to call out the names of the stations as the train approaches. These conductors are the modern equivalent of a town crier. Each stop is sung out, "Manhasset. Next stop, Manhasset" or my favorite, "Douglaston. Next stop, Douglaston."

When you reach the end of the line, you hear, "Penn Station. Last stop, Penn Station."

When Dad retired, he had been riding the Long Island Rail Road, commuting to and from Penn Station, for forty-nine years. Every workday he had heard the conductors yell, "Last stop, Penn Station."

Mr. Schneider Knows This Will Hurt

My father could tolerate pain.

For years he had a big black spot under his thumbnail, the result of closing the door of a 1938 Pontiac on his hand. Finally Dad asked our family doctor about getting rid of the black spot. Answer: "We'll just pull out the thumbnail, and a new thumbnail will grow back without the black spot."

Dad agreed, and out came the medical pliers. The nurse was aghast, "Doctor, aren't you going to give Mr. Schneider an anesthetic?" "Oh, no, Mr. Schneider knows this will hurt." The pliers gripped Dad's thumbnail, and out came his thumbnail without anesthesia.

My father was one tough guy.

One day, after grocery shopping, Dad dropped Mom off at the beauty parlor

317

Death

and went home to unload the groceries. Sitting in the beauty parlor, Mom heard an ambulance go by. Whenever she heard an ambulance, Mom would make a little silent prayer for the person being carried to the hospital. Little did she know it was Dad in that particular ambulance.

The driveway was on an incline, and when Dad reached in the car to unload the groceries, he hit the gearshift. The car rolled backwards, scooping him up with the open door. Dad fell to the ground; one tire rolled up on his chest, pinning him. Some neighbors saw Dad's legs protruding from underneath the car and got the car off of him.

Turns out that Dad had a few sore ribs, nothing more.

Within Seven Minutes

My father lived with a persistent stomach ulcer for five decades and survived. My father was diagnosed with skin cancer and survived. He was diagnosed with prostate cancer and survived. A doctor pulled out his thumbnail and he survived. A car sat on Dad's chest and he survived.

Dad's death came suddenly and unexpectedly. He had a heart attack and did not survive.

The heart attack came when Dad was running an errand for a friend --- an errand that involved riding the Long Island Rail Road. The heart attack came while Dad was in Penn Station. He was dead within seven minutes.

He died in a place he knew so well. He died on St. Patrick's Day, 1980, four days short of his seventy-seventh birthday.

For Dad, Penn Station really was the last stop.

Death

THE BLUE-EYED GIRL DID HER JOB WELL

Passing Enzo's Book Around

Enzo's book was remarkable, and we passed it around.

The cover of *The Art of Racing in the Rain* says that it was written by Garth Stein, but the book was really written by a dog named Enzo. Enzo lived in Seattle and wrote about his life and his death.

We were in a group of six Americans vacationing in Europe together in August 2008. We read books while flying across the Atlantic; we read while staying in hotels; and we read while riding on trains in Switzerland, Austria, and Italy.

My buddy Randy and I both read Enzo's book on this vacation. Little did we know then that our dog, Skye, would be dead from cancer in less than a year.

She hid her cancer from us. Before we went on vacation, she developed a limp; we thought it might be arthritis. The vet did not detect the leukemia that was settling into her joints.

After we returned from vacation, Skye started lagging behind on our daily walks. She kept up a cheerful face, but she was not her old self.

Eyes as Blue as My Mother's

Skye was an Australian shepherd.

We picked her out from a digital photo e-mailed to us when she was one day old. Her eyes were closed in the photo, but when they opened they were intense blue --- the same blue as my mother's eyes.

Skye's job in life was to give affection.

She did her job well. She would shine her blue eyes and her limitless affection on people; she would get compliments on her eyes in return.

Her appetite started to diminish. By the time the vet detected the cancer in Skye, the odds were against her. She grew thin; we had to force food into her mouth.

On Easter morning, I gave her a bath. With her fur all wet, she was disturbingly thin. I kept my spirits up by singing to her: "You'll be the prettiest

Death

doggie in the Easter parade."

But there was no Easter parade for Skye. I believe that the dog knew that she was dying, and she knew that if she died on Easter, it meant being taken to a strange 24-hour emergency clinic where a strange veterinarian would put her to sleep. I believe the dog waited until the day after Easter to give us the signal.

We were at work on that day. A friend stopped by the house to check on Skye. He found six puddles of unidentifiable body fluids sprinkled around the house. The dog had wanted to get up the stairs but had collapsed on the next-to-the-top stair, her legs feebly moving in the air, trying to make it up one more step.

Skye had given the signal: It was time.

Do You See the Field That Enzo Saw?

We left work and took Skye to our veterinarian to be put gently to rest. She was only five-and-a-half years old.

In *The Art of Racing in the Rain*, Enzo described what it was like to die. Enzo saw a field: no fences, no buildings, and no people --- just grass, like the grass that tickled his stomach when he was a little puppy. Enzo headed toward the field.

I looked at Skye on the vet's examination table.

Skye, do you see a field? Do you see the field that Enzo saw? You can get up now, Skye. You can walk; your limp is gone.

I kept on looking at Skye on the examination table.

See that field of grass up ahead? You can head toward it. Your body does not hurt anymore; you are free of cancer.

You can run now. Run, Skye. Run!

320

Death

TAKING ON HUMAN FORM

His Corpse is in New York City

My mother and I were nervous. We were both afraid of what the State of New York would do.

I was with my mother when she presented a bank teller with a withdrawal slip for an unusually large sum of money. It was a withdrawal from a joint bank account for my mother and my father.

The teller hesitated and looked at Mom. "Where is your husband?" I did some quick thinking and said: "He is in New York City."

The teller then handed my mother the money. My father wasn't really in New York City; his corpse was in New York City. Mom was withdrawing money for his funeral before the State of New York froze the bank account.

Mom and Dad lived seventy-six miles from New York City, and Dad had gone there to run an errand for a friend. Dad never returned; instead, Mom got a phone call telling her that Dad had died suddenly from a heart attack.

I was driving my mother to the funeral home, where we would wait for my father's corpse to arrive.

The Crushing Hug

It was weird standing in a viewing room in a funeral home with no body to view.

My cousin, a New York City policeman, was working his way through the red tape to verify my father's identity and to get his body out of New York City to the funeral home. Lunchtime came, and Dad's body had not arrived yet. My mother, my two brothers, and I went to a nearby restaurant.

When we got back from lunch, my father's body was in a casket in the front of the viewing room. The three sons held back and let Mom approach the casket by herself. Up to this point, she had received a telephone call, but she had no physical proof that her husband of fifty years was dead.

She stood there gazing at Dad. Then, finally, she turned to walk back to join her three sons.

She never got that far. A woman swept down on her.

321

Death

Mom was on the receiving end of a big crushing hug. The woman hugging her was taller than Mom, bigger than Mom, and kept on saying, "Edith, I am so sorry." Mom looked bewildered and was finally released from the embrace.

The three sons then went to view their father's body. I had brought a lapel pin that I had seen Dad wear every day of his working life. It was a pin for a professional printers' organization. I reached in the coffin and put the pin in Dad's lapel.

Later, the three sons asked each other: Who was the woman who gave Mom a big crushing hug? We did not know. We asked Mom; she did not know. We checked the funeral parlor guest book; the woman had not signed it.

After the Death of a Fire Jumper

On the second day, the funeral parlor had a little ceremony for Dad, and then people filtered away. I was the last person in the room. I reached in the casket and removed the pin from Dad's lapel. I did not want it to melt when Dad's body was cremated.

I walked up the empty aisle toward the door holding his lapel pin in my hand. I was still puzzled by the mysterious woman who had appeared so shortly after Mom saw Dad's corpse for the first time. No one had any idea who she was.

Years later I watched Steven Spielberg's movie *Always* about a fire jumper who dies in a forest fire. After the fire jumper's death, he sees Audrey Hepburn. She is his guide, and her task is to guide him with his transition into the afterlife.

I had never heard of guides before.

What about the woman with the crushing hug? Was she a guide? She looked nothing like Audrey Hepburn, but it would be nice to know that Dad had a guide to help him transition into the afterlife.

And it would be nice to know that the guide took a few minutes to take on human form and comfort my mother as my mother transitioned into widowhood.

FINDING SOLACE

My Grandmother's Death

I usually seek entertainment in the darkness, but sometimes I need solace.

Going to graduate school in London, England, sounded ideal. Since I was an army veteran, the GI Bill covered my tuition and my living expenses. I got to spend two years in London and relished every day there until I got a letter from my parents.

The letter said that my dear grandmother had died and had been buried. She had been buried three weeks before the letter was written. Suddenly, I felt isolated. My parents knew I did not have the money to fly back to the United States for the burial, so they were in no hurry to tell me about Grandma's death.

Living in London meant I had lost the chance to say goodbye. I needed to deal with my sadness, and I turned to the movies.

I knew there was a movie playing that celebrated old age. I went to the movies and saw *Harry and Tonto*. I sat in the darkness watching an aging Art Carney on the screen, but my thoughts were with my grandmother.

This may not have been traditional grieving, but it comforted me. I had done something that was a tribute to my grandmother.

My Mother's Death

I learned of my mother's death via a phone call in December 1992. I was living in Minnesota; she had died in Ohio. No burial. She was cremated, and my brother was arranging a memorial service for her. Attending the memorial service would be a way for me to say goodbye.

But I needed something more immediate.

I turned to the movies. I knew there was a movie about people who had faced misery. My mother's life had some ups and downs, but she did not have to face misery. I went to the movies and saw *Schindler's List*. I sat in the darkness watching a black and white movie about concentration camps, but my thoughts were with my mother. The grimness on the screen contrasted with the life she led, and the contrast comforted me.

Death

At the end of the film, the movie switched from black-and-white to color, and switched from the past to the present. It showed people at Schindler's grave, paying tribute to him.

I was comforted again because I knew I would be able to pay tribute to my mother: There would be a memorial service, and when the weather got warmer, there would be a scattering of her ashes.

Nearly 3,000 Deaths

September 11, 2001. I needed the darkness again.

The untimely deaths of nearly 3,000 people in the terrorist attacks had made me somber. I needed a movie that would purge the gloom that permeated my mind.

I went to the movies and saw *Rat Race*. The movie, a slapstick comedy with Cuba Gooding, Jr., was about a race to some treasure where everything that could go wrong did go wrong. The movie struck a chord with me and I laughed. I laughed so vigorously I was afraid that an usher would come and try to shush me up.

The movie had made the gloom disappear, at least for a few hours.

When I read the review in the *St. Louis Post-Dispatch,* it made me fire off a letter to the reviewer. I chided him for not rating the movie high enough. After reading my letter, he actually upped his rating by a half star.

For those times when I needed to sit in the darkness and find solace, the movies did not disappoint me. *Harry and Tonto*, *Schindler's List*, and *Rat Race* were the right movies at the right moment.

Death

US SCHNEIDERS ALWAYS DIE ON HOLIDAYS

A Death in the Family

I have a short note that my father mailed to me when I was living in Minneapolis. I treasure the note for two reasons. One, it is a sample of his meticulous handwriting. Looking at anything Dad wrote, you would swear it was on lined paper, but when you took a second look, there were no lines.

Two, I treasure it because Dad ends the note by saying "Happy St. Patrick's Day." The note was written a few days before Dad died of a heart attack on St. Patrick's Day, 1980.

I was also living in Minneapolis when I got a phone call on a Friday in 1983 saying that my middle brother was in Intensive Care. He and his wife were living with my mother, on Long Island. When I called up United Airlines to book a flight, I found out that all the New York airports were snowed in until Sunday. All the flights from Minneapolis to New York on Sunday were fully booked. The airline agent mentioned that there were 11 seats available from Chicago to New York on Sunday.

I booked a flight from Minneapolis to Chicago on Saturday, stayed overnight in Chicago, flew to New York on Sunday, got a bus to a subway station, took a subway to Penn Station, took a train to my mother's town. It was Sunday evening.

The hospital only allowed visitors into the Intensive Care Unit for five minutes, every hour on the hour. My brother was in a coma, no sign of activity except for a screen showing that his heart was still beating. I leaned over and spoke. I told him that I had come to Long Island from Minneapolis. I told him I would be taking care of Mom and his wife.

He died 12 hours after I spoke to him. It was Valentine's Day, 1983.

Choosing Your Time

Pope John Paul II was on his deathbed in April 2005. I stopped by a co-worker's desk and predicted that the Pope would die on a Saturday. He died on Saturday, April 2.

On the following Monday, my co-worker asked me how I knew when the Pope would die. It was a matter of timing. Dying on a Saturday meant that Catholics around the world would react to the news at Mass the next day.

325

Death

And then they would have one week to prepare for celebrating the Pope's life at the next Sunday's Mass.

I believe that some people get to choose when they will die.

A friend in Wisconsin married a much older man. They had never spent a night apart during their marriage until she went off to Texas without him for a high school reunion. He died in his sleep from natural causes while she was in Texas.

My friend was distraught, feeling helpless because she had not been there in Wisconsin when he passed. I tried to explain to her that her husband was too much of a gentleman to die in front of her. Her husband was from a generation where the husband's duty was to protect his wife. I believe that he had chosen to die while she was away.

I believe that my brother was holding onto life, and he chose to die once he knew that I had come from Minneapolis to be with our mother and his wife.

Through the Snowy Town

St. Patrick's Day. Valentine's Day. My mother told me: "Us Schneiders always die on holidays."

I believe my mother got to chose when she would die.

She spent her final years in a nursing home in Hudson, Ohio, the town where my older brother lived. She spent her final months dealing with a broken hip, a condition which reduced her life to lying in bed and being turned hourly --- face the wall for one hour, face the window for one hour.

Mom had spent her married life as a minority in a household consisting of four men and one woman. I believe she wanted to out-do the Schneider men who had died before her. Mom died on Christmas Day, 1990.

This was the day when my brother's children and grandchildren would be gathered at his house. They would be busy opening presents in the morning. Mom died at midday.

Midday on Christmas ---- when there was very little traffic on the roads. My grieving brother and his family drove to the nursing home to acknowledge Mom's death. Snow had fallen and the town looked like a Christmas card.

Mom had chosen to die on the biggest holiday of all.

SIGHTING A DOE

Juanita: Truly, a Nice Lady

Juanita died on a Monday in 2005. She was my buddy Randy's mother.

She was in home hospice care, and her five children set up a schedule, taking shifts to tend to her. A hospice nurse came every other day and checked up on things. Hospice is a wonderful thing.

Juanita Pulliam had an inner cheerfulness that drew people to her. I cannot imagine anyone not liking her. She truly deserved the description: "nice lady."

She is missed.

Rocky: Finding a Good Home

While Juanita was sick, we took Rocky, her dog, into our house. Our plan was to put Rocky up for adoption once Juanita passed away.

I built an adoption website for Rocky. In order to make a good match, I listed his minuses as well as his pluses.

Plusses = affectionate, intelligent, good manners, pearly-white teeth.

Minuses = overprotective, hates most dogs, chases most cats, and is too slow to be one of those agility dogs you see on "Animal Planet."

But I knew it was Rocky's eyes that would get him adopted. Each eye was divided vertically: outside half brown, inside half blue. A nice close-up of his eyes was the first photo on the website.

Juanita Pulliam was buried on a Thursday.

On Friday morning, I announced Rocky's website via e-mail to friends and coworkers. By 5:30 PM Friday evening, he got adopted.

Rocky now has a good home: He lives on five acres out in the country with a couple who wanted an affectionate dog, but also wanted an overprotective dog because the husband is often away on business trips.

I was elated. I felt that we had fulfilled a covenant with Juanita: We found a good home for her dog.

Death

Shannon: Sighting a Doe

Shannon, Randy's daughter, adored her grandmother. Shannon would glow any time someone pointed out the similarities between her and her grandmother Juanita.

Shannon believes that after a loved one dies, if you see a deer, it is an omen that the loved one's soul has found peace in the afterlife. This idea came from a very touching movie about a young boy with stunted growth, called *Simon Burch*.

On Saturday, Shannon phoned us. She had sighted a doe. The doe was in a patch of woods where no deer had ever been seen before. Shannon was convinced that Juanita's soul has found peace.

When did Shannon sight the doe? Turns out it was on Friday evening, just about 5:30, the time that Rocky got adopted and was being transported to his new home.

Finding a good home for Rocky must have been the last loose end that needed tidying up. So I also became convinced that Juanita's soul had found peace in the afterlife.

328

Death

UNSPEAKABLE THINGS AT THE END OF ROAD K

Get Out the Tire Iron

It was clear that we should scatter my mother and father's ashes in Shinnecock Bay at the end of Road K. Road K is about twenty yards long, a spur off Dune Road. Dune Road runs along a long barrier island off the southern shore of Long Island.

The beach at the end of Road K was off the beaten track, and few people went there. But my middle brother, John, loved solitude and enjoyed spending time at that beach. He often took the dog there and went clamming at low tide.

This is where my sister-in-law decided to scatter my brother's ashes.

She went by herself to Road K, parked, and opened the package that held the can with my brother's ashes in it. She expected the can to have a twist-off lid, but the can was sealed tight. Of course, she had not brought a can opener.

At this highly emotional moment, my sister-in-law got out her tire iron, punctured the can, and managed to scatter my brother's ashes while trying to maintain her composure.

Please Grind Dad Smaller

I was living in Minnesota when it came time to scatter my parents' ashes on Long Island.

My sister-in-law's experience with the tire iron was a lesson to me. My father had died first; his ashes were in a can. My mother had died a decade later; her ashes were in a plastic bag.

I took the can of Dad's ashes down to the Cremation Society and asked them to put him in a plastic bag. They told me he was in large chunks, so I asked them to please grind Dad smaller so that his ashes would resemble Mom's ashes.

I then flew to Long Island with two plastic bags under the seat in front of me. Dad was in the bag on the left and Mom was in the bag on the right. I arranged them like that because that was how my parents used to sleep in their bedroom --- Dad on the left and Mom on the right.

Death

Discarded Socks

One day before the scattering, I went to the beach at the end of Road K. I was afraid that the beach was a teenage party spot and was full of unspeakable things and discarded clothing.

I had some garbage bags but quickly discovered that there were no unspeakable things, just lots of empty clamshells from clambakes. There was some discarded clothing --- socks, to be exact. I guessed that people threw away their socks to they could spend their time on the beach barefoot.

I was stuffing discarded socks in a garbage bag when a car pulled up and parked on Road K; two people jumped out, holding garbage bags. They started to pick up discarded socks and other debris. A second car pulled up, and two more people jumped out with garbage bags and started to pick up discarded socks and other debris.

My heart sank. These other people might be picking up stuff because they were planning an event at the end of Road K. That event might interfere with the scattering of my parents' ashes the next day.

Suddenly, another car pulled up and parked on Road K. A newspaper reporter jumped out with a camera, and she asked us all to pose for a photograph. Turns out it was National Coastal Cleanup Day, sponsored by the American Littoral Society, and these other people were cleanup volunteers.

We all posed for the photo.

The first couple told the reporter they were from Hampton Bays, Long Island, and the reporter nodded her head.

The second couple told the reporter they were from Riverhead, Long Island, and the reporter nodded her head.

I told the reporter I was from Minneapolis, Minnesota, and her head stopped nodding.

I let her believe that I had flown in from Minnesota to Long Island to volunteer for National Coastal Cleanup Day. I did not tell the reporter that my parents' ashes were being scattered the next day, and I was there because I was afraid of unspeakable things at the end of Road K.

330

CLOSING

332

SAY GOOD NIGHT, NOT GOOD-BYE

The Letter from Cambridge, England

The letter from Cambridge, England, arrived in the mail. It was from Marion.

I had been in classes with Marion when I did my graduate studies at the University of London. Her mother was English, but her father was Greek; Marion had jet black hair that distinguished her from most of the English women I met in London. She had spent a year in New Jersey as a young teenager, which distinguished her even more because she understood Americans. We became good friends, even kindred spirits.

The letter from my English kindred spirit started with, "Dear Doug, I am dying." The letter ended with, "Keep me in your heart and your head, and I will live on."

I was caught off guard; this was totally unexpected.

Marion never said what she was dying from. No one ever said what my good friend was dying from.

Punting on the Cam

I remembered back to the 1970s when I lived in London and I relied on Marion.

Many times I was lulled into the false impression that I fit in with the British because we spoke the same language. But I wasn't British.

I needed Marion to explain things to me --- like how I should say "Excuse me" instead of "Pardon me" because the British considered "Pardon me" to be arrogant.

She explained why a bookstore clerk got upset with me. She explained why I didn't have to do every homework assignment. She was my guide.

When I heard that my grandmother had died back in the United States, Marion was one of the people I turned to. I told her that I did not feel like being alone; could I just come over to her flat and sit in her living room. She didn't have to entertain me; I just needed to be around people doing their daily activities. That was fine with her.

Being her friend also meant getting to visit Cambridge, where her mother lived. Marion showed me a Roman road. She showed me the house where Charles Darwin had lived. And she took me punting.

A punt is the English equivalent of a gondola. You stand on a small deck in the rear of the boat and propel the punt using a pole. Marion handed me the pole, and I managed to get the punt moving forward. The River Cam is small and meandering, and I was punting along quite nicely.

Quite nicely --- until we came across a punt coming toward us on the river. I tried to avoid the other punt, but we collided. The guy in the other punt fell in the river and lost his pole.

I felt like laughing, but I was too busy apologizing.

The Blossoming of the Internet

Marion's letter was written in 1999. The Internet was about to blossom, and the Internet allowed me to become part of Marion's support group.

A friend of Marion's e-mailed out reports on Marion's health, her fortitude, and her emotions. These e-mails always began with the same salutation, "Dear Everyone."

"Marion has to conserve energy, even to be ordinary." "She retains her grace, if not her bounce." "Marion walked to the pharmacy today. It tired her out, but she also feels tired doing nothing." "It must be a terrible strain to live as if there is a future, while attending to all the details of the end of life."

Marion held on for a year. She managed to put together a Christmas e-mail: "My energy is very low. My husband's energy is even lower because he is my caregiver. I send you my love. I have had an amazingly rich and rewarding year, despite the illness. I am attaching a photo: The holly was stunning last month. And my fourteen-year-old daughter is always, and ever increasingly, stunning."

Marion died two days after Christmas; she was forty-seven years old. She had planned all the details of her memorial service.

At the end of the service, there was an American song by Beth Nielsen Chapman. Marion's family and friends filed out of the chapel listening to the loudspeakers: "You are everything you want to be. So, just let your heart reach out to me; let my light shine in your eyes. Say good night, not good-bye."

I knew Marion during her life, and I knew her while she was dying. With that song, I continue to know her.

ACKNOWLEDGEMENTS

My journey in writing true-life vignettes began in January 2001, with the tragic news that Louis Javelle had been killed in a workplace massacre (see the Opening story in this book.) From there, I wrote one true-life vignette (which I called an ELetter) every week until January 2011, e-mailing the three-tiered pieces to the inboxes of friends, family, and well-wishers.

When I switched to blogging in 2011, I wanted to compile ten years of e-mail vignettes into book form. I scoured the globe from Singapore to St. Louis to Norway and beyond, asking people to judge the stories, giving them a thumbs-up or a thumbs-down. What you read in this book is their final master list: 145 of their favorites, culled from 520.

My thanks go out to my book coach Christine Frank (of Christine Frank and Associates), my editor Lois Rosenfeld, my colleagues at the Grand Glaize Writers Group, all my book judges, and my buddy Randy who has had to live with a puppy out of breath all these years.

OTHER BOOKS BY DOUGLAS E SCHNEIDER

Wee Hoose on the Prairie
     (Co-written with Todd McCall of Nova Scotia)

Wee Hoose on the Mississippi
     (Co-written with Todd McCall of Nova Scotia)

A Tourist Guide to Sokoto State, Nigeria